THE "HOW TO" GRANTS MANUAL

The "How To" Grants Manual

Successful Grantseeking Techniques for Obtaining Public and Private Grants

Fifth Edition

David G. Bauer

AMERICAN COUNCIL ON EDUCATION
PRAEGER
Series on Higher Education

Library of Congress Cataloging-in-Publication Data

Bauer, David G.
   The "how to" grants manual : successful grantseeking techniques
for obtaining public and private grants / by David G. Bauer.—5th ed.
     p. cm. — (ACE/Praeger series on higher education)
   Includes bibliographical references and index.
   ISBN 0–275–98070–7 (alk. paper)
   1. Fund raising. 2. Grants-in-aid. 3. Nonprofit organizations. I.
Title. II. American Council on Education/Praeger series on higher
education.
HG177.B38   2003
658.15′224—dc21   2003052886

British Library Cataloguing in Publication Data is available.

Library of Congress Catalog Card Number: 2003052886

ISBN: 0–275–98070–7

First published in 2003

Praeger Publishers, 88 Post Road West, Westport, CT 06881
An imprint of Greenwood Publishing Group, Inc.
www.praeger.com

Printed in the United States of America

The paper used in this book complies with the
Permanent Paper Standard issued by the National
Information Standards Organization (Z39.48–1984).

10 9 8 7 6 5 4 3 2 1

CONTENTS

LIST OF EXHIBITS, FIGURES, AND TABLES

PREFACE

This fifth edition of *The "How To" Grants Manual* reflects the changes and challenges that have occurred in the grants marketplace since the fourth edition was published in 1999. The exhibits and tables have been updated to reflect advances in technology and computer usage, and are available on a CD-ROM inside the back cover of the book.

Changes in the grants marketplace have occurred at a faster pace than I have ever seen in my 30 years of experience in grant seeking and fundraising. We have moved from a rapidly increasing stock market driven by technology and industrial strength to a recession and record stock losses. Foundations are having trouble maintaining assets and grants in this new marketplace, and corporations have decreased grants dramatically. These forces, plus the impact of the September 11 attack on the World Trade Center, have markedly changed the not-for-profit field and all of us. However, the grants marketplace has weathered recessions and wars before, and many of the lessons we can learn from these events are shared in this fifth edition of *The "How To" Grants Manual*.

If asked what percentage of the book I have changed since the 1999 fourth edition, I would have to say well over 50 percent. The purpose of these changes is not to sell a new book but to enhance your ability to compete in the grants marketplace, and to avoid failure and the waste of time involved in proposal rejection.

What is amazing to me, looking back over the previous four editions, is the consistency in the basics of effective grantseeking. The constants remain the same, and two of the basics are that you cannot succeed unless you try, and that trying will always involve some degree of failure and rejection. The trick to grantseeking, if there is one, is to make every experience a learning opportunity. From acceptance of your proposal or to rejection of your proposal, attempt to learn as much as you can about what worked and why, and what didn't work and how to avoid these mistakes next time.

This edition also contains several new concepts that were not included in previous editions. The inclusion of these concepts was driven by advances in technology and the growing desire of grantors to fund consortia that hold the promise of new and fundamentally different interdisciplinary opportunities, and provide for cost efficiency through the use of shared resources. Since the last edition of this book, I have instructed approximately 10,000 grant seekers in over 200 grants seminars, and time and time again, the concept of consortium grants surfaced. In fact, it was so prevalent, that in addition to including the how to's of consortium grants in this edition, I also developed a new seminar, *How to Increase Grant Productivity through Effective Consortia and Team Building.*

While my teaching experiences have had an impact on the changes in this edition, so has my development of the companion book to The *"How To" Grants Manual, How to Evaluate and Improve Your Grants Effort* (Westport, Conn.: American Council on Education/Oryx Press/Greenwood Publishing, second edition, 2001). When researching and writing *How to Evaluate and Improve Your Grants Effort,* and then helping universities and nonprofit organizations apply the techniques presented in it, I continually received feedback on what you, the grantseeker, needed to be able to produce a winning proposal, and have included and addressed this important data in this edition of The *"How To" Grants Manual.*

The format for this edition is similar to that used in past editions. Because there is a basic scope and sequence to successful grantseeking, the order of the book remains the same. However, there are new sections within each part of the book, and part 3 of the past edition (Private Funding Sources) has been divided into two separate parts (foundation and corporate).

Part 1, "Getting Ready to Seek Grant Support for Your Organization," will show you how to organize your effort to produce a winning proposal, and provide you with the best and latest techniques to simplify your grants quest and use your time efficiently. Part 2, "Public/Government Funding Opportunities," is devoted to understanding the federal and state grants process, and includes strategies for procuring and utilizing information on funding opportunities through the latest computer assisted technologies. Part 3, "Private/Foundation Funding Opportunities," takes a comprehensive look at the foundation grants marketplace, and assists the grantseeker in developing a grant-winning approach to foundation funding sources. From procuring a grant, to performing a need's assessment, to developing preliminary data, to planning an affordable model or research project, part 3 is designed to increase your chances of success with foundation grantors. Part 4, "Private/Corporate Funding Opportunities," recognizes recent setbacks in the corporate segment of the private marketplace, but acknowledges the fact that as economic recovery continues it will be more and more important for grantseekers to know how to select prospective corporate grantors, and to create a tailored approach to meet the needs of corporate funding sources.

If you are involved in evaluating and improving your organization's grants effort, you will find the book *How to Evaluate and Improve Your Grants Effort* particularly helpful. If you are interested in learning more about the grantseeking process, you may find the videotape training program *Winning Grants 2* useful. If you are interested in instructing others in grantseeking, you may find the videotape training program *How to Teach Grantseeking to Others* invaluable. (See the Bauer Associates ordering information at the end of the book for both of these resources.)

Special thanks must be given to Donna Bauer, wife, vice president, and indispensable partner, and to my son, Karl Bauer, for his illustrations. A special thank you also goes to Jim Murray, retired Vice President for External Affairs, American Council on Education (ACE), for providing me with the opportunity to produce the first four editions of this book, and to Wendy Bresler, ACE Director of Publications, for publishing the fifth edition.

The experiences I have had at the universities where I have held positions and guest lectured at are an integral part of this book. While all of these institutions deserve credit, they are too numerous to mention individually.

Special thanks must be given to Oakland University and in particular to Dr. Randy Hansen and Pat Beaver for their support, and the support of their information technology staffs in creating the CD-ROM that accompanies this book. Steven King and Steve Sapelewski have my thanks as well for their technology genius.

INTRODUCTION

This book has been created for novice grantseekers who need instruction on how to begin the grants process, as well as seasoned grantseekers who want to learn new techniques to save time and increase their success rates. While competent grantseekers tailor their proposals to prospective funding sources, they use the same basic process time and time again to procure funding for their projects. This book will help you join the ranks of the competent grantseeker by providing you with a grantseeking process or system that goes far beyond how to create a proposal. The system is very simple to follow but that does not mean it is easy or quick; and, while successful grantseeking is hard work, it need not be overly time-consuming. The information you derive from this book will help you work smarter, not harder, in the pursuit of grant support. Several colleges who use the system presented in the preceding chapters report success rates of 75 percent. This edition of *The "How To" Grants Manual* seeks to improve your success rate even more.

For those of you just learning about grantseeking, you are about to embark on an exciting journey. Being skilled in securing grant support will have a dramatic impact on your career, and to some of you, securing grant support will become your career. The ability to attract grant funding accelerated my original career in health education, and was responsible for the tripling of my salary in three years! However, an increase in my personal salary was not then, and is not now, the most satisfying aspect of my grants career. The best part is the difference my work makes in people's lives.

Individuals pursue grant funding for many reasons besides money. In fact, one study on what first-time federal grantees found satisfying about grant procurement reported thirteen factors[1] that more than offset the hard work that grantseekers often complain about. These included:

- praise and personal recognition
- satisfaction from working with a research team
- satisfaction from immersion in research
- satisfaction from commitment of subjects
- salary, space, travel, and equipment
- speaking opportunities
- opportunity to review proposals
- familiarity with federal agency personnel
- recognition in university publications
- increased awareness of research among students and colleagues
- increased responsiveness from campus research officials

In many respects, the quest for a grant in the nonprofit world is equivalent to efforts in the for-profit world that are associated with superior performances and super achievers.

While the current grants marketplace is rife with changes, the intent of this book is not to just provide you with the most current data. The intent is to provide you with techniques that will help keep you current and ahead of these changes. This includes an historical perspective of the grants marketplace and insight on what to expect in the next few years.

With the current problems in stock performance and profitability, many grantseekers are moving away from foundation and corporate grants support. Don't get caught following the crowd. The smart grantseeker sees this as the best time to get to know private grantors. Right now there is less competition for their time, and private grantors appreciate the professional who understands the pressure they are under. Yes, you do need to adjust your request to private funders based on the current financial situation, but you don't need to leave the marketplace altogether. I believe that the cyclical trends of the past will be at work again and that these funders will be back on top in short order.

The federal grants marketplace may look good as we face another presidential election, but there are problems in this sector as well. As federal budget deficits go up, grant-funding allocations will go down.

Flexibility and anticipation are the operand terms for both the private and public grants marketplaces and your grantseeking strategies. Proactive grantseeking that incorporates research on the funding trends of grantors has never been more important. Figuring out where to go for your best chance of grants success will take some work but also will pay off handsomely.

As long as your budget does not allow you to fund your own projects and make personal contributions to your field, you are left with the alternative called grantseeking. I hope you find the system and strategies outlined in this book helpful and that your grantseeking has an as positive and dramatic effect on your career as it has on mine.

NOTE

1. Sharol F. Jacobsen and Mary Elizabeth O'Brien, "Satisfying and Stressful Experiences of First-Time Federal Grantees," IMAGE: *Journal of Nursing Scholarship*, 24, no.1 (Spring 1992): 45–49.

PART ONE

....

Getting Ready to Seek
Grant Support for
Your Organization

CHAPTER 1

Setting Yourself Up for Grants Success

Developing a Proactive Grants System

One of the biggest problems in grantseeking is that most proposal writers do not begin the process early enough and are forced into a reactive grants process driven by an impending deadline. In this chapter you will explore techniques to help you begin the grants process in an orderly and proactive manner resulting in higher quality proposals and an increased success rate.

If you have a set of proposal guidelines or an application package in hand, and a deadline in two or three weeks, you may as well skip this chapter and part 1 of this book, and move quickly to proposal preparation. However, before you rush off, consider the fact that when you write your proposal before researching and making preproposal contact with your potential grantor, you reduce your chances of success three to five times. Because of this, I urge you to consider submitting your proposal in the funding source's next grants cycle instead of the current one, even if this means putting your project off for one year.

The suggestions in this chapter are aimed at helping you produce a winning proposal that reflects your thoughtful consideration of how your project or research fits into your personal development, the fulfillment of your organization's mission, and the needs of the prospective grantor. When you approach proposal preparation in this win-win-win manner, the writing of the proposal will become easier and your finished product will reflect a confident, positive, quality and tone.

DEVELOPING YOUR CAREER GRANTS PLAN

Whether you are working in higher education or a nonprofit organization, grant-funded projects and research provide you with a variety of opportunities, choices,

1. Where do you want your career to be five years from now? What projects, programs, and/or research will you be performing? How do these projects, programs and/or research fit into your vision of success in your field?

2. What percent of your time will be devoted to these projects/programs/research as opposed to your current job responsibilities? _____%

    Based on the percent of time you will be devoting to projects/programs/research, what is the estimated cost of your *grant related* salary/wages including fringe benefits? $_____

3. What personnel will you need to help you perform the tasks you would like to accomplish in the fifth year of your vision?

	Number	Estimated Cost
Project coordinator(s)		
Laboratory assistant(s)		
Graduate student(s)		
Work study student(s)		
Other (please list)		

4. What facilities will be required to house these individuals? In-house, on-campus, off-campus, etc.? What do you estimate the required square footage to be?

5. What new equipment (computers, software, machines, vehicles, etc.) will you and your staff need to accomplish the projected task?

Equipment Item	Estimated Cost

6. Based on salary/wages, personnel, and equipment, what is the total amount of resources needed in year 5? $_____

    Of this total, how much will be needed from your organization/institution? $ _____

    How much will be needed in grants? $_____

YOUR PERSONAL GRANTS PLAN

EXHIBIT 1.1

and directions. Grantors want to believe that the projects you present to them for funding will move you toward your predetermined career goals, and your organization's stated mission and goals. One must not appear to be following the grant money; willing to do anything for the grantor regardless of where it takes you or your organization.

While chapter 6 asks you to examine your organization's commitment and its available resources, this chapter asks you to reflect on your career and how grantseeking works into your professional development. To do so, you must first

1. What steps can you take in the next twelve months to move you toward your 5 year vision? (These steps could include procurring smaller start-up or initiation grants, need assessment grants, grants to develop preliminary data, or grants for a minimal amount of essential equipment or software.)

2. What resources do you need to help you initiate these first steps? (These resources should include a list of potential advisors, mentors, colleagues, etc. who you can brainstorm your topic with, enlist support from, and/or develop a consortia approach with.)

3. Who will you contact, and when?

Who	When
_____	_____
_____	_____
_____	_____
_____	_____

SETTING YOUR GOALS AND ENLISTING SUPPORT

EXHIBIT 1.2

do some *visioning*. Where do you want to be in your field in five years? What type of work would you like to be doing? Your answers to these questions define your image of personal success. If your current budget will cover all the costs of attaining your vision, you do not need to pursue grants. If your vision requires grant funds from outside of your institution or organization, you must define how you will use these external resources.

Exhibit 1.1 helps you refine your vision by asking what resources you think you will need. For example, will you need special release time or time specifically allocated to your grant as opposed to your regular workload or schedule? If so, how much time will you need to achieve success? Partial release time for your grant-funded project or full time? Continue to answer the questions regarding your five-year vision. What personnel will you require? Project coordinator? Lab assistants?

Support staff? Work study students? Graduate assistants, and so on? What software, equipment, transportation, and so on will you require? By estimating the cost of the components you need to fulfill your five-year plan you can come up with a total cost, and then determine if any of the cost may be covered by your normal budget process. If so, subtract this amount from the total so that you can come up with a more accurate estimate of the amount you must procure through grants.

This visioning process is critical in that it will help you develop benchmarks to keep your five year plan in focus as you start out toward your first year goals. Setting up your goals in a tangible written format follows the philosophy presented in Dr. Denis Waitley's book *The Psychology of Winning*.[1] You must first conceive it, then believe it, before you achieve it.

Exhibit 1.2 will help you break your five-year plan into a one-year plan and assist you in determining what resources you will need. First, review your five-year plan and write down what initial steps are critical to begin movement toward your vision. What smaller steps must you take now to begin the process? What components will require grant funding? Second, determine who might be able to help you achieve the initial steps. You might even consider organizing a small group of individuals who are interested in your project or research area and have had experience working with you. Potential group members could include individuals from your undergraduate, graduate, and postgraduate work. Consider advisors, mentors, and colleagues as potential project consultants, co-investigators, or consortium partners.

DEVELOPING A PROACTIVE SYSTEM

Once you have your five-year grants plan written, you are ready to begin the process of developing grant support. Many well-intended grantseekers begin the process by creating a proposal and searching for a grantor, or they learn of grants with a fast approaching deadline and try to get a proposal completed quickly. Advances in technology such as electronic proposal submittal actually encourage last minute proposal preparation. However, this is called reactive grantseeking, and results in high rates of rejection (80 to 90 percent).

By contrast, proactive grantseeking is a positive step toward success. By spending a little time researching a prospective grantor before writing and submitting a proposal, proactive grantseekers will uncover information that will help them increase their chances of acceptance by

- determining what the grantor is really looking for (the grantor's hidden agenda)
- predicting their likelihood of success before investing additional time
- tailoring their proposal to the funding source's needs

The difference between reactive and proactive grantseekers is *when* and *how* they invest their time and how these variables influence their success rate. Proactive grantseekers put in small amounts of time *throughout* the grantseeking process. The analogy to the age-old story of the rabbit and the turtle applies here. The reactive grantseeker (rabbit) make a Herculean attempt at developing a proposal, racing against time (and the deadline), only to lose to the proactive grantseeker (turtle) who has been plodding along the grants trail using an energy-efficient and ultimately successful strategy.

The first step in taking a proactive approach to grantseeking is for you to extricate yourself from the notion that your proposal's approach is the only one (or at least the best) way to move ahead. In reality, there are many approaches that could result in the changes your proposal suggests. By neglecting to develop several approaches to discuss with the potential grantor during preproposal contact, grantseekers limit their ability to uncover any preferences or hidden agendas that the grantor may have. Those grantseekers who have rigid ideas about their projects and exactly how they will be carried out miss the opportunity to learn what the grantor is really looking for. In addition, their proposals often suffer from a narrow viewpoint, focusing on what the grantseeker wants instead of the needs of the prospective grantor. This myopic approach can be contrasted with the equally ill-fated general approach. General proposals are designed to fit almost any possible grantor's guidelines, lack specificity, and are not targeted to the needs of the grantor. Whether myopic or general, proposals resulting from these approaches are easily recognizable because of a preponderance of statements beginning with "We want," "We need," "We propose to do."

Unfortunately, this self-focus has been aided by the use of computers for researching grantors. In many cases the overzealous and self-focused grantseeker will secure printouts of all the grantors who have funded projects even remotely related to theirs and then send the same proposal to every grantor on the list. What these grantseekers overlook is that the shotgun approach results in high rates of rejection and negative positioning with funding sources.

Whenever your proposals (or those of your nonprofit organization) result in failure, you risk positioning your organization in a negative manner. Of course, grantseeking will always result in a certain percentage of rejection. That is bound to happen. But how much rejection can you, the grantseeker, and your organization afford before the very appearance of your name on a proposal elicits a negative reaction from grantors? What is the success rate you need to achieve to avoid negative positioning? Anything less than a 50-percent success rate could result in negative positioning. An 80- or 90-percent failure rate could not possibly create a positive image for your organization with the grantor's staff or reviewers.

Embracing a proactive approach to grantseeking means starting the process early. This enables the grantseeker to employ quality assurance techniques to increase success and avoid negative positioning. A proactive grantseeker has enough time to conduct a quality circle exercise or mock review of his or her proposal before submittal, using the same review system that is to be used by the grantor. This technique helps to insure that the submitted proposal represents the grantseeker's best effort. By starting early and finishing your proposal a week before the grantor's deadline, you will be able to have your proposal read and scored by friendly role players who can pick up any errors before your proposal is submitted for its real review. While chapter 12 provides details on how to use a grants quality circle to improve a proposal, the simple fact is that you will not have enough time to use this invaluable technique unless you become a proactive grantseeker! Exhibit 1.3 shows what kinds of reviewer comments are likely to be received when proactive grantseeking is abandoned.

Many reactive grantseekers resort to a "one proposal fits all grantors" strategy because they run out of time and mistakenly believe that the shotgun approach will be time efficient. After all, if you shoot enough times, you've got to hit something eventually, right? In reality, the shotgun approach seldom works in hunting or grantseeking, and ends up meaning nothing when proposal after proposal is rejected. In my early attempts at grantseeking, I quickly learned that the best strategy for winning grants was to tailor each and every proposal to the perspective of the potential grantor. After a reactive grantseeking failure, I remembered a theory I learned as a psychology major and applied it to grantseeking. Thirty years later, I can say unequivocally that this theory has helped me develop millions of dollars in successful projects and research for nonprofit organizations. I share this theory with you to help you approach grantseeking from the grantor's perspective, and to provide you with the basis for developing a tailored proposal to each grantor.

FESTINGER'S THEORY OF COGNITIVE DISSONANCE

Leon Festinger developed the theory of cognitive dissonance[2] to explain how individuals learn and assimilate information. In brief, Festinger states that each of us sees, hears, and remembers what we already believe to be true. When we are presented with information that is contrary to what we believe to be true, dissonance or static is created in our information-receiving systems. To reduce this static and maintain homeostasis, we discount the new information. While Festinger was interested in how individuals learn, the theory of cognitive dissonance has great application to grantseeking.

VALUES-BASED GRANTSEEKING

By expanding Festinger's theory, I developed the values glasses theory and the concepts of values-based grantseeking. A common mistake of grantseekers is to write their proposals based on their own values. They assume that their prospective

---

APPLICATION NUMBER:

Technology Innovation Challenge Grant Program
Individual Technical Review Form - <u>Tier 1</u>

<u>SUMMARY ASSESSMENT</u>

Please summarize your overall thoughts about the application in light of your previous
comments on "significance" and "feasibility", and mention any important points on
which the application is unclear so that these points can be raised with the applicant.

   The conversational style was welcome and easy reading. For once there was an absense
of educational "buzz words." However, watch out for too much informal style. (The phrase
"parents don't have a clue.")
   Don't forget to identify acronyms, GSAMS was only identified in a letterhead in the
appendix.
   It is extremely important to proofread your application. There were no less than nineteen
grammar and punctuation errors. If simple details like these are not corrected as a matter of
professionalism, can one reasonably be expected to properly manage several million dollars?

OVERALL GRADE _____ B_____
A=high, B=medium, C=low

SAMPLE REVIEWER'S COMMENTS

EXHIBIT 1.3

---

grantors have similar values to themselves, and that they will read their proposals from their (the grantseeker's) point of view. This is a mistake. Using a proposal to try to change the values of a grantor or to show that the funding source's
granting pattern is unenlightened is another mistake that usually results in dissonance and rejection. Some grantseekers also make the mistake of using their own
vocabulary in proposals, forgetting that grantors will read and react to proposals
based upon their (the grantors) vocabulary.

Figure 1.1 illustrates the grantseeker's predicament. As a proactive, values-based
grantseeker he or she must strive to get the facts through the lenses (filters) of the
grantor over to the brain of the grantor that controls the hand, arm, and money
(check) the grantseeker wants.

The ensuing chapters are all based on uncovering the information you need to
understand the values of the grantor so that your proposal can be written and presented in such a way that it reinforces your prospective grantor's values. Values-
based grantseeking entails uncovering information about the grantor that will help

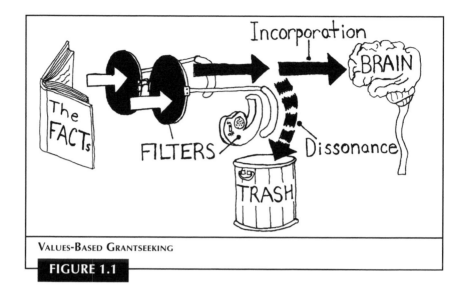

VALUES-BASED GRANTSEEKING

FIGURE 1.1

you develop an appreciation and understanding of the grantor's values glasses. Once you have this information, you can use it as a guide to your approach, helping you select the right needs data and vocabulary to include in your proposal and insuring that you present a compelling case for funding.

Successful grantseekers avoid jeopardizing their chances at being funded by being sensitive to the values of the grantor. They do not pander to the reviewer, or wrap a wolf in sheep's clothing, but their approach to proposal preparation does reflect their knowledge of the grantor and ultimately, respect for the grantor's values.

If you follow this theory through, it will be obvious to your prospective grantor that you know what the grantor values and that rejecting your proposal would be a repudiation of their (the grantor's) own values. In fact, not funding you would be unpleasant, create internal static, and produce dissonance!

This theory does not apply just to private funding sources (foundations and corporations). Proposals to federal and state grantors are read by staff and peer reviewers who are also likely to give the best scores to proposals tailored to their beliefs. In fact, reviewers selected by government bureaucrats are likely to be professionals who have perspectives and values similar to those of the government bureaucrats.

To be truly successful, your proactive grants system should be based on a triple win—meeting the needs of the grantor, your organization, and you, the proposal developer. You need not invest more time in the process than the reactive grantseeker; you just need to invest your time earlier and more wisely. Instead of a 72-hour, last-minute, Herculean proposal effort, invest 10 hours per month for seven months. This will give you plenty of time to research the grantor, make preproposal contact, and construct a tailored proposal—all without the stress of a last-minute effort!

Now that you know some of the advantages of proactive grantseeking, you have come to your first major grantseeking crossroads. Yogi Berra once said, "When you come to a fork in the road, take one,"[3] and you will. I have always preferred having a plan and have told all my students that if you don't have a plan, any road will get you there. The only problem is you won't know when you are there. I hope you have a plan and are ready to move into the next phase of successful grantseeking. The projects, programs, and research you propose are important to you, your career, and to the fields you will impact.

If there is one lesson that grantseeking has taught me in the millions of dollars of grant-funded projects I have completed in my 30-year career, it is that you can make a living doing a lot of things, but what is truly important is making a living while making a difference. If the strategies outlined in the following chapters help you move toward your vision then I have reached my goal in writing this book.

NOTES

1. Denis Waitley, *The Psychology of Winning* (New York: Berkley Books, 1984).
2. Leon Festinger, *A Theory of Cognitive Dissonance* (Stanford, CA: Stanford University Press, 1962).
3. Yogi Berra, *The Yogi Book* (New York: Workman Publishing, 1999), p. 48.

CHAPTER 2

Developing and Documenting
the Need for Your Project
Creating Urgency and a
Compelling Proposal

Before you become overly involved and focused on your project or research, step back and look at the larger picture. Your proposal will be evaluated against hundreds, sometimes thousands, of others. Yours must cause the grantors/reviewers to motivate themselves to select it over the others. Your proposal must present a clear vision of what exists now compared to what ought to or could be in the problem area you seek to reduce. The motivation for funding your proposal over another's is directly related to how well you document the gap that exists and how compelling you make the case for closing or reducing the gap. Sometimes referred to a search of relevant literature, this is not a list studies but, rather, a carefully laid-out plan that demonstrates what has been done in the field to date, and documents the need to take the next step to move ahead.

Failure to document need most often results from the self-focus of the proposal writer. Committed proposal writers frequently believe that everyone, including the potential grantor, is as highly motivated as they are to solve a particular problem, so they move directly to presenting the project/solution before ever establishing the need for a solution. Do not assume that the grantor knows the need in your field. Even if the proposal reader is an expert, your efforts to describe the most relevant studies and advances demonstrate *your* expertise and command of the most current data and reinforce the motivation for the grantor to reduce the problem.

To begin developing the need or problem statement for your proposal, answer the following questions:

- What is the problem that requires a solution?
- What will happen if this needs area is not addressed?

- What is the gap between what exists now and what ought to be or would be if the knowledge existed to solve the problem?
- Why should grant funds be used *now* to solve the problem and reduce the gap?

Many grantseekers make a fatal error when answering these questions. While they are well intended, they often are so over zealous that they look at the problem in a myopic manner. For example, a grantseeker who sought funds for computers to bring technology and the Internet to her school felt she had documented the gap and developed a compelling need by stating the age of her school's existing equipment and mentioning how other schools already had the computers her school needed. What she didn't realize is that she couldn't possibly show a compelling need by simply documenting what kind of and how many computers her school currently had and what and how many they wanted. In brief, all equipment, from technological to playground, is a means to an end, not the end. The gap was not what her school didn't have compared to what it needed. The true need for the computers and for technology should have been documented through an explanation of how the equipment and technology would allow her school and its students to function in improved ways. The end should not have been presented as a room full of equipment but, rather, increased reading or math scores or better preparation for the job market.

While the above example may seem obvious, the same problem often occurs when the prospective grantee desires a building. Architecture plans and the documentation of a leaky roof in the existing building are not reasons enough for a grantor to fund a new building. In this instance, the gap should be created by documenting the difference between what can be done in the existing facility and what more a new facility would enable the organization to do. In other words, how would a new building facilitate increased programs and services, and better solve the problems of the organization's clients? The building (or lack of it) is not the problem. It is the means to an end, and the end is what needs to be documented.

Even a grant for playground equipment can fall prey to mistaken needs documentation. The need is not the absence or condition of existing equipment. Again, equipment is a means to an end—whether its playground equipment or computers. What needs to be demonstrated is what the new playground equipment will allow kids to do that they cannot do now. To create a compelling need, the grantseeker needs to demonstrate things like how many kids will be affected, how the playground equipment will impact their physical and mental health, and what alternatives for their time exist now.

Researchers are faced with a similar dilemma. The need is not the research they propose to accomplish but, rather, the benefits of their research and the problems it can be used to solve. Even pure bench research must seek to close a gap of knowledge in the field. The documentation of the need must include a cohesive explanation of how current research has driven the researcher to ask additional questions, seek to test other relationships and advance the field so that new and even more poignant questions can be asked.

Researchers may focus on studies, facts, and/or statistics to document need, while those seeking project grants may have to look beyond facts and statistics to case studies or examples to present a clearer picture of the problem and the benefits to be derived from solving it. In either instance, needs documentation should be gathered before contacting a funding source or writing a proposal. Just remember, your opinion does not count. You have to *prove* that something must be done.

Researchers should be wary of becoming so impassioned in the documentation of their project that they run the risk of being perceived as arrogant or disrespectful of their fellow scientists. Imagine you are writing a proposal for a research project, and you have decided to document the need by citing relevant research in the field (search of the relevant literature). This is not difficult for you to do because you consistently read the journals and major publications in your field and you actually set aside a specific time each week to review them. After performing a thorough search of the studies and articles in your field and gathering many resources, it is now time to select the citations to include in your proposal. You want to select only the best citations (those that present a clear, concise, and current picture of the problem) and be careful not to include so many that you overwhelm the reader and cloud or confuse the real issue or problem. Besides making sure that your search documents both the urgency of the problem and your command of the current knowledge in the field, consider which of the following two statements to include.

- Statement 1—In their research, both Smith and Jones overlooked the importance of "X" and failed to explore its relevance to "Y."
- Statement 2—Smith and Jones's pioneer work brought a focus to the field and advanced the understanding of "ABC." Their work also revealed several new factors that, while not the main focus of *their* research, now present a potential link to "D, E, and F."

The first statement tends to minimize the work of Smith and Jones and even makes them appear ignorant because they either didn't see the variable or understand its importance. The second statement tries to depict the work of Smith and Jones as advancing the field and ultimately allowing other researchers to push forward. Before you make your decision, remember that the real Smith and Jones or one of their graduate students, doctoral students, or friends may be on the grantor's review committee. Keep sight of the fact that the last thing you want to do is cause dissonance in the reviewers.

Be aware also that you could cause dissonance by citing references, researchers, or data that the reviewers do not favor. While the reviewers' reactions to specific information are not totally in your control, the more you know about the values

What data do we have to document the problem? (What exists now)

What information do we need to create a compelling and accurate assessment of the problem?

What information do we have to provide a clear picture of the desired state of affairs that should or could exist? (What ought to be in the future)

What will happen in the field if the problem is not addressed in a timely manner? (The urgency and motivation)

Which of the following approaches to assessment and documentation of need do you think appeals the most to the grantor?

Key Informant:	_____	Statistical Analysis:	_____
Community Forum:	_____	Survey Data:	_____
Case Study:	_____	Studies:	_____

Data to be gathered	How data will be gathered	Who will do it	Date due	Cost	Consortium agencies involved

NEEDS ASSESSMENT WORKSHEET

EXHIBIT 2.1

and background of the reviewers and decision makers, the better able you will be to avoid this problem.

CREATING A GAP BETWEEN WHAT EXISTS NOW IN THE FIELD AND WHAT COULD OR SHOULD BE

The statement of the problem that your project seeks to impact must be clear, concise, and possess a futuristic reference to why the problem needs to be addressed

TABLE 2.1

NEEDS ASSESSMENT TABLE

Key Informant - Solicit information from individuals whose testimony or description of what exists for the client population or state of affairs is credible because of their experience and/or expertise. Includes elected officials, agency heads (police chiefs, juvenile delinquency case workers, parole officers, etc.) Funders may value their opinions/insights.	• Easy to design. • Costs very little. • You control input by what you ask and whom. • Excellent way to position your organization with important people (shows you're working on common problems/concerns).	• Most funding sources know you have selected and included comments from those individuals sympathetic to your cause. You may be leaving out parts of the population who have not been visible and caused problems that were noticed and commented on.
Community Forum - Host or sponsor public meetings. You publicize the opportunity to present views of the populace and invite key individuals to speak. Funder may like the grassroots image this creates.	• Easy to arrange. • Costs very little. • Increases your visibility in the community. • Promotes active involvement of the populace.	• Site of forum has profound effect on amount and type of representation. • You can lose control of the group and have a small vocal minority slant that turns meeting into a forum for complaints.
Case Studies - An excellent approach to assist the funder in appreciating what representative members of the client population are up against. Select individuals from the needs population or client group and provide an analytical, realistic description of their problem/situation, their need for your services, etc.	• Easy to arrange. • Costs very little. • Increases sensitivity to the client's "real world." • Very moving and motivating.	• Your selection of a "typical" client may be biased and represent a minority of cases. • You must describe one "real" person - not a composite of several. The anonymity of the person must be ensured.

TABLE 2.1

NEEDS ASSESSMENT TABLE *(continued)*

Key Informant - Solicit information from individuals whose testimony or description of what exists for the client population or state of affairs is credible because of their experience and/or expertise. Includes elected officials, agency heads(police chiefs, juvenile delinquency case workers, parole officers, etc.) Funders may value their opinions/insights.	• Easy to design. • Costs very little. • You control input by what you ask and whom. • Excellent way to position your organization with important people (shows you're working on common problems/concerns).	• Most funding sources know you have selected and included comments from those individuals sympathetic to your cause. You may be leaving out parts of the population who have not been visible and caused problems that were noticed and commented on.
Community Forum - Host or sponsor public meetings. You publicize the opportunity to present views of the populace and invite key individuals to speak. Funder may like the grassroots image This creates.	• Easy to arrange. • Costs very little. • Increases your visibility in the community. • Promotes active involvement of the populace.	• Site of forum has profound effect on amount and type of representation. • You can lose control of the group and have a small vocal minority slant that turns meeting into a forum for complaints.
Case Studies - An excellent approach to assist the funder in appreciating what representative members of the client population are up against. Select individuals from the needs population or client group and provide an analytical, realistic description of their problem/situation, their need for your services, etc.	• Easy to arrange. • Costs very little. • Increases sensitivity to the client's "real world." • Very moving and motivating.	• Your selection of a "typical" client may be biased and represent a minority of cases. • You must describe one "real" person - not a composite of several. The anonymity of the person must be ensured.

now! Complete the Needs Assessment Worksheet (exhibit 2.1) to help you develop your statement of the problem.

Grantors seek out and select those proposals that show the greatest potential for impacting the problem they are interested in, and closing the gap between what exists now and what could or should be. Whether it is subjects that are affected, or time, resources, or effort, you must document the importance of moving toward closing the gap.

Most government grantors, and some private grantors who have a required proposal format, place a specific value on the different proposal components including need documentation. Government grantors usually have a scoring system that they instruct their reviewers to employ in evaluating proposals. While research-ing these review systems and point values will be discussed in detail in part 2, needs documentation is infamous for costing prospective grantees valuable points.

In one proposal I worked on and submitted to a foundation, I demonstrated how the problems related to new teachers, improperly trained in technology could magnify significantly over a few years. By graduating 600 new but improperly trained teachers each year, there would be 3,000 improperly trained teachers in the workforce in five years. Each of these teachers could impact an estimated 300 students in one year, for a five-year total of 90,000 students. Imagine, this is 90,000 students who will not be exposed to technology that could enhance their interest in learning and their future employment!

Does your gap have the potential to grow with time? Will the costs increase if not dealt with now? How important and compelling is it to act now in solving your problem of interest?

NEEDS ASSESSMENT APPROACHES

There are six basic approaches for assessing and documenting need:

1. Key informant: Quotations from people who know about the problem or are experts in the field.
2. Community forum: Public meetings to get testimony on the problem.
3. Case studies: Examples of clients in a need population.
4. Statistical analysis: Use of data from public records.
5. Survey: Random selection of population to answer questions related to the need.
6. Studies: Literature search of published documents on the subject.

The needs assessment table and needs assessment worksheet (see table 2.1 and exhibit 2.1) will help you decide which approach to adopt for your project. Cor-porate and foundation grantors may respond to best case studies or examples of the human side of the need, while government funders usually prefer a needs state-ment based on facts and studies. By having a variety of needs assessment tech-niques at your disposal, you will enhance your ability to tailor your proposal to a specific grantor.

Whether the potential grantor understands the importance of addressing the problem and ultimately enacts your solution is a function of how compelling your needs documentation is.

After you, the grantseeker, document a need, ask yourself the following ques-tion: Would you dedicate your own money to closing this gap between what we know now and what we could know or do? Many grantseekers say no to this ques-tion, but they are happy to take someone else's money. Compelling and motivating proposals come from grantseekers who truly believe that their project is critical to closing the gap, and would use their own money if they had it.

NEEDS ASSESSMENT GRANTS

If your completion of exhibit 2.1 demonstrates that your proposal is weak in the area of needs documentation, or if it becomes difficult to locate studies, literature or data to document the problem you seek funds to solve, you may find that you need to attract a small foundation or corporate needs assessment grant to help you. Yes, it is possible to locate a funding source that will value the fact that its modest investment will allow you to develop an excellent needs statement and ultimately make it possible for you to attract larger grants from other funding sources for conducting your project. A needs assessment grant also can help to position you as the resident expert in your field and provide you with valuable insights into the problem. Since you are only able to measure the success of your project on how much of the gap is closed because of your intervention, a needs assessment grant also may provide you with an improved tool to use in the measurement of the need. See chapters 19 and 20 for information on how to locate potential funding sources for small needs assessment grants.

CHAPTER 3

Finding Time to Write Grant Proposals
Organizing a Proposal Development Workbook

After working with nonprofit organizations for 30 years to increase staff involvement in grantseeking, I have determined that the two major obstacles to grantseeking are finding the time to get involved and developing a proactive approach. Most grantseekers are expected to prepare proposals in their spare time and carry out all their existing job responsibilities until the proposal is funded. While there are some job descriptions that include proposal preparation as one of the job responsibilities, these are usually jobs in state or regional government agencies, where federal grant moneys are passed through to local grantseekers. There are rarely personnel at nonprofit organizations, including colleges and universities, whose main job responsibility is to write grants for other staff members, faculty, and so on. Even when individuals are expected to attract outside funding for tenure or advancement, they hardly ever get release time to write their proposals. The way the system seems to work is that the grantseeker writes the proposal, gets it funded, and then is given release time to carry it out. Then, while carrying it out, the successful grantseeker is expected to find the time to create yet another proposal!

Many creative and well-intentioned grantseekers develop innovative approaches to solving problems. They can often cite the literature that documents their command of the current state of knowledge in the field, but they have a problem putting the need and their idea together in a proposal. When asked why, they often say they cannot find the time.

The steps necessary to produce a grant application are logical and follow a definite order. However, many people are overwhelmed by the *total* amount of work involved in proposal preparation. Because of this, they procrastinate and avoid approaching proposal development until it is too late to do an adequate job.

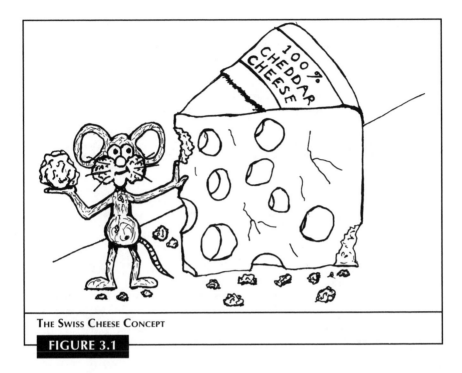

THE SWISS CHEESE CONCEPT

FIGURE 3.1

Allen Lakein was one of the early leaders in time management. In his book *How to Get Control of Your Time and Your Life,* Lakein presents a technique that you can use anytime you face a large task such as getting your grant writing process under control and organized.[1] His Swiss cheese concept suggests dividing a difficult task into smaller, less overwhelming parts. Lakein's example of a mouse confronted by the job of carrying away a huge piece of cheese is analogous to a grantseeker presented with the prospect of creating a grant proposal. Both the mouse and the grantseeker feel overwhelmed! To avoid this feeling, Lakein suggests that the mouse should divide the big piece of cheese into smaller parts. By eating small pieces of cheese at a time, making the cheese into Swiss cheese, the mouse can divide the task into manageable parts so that final task of carrying the cheese away is less onerous (see figure 3.1).

I have applied this concept to grantseeking and developed a set of tabs that can be placed in a three-ring binder to create a Swiss cheese book (referred to professionally as the proposal development workbook; see exhibit 3.1). I have divided the task of developing a proposal into steps, with each step corresponding to one tab in the Swiss cheese book. By addressing each step in the grantseeking process, you, the proposal developer, can organize your approach, control the process, and lower your anxiety level. By nibbling at your proposal a piece at a time, you will not be overwhelmed by the process and you will ultimately save time and increase your success rate.

**INTRODUCTION TO YOUR
YOUR PROPOSAL DEVELOPMENT WORKBOOK
(SWISS CHEESE BOOK)**

The grants mechanism is one method to unlock the world's largest reserve of collective and specific genius and pits that reserve against the multitude of problems that plague the modern world.

By supplying moneys to solve a problem, funding sources, be they federal, foundation or corporate, benefit from competition amongst the best minds and groups who seek their funds and ultimately create innovative solutions and new research techniques, and apply their methodology to the test of reality.

Funding sources exist because individuals have created them by acts of commission that represent various motivations and bias views of what the needs are. **Each funding source has a certain perspective** on what it **wants for its money** - a perspective based on its values and how it interprets its charge as a granting entity. Each funding source (corporation, foundation or government agency) has determined that there is a **NEED** to invest the money entrusted to it in ways that reflect the goals of the organization.

You, as a grant seeker, have a **NEED** for financial resources to support projects aimed to address specific and critical problems. The key to successful grant seeking is matching up your particular need for financial resources with the need (s) of funding sources to invest their financial resources in projects such as yours and produce the mutual desired results. Successful grant seeking requires that you carry out your "homework" **before** you write your proposal. All to often, grant seekers begin the process with a proposal outlining **what they want**! Successful grant seekers know that the writing of the proposal occurs much later in the process - after they know what the funding source **wants**.

Your grant Proposal Development Workbook is your Swiss Cheese Book. The steps involved in preparing for and producing a grant application or proposal are simple and follow a definite order. The design of this notebook is based upon a systematic approach to grant seeking described by **David G. Bauer** in his *"How To" Grants Manual.*

The "Swiss Cheese" Concept
Many individuals find the grant seeking process complex, tedious and difficult to deal with. They just want the grant money to do what they want! They get overwhelmed with the enormity of the total task and the time and planning required. They frequently delay starting the application process until it is too late to do an adequate job.

One way of approaching the task of applying for grants is to be proactive. Allen Lakein, the author of *How to Get Control of Your Time and Your Life* uses the analogy of a mouse confronted with a large piece of cheese. The mouse does not attempt to eat or move the cheese in one large piece. Instead, it eats holes in the cheese, devouring a little at a time until it is all gone. The same applies to grant seeking. **APPROACH EACH PART OF THE GRANT SEEKING PROCESS A LITTLE AT A TIME AND BEFORE YOU KNOW IT, THE PROCESS WILL BE COMPLETED!**

INTRODUCTION TO YOUR PROPOSAL DEVELOPMENT WORKBOOK

EXHIBIT 3.1

I have found the Swiss cheese concept a great help in making the grants process more understandable and manageable. In fact, I suggest that you construct a proposal development workbook for each of the major problem areas for which your organization is planning to seek grant funding.

For example, imagine that your program is working with senior citizens. You might construct four proposal development workbooks: one for the elderly and transportation, one for the elderly and health, one for the elderly and nutrition, and one for the elderly and recreation. Each proposal development workbook would be placed in a three-ring binder with each tab acting as a divider for one of the tasks involved in developing a full-scale proposal. When you read a research article on nutrition and the senior citizen, you would make a copy of the article, abstract, or summary and place the copy under the tab for "Documenting Need." To avoid making this section of your workbook too voluminous, place a copy of the summary or abstract of the article instead of the entire article in your workbook, but be sure to include a reference as to where the entire article has been filed.

When politicians or community leaders visit your organization and express their concern for the elderly, you could ask them for a letter of support for your group's work and whether they would be willing to serve on your advisory committee. Copies of their letters of support would be filed under the tab labeled "Advisory Committees and Advocacy," as would their names, addresses, and telephone numbers.

As you can see, proposal development workbooks act as files for proposal ideas. Most potential funding sources would be very impressed by a prospective grantee who responds to a question by referring to a proposal development workbook instead of fumbling through a tattered pile of file folders and loose pages of notes.

One grantseeker using this process called our offices to tell us how helpful her proposal development workbook was during a visit with a funding source. When asked why the funding source should give the money to her organization instead of one of the hundreds of other applicants, she opened her proposal development workbook to the tab on uniquenesses and presented a list of 50 reasons why her organization was uniquely suited to carry out the proposed project, with the top five reasons circled. The grantor was quite impressed.

The proposal development workbook is one step in the process of making your grants effort more cost- and time-efficient. If you thought that proposal preparation was a Herculean last-minute task, a 72-hour miracle, think again. You will find that the application of the Swiss cheese concept and the development of proposal development workbooks will provide you with an organized approach to proposal preparation, an approach that makes effective use of your time. In addition, this approach will help you improve your organization's image with funding sources (known as *positioning* in marketing talk) by enabling you to present your organization as an honest, organized, well-planned agency.

Those grantseekers who prepare proposals overnight run the risk of damaging their organization's image in the eyes of funding sources. One hastily written proposal with budget transpositions and typographical errors can affect your organization's image for many years.

The construction of proposal development workbooks is a proactive process that can work for you and your organization. Once this approach is initiated, I am sure you will find it invaluable for promoting the development of project ideas, locating funding sources, and writing proposals. I have personally found that, in addition to impressing funders, the use of a Swiss cheese book reduces the time it takes to create a proposal by approximately 50 percent.

Review the list of suggested proposal development tabs after you have read this manual. You may want to change, eliminate, or add some areas to tailor the concept to your organization. The following are suggested tabs:

- Introduction
- Documenting Need
- Organizing the Process
- Developing Ideas
- Redefining Ideas
- Uniquenesses
- Advisory Committees and Advocacy
- Choosing the Marketplace

In addition, you will want tabs to organize the research and contacts in the marketplace you choose.

For government funding sources, consider the following additional tabs:

- Researching Government Marketplace
- Characteristics: Government Grants
- Contacting Government Sources
- Planning Federal Proposals
- Improving Federal Proposals
- Submission: Public Sources
- Decision: Public Sources
- Follow-up: Government Sources

For private funding sources, you also may include the following tabs:

- Differences: Public versus Private Sources
- Recording Research
- Foundation Research Tools
- Researching Corporate Grants
- Contacting Private Sources
- Letter Proposal
- Submission: Private Sources
- Decision: Private Sources
- Follow-up: Private Sources

The following chapters include worksheets, letters, and forms that could be placed behind each of the tabs in your proposal development workbook.

Grantseekers also can create a computer file for each of their proposal development tabs. While some may prefer to do this, a computer disk may be difficult to use with a potential funding source during a visit. You will still need a hard copy of your proposal development workbook. In addition, some proposal developers may find that arranging hard copies of certain sections of their workbook, like the studies to be included under the "Documenting Need" tab, will help them develop their approach.

NOTE

1. Allen Lakein, *How to Get Control of Your Time and Your Life* (New York: American Library, 1974).

CHAPTER 4

Developing Grant-Winning Ideas

From Research to Model Projects

The underlying theme of this manual is that when you ask a funding source for grant support you must look at your organization and your request from the funding source's perspective. This concept supports the golden rule of grantseeking: he or she who has the gold rules. The least the prospective grantee can do is try to determine what the grantor values, likes, and dislikes, avoiding those areas that are potentially negative and highlighting those that appeal to the grantor's interests and make the prospective grantee look competent.

The process outlined in this chapter recommends that you develop several alternative approaches to the problem you have documented. There is usually more than one way to perform your research or develop your model project. To increase your chances of selecting the right approach for inclusion, you should be able to discuss more than one way of solving the problem with the prospective funding source before submitting your proposal. Even the briefest preproposal contact could give you the insight necessary to tailor your approach to the funding source. In addition, discussing several approaches with the prospective funding source before selecting one for your proposal will increase your credibility and demonstrate that your favored approach is based on careful analysis, not the personal biases and preferences of you or your staff. The worksheets in this chapter will help you

- generate more thought out and fundable ideas by brainstorming your approaches with colleagues and key individuals on your grants advisory committee

- develop a system to summarize your best ideas and assess organizational commitment to the project

- conduct a cost-benefit analysis of your best ideas that highlights the differences, strengths, and weaknesses of each approach
- develop institutional support for your proposal early on in the grantseeking process so that you can avoid last-minute problems at submission time

BRAINSTORMING MORE FUNDABLE PROPOSAL IDEAS

One of the best techniques for developing sound proposals and alternative solutions to problems is to brainstorm proposal ideas with staff, peers, and advisory committee members. Inviting others to share in idea generation taps the collective genius of the group and builds support for your proposal. In fact, the brainstorming process can even promote the feeling that your project is "everyone's" project, so that colleagues and volunteers will me more willing and eager to work at night and on weekends in your effort to promote a proactive approach that exceeds the deadline.

Many researchers are reluctant to share their ideas and creative solutions because they fear that they will be stolen by colleagues. In the majority of the cases this fear is unwarranted. Most colleagues can be trusted, and discussing proposal ideas and solutions with them can help eliminate the development of narrow, self-focused grant ideas. In addition, more and more funders are interested in funding consortium grants, and brainstorming ideas can provide an ideal way to foster the development of joint funding.

Brainstorming is a simple technique for quickly generating a long list of creative ideas. Since you may be employing this technique as a vehicle to create partners and consortia, it is critical that you share ideas in a noncompetitive forum. To obtain maximum benefit from the process:

1. Break your participants into groups of five to eight.
2. Appoint a neutral group leader to facilitate the process (encouraging and prodding other members, checking the time).
3. Appoint a recorder.
4. Set a time limit (10 minutes will be plenty).
5. State one question or problem (e.g., reducing the number of high school dropouts, nutritional needs of pregnant adolescents, reducing alcoholism in the elderly, increasing awareness of wildlife preservation).
6. Ask group members to generate and present as many possible solutions to the problem as they can within the time limit.
7. Encourage group members to piggyback on each other's ideas (suggesting a new idea that adds to one already given).
8. Record all answers, combining those that are similar.
9. Avoid any evaluation or discussion of ideas until the process is over; this rule is critical for productive brainstorming. The recorder can ask to have an idea repeated but should allow no comments, negative or positive (e.g., "We can't do that!" "That's stupid!" or "I love your thinking.") from others.

COST-BENEFIT ANALYSIS WORKSHEET

An important aspect of any fundable idea is its economic feasibility. Funding sources want to know that you have chosen methods that will produce the best results for the least amount of money. The cost-benefit analysis worksheet (see exhibit 4.1) will help you demonstrate economic accountability.

Column One. Place brief descriptions of each approach you are considering in column one. For example, a project to feed senior citizens could range from a meals-on-wheels program, to group meals, to a food cooperative of the elderly. Choose two or three possible approaches that will meet the goals of the project from your brainstormed list of ideas.

Column Two. Record the estimated price or cost of each idea or set of methods in column two. This figure can be taken off of your preproposal summary and approval form (see exhibit 4.2) and is intended to be an estimate of the cost of the approach, not a final budget. One way to ensure variety in the approaches and in the amount of funds required is to select the approach you favor and determine how you would have to alter if you could have only one-half of the amount requested.

Column Three. Use columns three and four only if your project involves subjects. For evaluating research protocols go directly to column five. Use column three to estimate the number of people who will be affected by a particular approach. Remember to roll out the benefits over several years and over the life of the equipment.

Column Four. Enter the estimated cost per person or client served. This is essential, since funding sources are apprehensive about sponsoring projects that possess an unrealistic cost per individual served. Projects with a high cost per person are considered a waste of money by many funders, so grantseekers may have great difficulty securing continued or follow-up funding for such projects.

Column Five. Summarize the advantages of each idea or set of methods in this column. By having this information on hand, some funders may actually consider supporting a more costly approach because they can see how the outlined advantages outweigh the expense.

Column Six. In this column, outline the disadvantages or drawbacks to each approach. This demonstrates your honesty, which will increase both your credibility with funders and their confidence in you. Funders know that each approach has pitfalls or variables that must be controlled.

Use this worksheet each time you refine your project ideas and bring completed cost-benefit analysis worksheets to preliminary meetings with funding officials. They will be impressed by the fact that you considered their financial interest while designing your project.

1 Summary of Idea and Methodology	2 Cost	3 No. of Persons Served	4 Cost per Person Served	5 Positive Points	6 Negative Points

COST-BENEFIT ANALYSIS WORKSHEET

EXHIBIT 4.1

Remember that many grant officials are executives of profit-making companies. They are very sensitive about maintaining cost efficiency in all of the investments they make. Take this into account when refining your project ideas; it will help you win more grants.

PREPROPOSAL SUMMARY AND APPROVAL FORM

The preproposal summary and approval form (see exhibit 4.2) could be subtitled "The Grantseeker's Insurance Policy." When you have an idea you would like to seek funding for, fill out this form before writing your full-scale proposal. Then have the form reviewed by your proposal review committee, staff, or administrators, and have it returned to you with their criticisms and suggestions. Make sure the form is reviewed by those people who must sign the final proposal. The purpose of the preproposal summary and approval form is to elicit comments from your organization's leaders and to have them endorse your solution. The form actually provides a vehicle to test the acceptance of your idea or project with your superiors. This is important because they should agree on the use of institutional resources before you invest hours of your time on proposal development. This is

1. Proposed Proposal Director/Project Director: _____

2. Statement of the Problem: _____
   _____

3. Brief Statement of Solution: _____
   _____
   _____

4. How this Project Relates to Our Mission/Goals: _____
   _____

5. Estimated:
   Cost of Project (Total): _____
   Project Duration (Number of Years): _____
   Matching Funds Needed: % _____ $ _____

6. Proposed Project Personnel   Released Time/New Employee
   _____   _____
   _____   _____
   _____   _____

7. Facilities Required:
   Square Feet: _____   Desired Location: _____

8. Equipment Needed for Project (Note if equipment on hand or provided by grant, and if
   any special maintenance will be required): _____
   _____
   _____

9. Signature/Approval (Your signature represents approval of any institutional support outlined
   above): _____

10. Conditional Signature/Approval: _____
   Approval to proceed with full proposal development as long as the proposal developer meets
   the following conditions: _____

   Attach a brief summary/concept paper to this approval form and a list of potential/probable
   funding sources.

PREPREPOSAL SUMMARY AND APPROVAL FORM

EXHIBIT 4.2

especially important when the grant will require matching funds. You need to get
a go ahead before you invest your valuable time. There are many benefits to using
the preproposal summary and approval form:

- Projects can be quickly summarized, so more ideas for projects are generated.
- The increase in the number of ideas lends itself to an increase in the number of fundable projects.

- By generating a number of ideas, you may enhance your ability to see the advantages of combining several good ideas into one great one. Comments from those reviewing the form also may lead the proposal writer in this direction.

- Because at this point in the proposal development process project designers have not invested a great deal of time in writing a proposal for their idea, they are less defensive when their project summary is criticized and suggested improvements are easier to make.

Many organizations find it useful to make the preproposal summary and approval form available electronically to the appropriate individuals as an e-mail attachment. Using this form can be beneficial when proposals must be approved before they are submitted. The preproposal summary and approval form can be used to make sure that the individuals who are required to sign your proposal at submittal time know (in advance) that the proposed project is coming. I recommend that you have key people comment on the areas they question or have a problem supporting. If they have no problems, they can endorse your idea by signing at number 9 of the exhibit. If they have a condition that must be met first, they can list the condition under number 10 of the exhibit and provide their conditional signature. This ensures that the time, money, and resources spent in your proposal preparation process will not be met with a negative response internally and result in failure to have your proposal signed when ready for submittal.

This preproposal summary and review process also allows decision makers to comment on important issues and requirements relative to:

- released time of project director/principal investigator to work on the grant when funded
- matching funds commitment
- space, equipment, support personnel, and resource allocations

Your grantseeking efforts are more likely to receive support and to provide a basis for matching funds and other resource allocations when you apprise your administration of your entrepreneurial grants effort and seek their endorsement in advance of submittal. This will reduce chances of getting a grantor excited about your project, and then not being able to submit your proposal because of internal problems, and a refusal to sign off later by your administration.

CHAPTER 5

Redefining Proposal Ideas
Improving Your Database Research and Finding More Funding Sources

While most grantseekers are well intended, some also tend to be overly self-focused. They develop a case of "we-we disease" as they begin seeking grants. Often their proposals start with, "We need this," or "We want to do that." What they need and what they want becomes the focus of their grantseeking. While a certain degree of self-focus is beneficial in helping prospective grantees move proactively toward proposal development, it also can be counterproductive in their search for appropriate grantors. The more zealous the grantseeker, the more he or she believes that the merits of their proposal will be obvious to just about all grantors.

One of the rudest awakenings in my grantseeking career occurred when a prospective grantor reminded me that his agency was interested more in what it wanted than what my organization wanted and suggested I develop a wider perspective. It's clear to me now that what I had was a case of tunnel vision and grantseeker's myopia! What I have since learned is that by looking at their projects from the perspective of funding sources, grantseekers can unearth more potential grantors and increase their chances of uncovering the less than obvious ones.

KEY SEARCH TERMS

The secret to uncovering the right grantor for your project is to take the time to determine the best key terms or words to use in your funding source database search. Consider the process used to create these databases. The process may consist of one or both of the following scenarios.

- The grantors select key search terms that best describe their project/ research interests, and then provide these terms to the database managers.

- When a grants opportunity is created and knowledge of it is conveyed by newsletter, news release, government publication, and so on, a database manager adds the opportunity to the database and chooses several selector or key words to link grantseekers' searches to the opportunity.

Whether the key search term selection is driven by the grantor or by the best efforts of data input personnel, the key words used may be quite different that the key search terms you would initially use. This is why it is so important to put your biases aside, and think about your project from the grantor's perspective, and how others would describe it. For example, when working with an organization assisting the blind, the grantseekers initially did not want to use the term *blind* as a search term. They did not like *visually impaired*, or *visually challenged* either, and preferred *people without sight*. However, when they used *people without sight* as their key search term, they found no hits. When they used *blind* they uncovered many opportunities. They decided that the use of the word *blind* was not so bad after all as long as it helped them find the money and the right grantor for their project.

You have already begun developing your grants plan, and in doing so, have looked at the values of your project/research. Determining how others would describe the benefits of your project is a natural extension of that exercise.

Redefining your project asks you to go beyond identifying the key terms to use in database searches to considering how you could alter your project slightly to relate it to new and different grantors. This step could significantly increase the number of grantors who could see how your project relates to their needs.

However, the process of redefinition is not intended to take you off track from your grants plan or to turn you into a grants mercenary who will do anything for money regardless of where it takes you and/or your organization. If you do not like the direction redefinition takes you, don't go there. But if redefinition even allows you to locate partial funding for a related project that keeps you, your career, and your grants plan operational, you may want to pursue it rather than be a purist with no funding!

Exhibit 5.1 will help you develop your list of key search terms and assist you in redefining and altering your project, if you so choose, so that you may find your less than obvious potential grantors. Question 1 requires that you revisit your professional grants plan and then list the terms that describe what you believe a funding source would need to value in order to support your project. Question 2 refers to subject areas and asks that you list the terms that could be used to define the topics or proposed areas of work that your grant-funded project could be related to. Question 3 asks you to list other potentially relevant fields. To do so, you need to redefine your project by considering how you could adapt it or change your approach slightly so that you could use terms describing other relevant fields or sub-

1. **Values**: What would a funding source need to value in order to support your project?

2. **Subject Areas**: Subject areas such as employment, environment, mental health, child development, etc. are used as key search terms in many of the computerized grantor databases. List the subject areas that your project can be related to, and/or impact.

3. **Other Potentially Relevant Fields**: How could you change the focus of your project so that it could be potentially related to more subject areas/fields, and what would these areas/fields be?

4. **Constituency Groups**: Many government and private funding sources focus their grant priorities by the constituency groups they want to impact, such as children, at-risk youth, elderly, economically disadvantaged, etc. What constituency group(s) would a funding source have to care about to support your project?

5. **Project Location**: What is the geographic location for your project, and how could you redefine it to better appeal to a grantor's geographic perspective?

   _____

   _____

   City/Community   Region
   County/Borough/Parish   Nation
   State   International

6. **Type of Grant**: What type of grant support are you looking for, and how could you redefine your project to attract funding sources interested in different types of support?

   _____

   _____

   Model/Demonstration Project   Training Grant
   Research Project   Discretionary
   Needs Assessment Grant   Unsolicited Proposal
   Planning Grant   Contract

7. **Consortia/Partners**: What potential partners/collaborators could you involve to assist in redefining your project, and enhancing your funding perspective?

   Potential Partner/Collaborator   Advantage

   _____   _____

   _____   _____

REDEFINITION/KEY SEARCH TERMS WORKSHEET

EXHIBIT 5.1

ject areas in your search, and ultimately provoke additional grantors to be interested in your project. For example, although your subject area may best be described as enhancing the engineering curriculum at your institution, you could decide to deviate slightly from your original approach by also looking at problems related to student ability in math and science. This would allow you to expand your search words to include other relevant fields (such as math and science), and enable you to uncover more potential grantors. Question 4 refers to your constituency groups. The grants mechanism is frequently relied on to solve problems occurring in distinct groups or populations. Through redefinition, your engineering enhancement project could be related to encouraging *minority* or *economically disadvantaged students* to pursue a career in engineering. Question 5 examines project location. Many grantors exhibit a pattern of giving based on a geographic predisposition as well as their granting interests. It is important that you determine where your project would be best conducted and why the geographic location or area you choose is a good place to perform your work. Once you have done this, you should then ask yourself if there are geographic areas similar in subject population, project uniqueness, and so on in other parts of your city/community/county, state, region, the nation, and/or the world. If your project could be redefined as having a national impact, your universe of potential grantors would increase substantially; and if you could make the project international in scope, you could even use the term *international* in your database search for funding sources. Question 6 looks at types of grants and encourages you to think about ways you could redefine your project to attract a different type and hence, more potential grantors. Finally, question 7 asks that you consider your potential collaborators as you redefine your project.

DEVELOPING CORPORATE KEY SEARCH TERMS

Searching for corporate grantors requires a special focus because of the unique way they (corporate grantors) view the grants process and its benefits. Two guiding principles to remember when searching for corporate grantors is that corporations usually prefer to support where they "live" and like to fund projects that can be related to their profits. Use exhibit 5.2 to list search terms associated with:

- hiring, retaining, educating, or training today's workforce as well as the future's
- employee benefits and resulting corporate benefits
- positioning of the corporation as a concerned partner in the field and in your geographic area

In addition, consider whether there is or could be a direct benefit between your project and increasing corporate profits through:

1.	How does your intended project/research relate to the concerns of corporate (for profit) grantors? What are your shared values?

2.	Does or can your project/research provide benefits to corporations in the areas of:
	
	• employee development/skill enhancement?
	  If so, how?
	
	• employee benefits (including health, quality of life, low costs or risks)?
	  If so, how?
	
	• public relations (promotion of a concerned and responsible image in the community)?
	  If so, how?

3.	Can you redefine your project so that it increases corporate profits by:
	
	• promoting a lead to new product development (possible patents, etc.)?
	  If so, explain.
	
	• enhancing current products through new application, redesign, etc.?
	  If so, explain.
	
	• increasing sales through product positioning with clients, students, etc.?
	  If so, explain.

CORPORATE REDEFINITION

EXHIBIT 5.2

- possible patents or new product development
- product enhancement, redesign, or reengineering
- product position/sales

After you have read this chapter and completed the accompanying exhibits, you will begin to understand how you could conduct a database search for grantors that could be as specific as what grantor(s), funded projects related to these key search terms, in the following Zip codes!

CHAPTER 6

Why Grant Funds to You and Your Organization?
Capitalizing on Your Capabilities

Why would a funding source select your organization and you, as the project director or principle investigator, to grant funds to? If your response is, "Because we thought up a fabulous project," you are not looking at your proposal from the grantor's perspective. Even if your approach to solving the problem is creative and dynamic, the grantor's ultimate decision is based on who it believes can best carry out the project. While grantors expect creativity and superior ideas, they make their final decision based on the grantee's *capability* to complete the project.

Most government grant applications will include review criteria that specifically address the capabilities of the project's key personnel and resources. Exhibit 6.1 provides some of the review criteria used by the Department of Education in selecting proposals for funding. The Department of Education, like many other federal agencies and departments, allocates points to how well the applicant documents the quality of its key personnel and the adequacy of its resources. While the points allocated to these two criteria will vary with the program, you will be asked time and time again to document why your organization's resources and you and your partners' skills and background, make you the perfect choice to carry the proposal; and how you have planned for the provision of training in any areas of weakness.

The importance of this documentation is even more evident when you compete for government contracts. In this very competitive process of bidding on the completion of a well-defined deliverable, you must actually include a capability statement that documents your capacity, resources, and related experience in producing the desired end product. Even if you are the lowest bidder for the contract, you can be passed over for a higher, but more capable, bidder.

Quality of Key Personnel   (15pts)

1)   Do the job descriptions adequately reflect skills needed to make the project work?

2)   Are the duties of personnel clearly defined?

3)   What relevant qualifications do the proposed personnel possess, especially the Project
        Director? (Focus on their experience and training in fields related to the objectives of the
        project, though other information may be considered.)

4)   Will proposed personnel need to be trained for the project?

5)   How much time will the proposed personnel actually devote to the project?

6)   To what extent does the applicant encourage employment applications from members of
        traditionally under-represented groups (ethnic or racial minorities, women, handicapped
        persons, elderly persons)?

Adequacy of Resources   (10pts)

1)   Are the proposed facilities adequate for project purposes?

2)   Is the proposed equipment adequate for project purposes?

3)   Does the applicant have access to special sources of experience or expertise?

DEPARTMENT OF EDUCATION PROPOSAL EVALUATION PROCESS

EXHIBIT 6.1

In many instances, making a grantor's first cut means that you are now on a
short list of potential grantees, which includes hundreds as opposed to thousands
of applications. What can you do to enhance your proposal in such a way that it
makes the final award list?

In fear of appearing boastful, many well-intended grantseekers are hesitant to
enhance their proposals by emphasizing their unique qualifications. This is wrong.
While you should not create falsehoods or go around "thumping your chest," you
do need to analyze your institution's capabilities and the characteristics that dif-
ferentiate you from the other applicants. Your prospective grantor needs to know
that your proposal has a greater likelihood of success because of your personal capabilities and your institution's distinct advantages. These advantages are not hy-
pothetical but, rather, the components involved in the successful completion of
the activities and methods that your project or research will utilize.

Every funding source will want to know why you are their best choice for funding, and developing a list of your organization's special qualities or uniquenesses
will go a long way toward convincing a grantor that yours is the right organization
to fund.

WHEN TO USE SIMILARITY AS A UNIQUENESS

In model or demonstration grants, as opposed to research proposals, you may need to consider varying the uniqueness approach slightly. If one of the desired outcomes of the grant is to develop a model that can be applied to other organizations, institutions, or colleges, then you need to demonstrate your similarity to others in your field that face the same problem. You do not want to highlight the *unique* qualities of your institution that are critical to the model's successful implementation. This would only weaken your case for the model's replicability. Instead, you want to identify the variables you share with others and focus on the uniquenesses that allow you and your organization/institution to develop, test, and produce materials that will be useful to those who will follow the results of your work or replicate your model.

The Department of Education has a selection criteria overview (see exhibit 6.2) that outlines what it is looking for in terms of project significance; and, as you can see, several of the items are related to the future use of project products, extrapolation of results, replicability, and so on. With this criteria in mind, a successful grants strategy would entail convincing the reviewer that while your organization/institution shares the similarity of the problem and its inherent variables with others, it has unique qualities that enable it to create valid approaches that others can benefit from. These might include special capabilities in the areas of testing, model development, evaluation, training, and dissemination, as well as past success in these areas.

Most foundation and corporations do not have as well a defined or documented review process as public funding sources. But they still have the same question in mind: "Why should they fund you and your organization?" Later, in parts 3 and 4, you will learn where to include these important credibility builders (uniquenesses) in your proposal. But why wait to identify them until you are filling out your application? Start now and be one step ahead of the game!

UNIQUENESS EXERCISE

Use the following brainstorming exercise to develop a list of your organization's unique features. This exercise will add a little excitement and flavor to meetings and can be done with a variety of groups such as staff, volunteers, clients, board members, and grants advisory committee members. Keep the information you develop in your proposal development workbook, where it will be ready for use in proposals, endorsement letters, and preproposal contact.

Please note that you may encounter some initial reluctance to this exercise because some individuals think it promotes bragging. However, these same individuals probably believe that humility and occasional begging will move grantors to take pity on your organization, and fund your proposals. They are wrong! From

---

Significance

- national significance
- significance of problem or issue to be addressed
- likelihood that project will result in system change or improvement
- potential of project to contribute to development and advancement of theory, knowledge, and practice in the field of study
- potential for generalizing from findings or results
- likelihood of project to yield findings that may be used by other appropriate agencies and organizations
- likelihood of project to build local capacity to provide, improve, or expand services that address the needs of the target population
- extent to which project involves development or demonstration of promising new strategies that build on or are alternatives to existing strategies
- effective use of product resulting from the project (i.e., information, materials, processes, techniques, etc.)
- dissemination of results in a manner that will allow others to use the information or strategies
- potential replicability of the project or strategies
- magnitude of the results or outcomes, especially improvements in teaching and student achievement

DEPARTMENT OF EDUCATION SELECTION CRITERIA OVERVIEW

EXHIBIT 6.2

---

the grantor's point of view, the humble approach does not highlight the reasons a prospective grantee should be funded.

To combat this problem, just remind all those participating in the exercise of its positive results. After the exercise, you will have a list of factors that make your organization unique, from which you will be able to select those uniquenesses that may appeal to a particular funding source. Also, the exercise will refocus those participating in the activity on the positive attributes of your organization and away from the negative.

1. Distribute the uniquenesses worksheet (see exhibit 6.3) to the group, remind the group of the rules for brainstorming (outlined in chapter 4), and set a time limit for brainstorming.
2. Record the group's answers to questions 1 and 2.
3. Ask the group to rank order the responses to the questions from a potential grantor's perspective with rank number one being the most positive uniqueness or qualification.
4. Have the group select the top three answers for both questions and combine them to develop a list of your organization's most positive uniquenesses/qualifications with respect to the adequacy of your institutional resources and the quality of your project personnel.

If your institution has a computer or decision lab, have the group meet there so you are in close proximity to the hardware and software necessary to provide instant rank ordering and frequency distributions.

Use the final list to select uniquenesses that will convince funders that their money will go further with you than with any other prospective grantee. For example, a particular funding source may be impressed with your total number of years of staff experience, central location of buildings, special equipment, and broad-needs populations and geographic coverage.

Your uniquenesses list will also prove valuable in

- selecting consortia partners or additional team members who can fill personnel voids and/or improve your capabilities
- recruiting and training staff, board members, and volunteers
- developing case statements
- using other fundraising techniques such as direct mail and wills and bequests

Do not forget to include yourself, the proposal initiator, project director, or principal investigator, as a uniqueness. Your previous work, publications, collaborative efforts, awards, and recognition are important components of your organization's overall uniqueness.

One culminating activity is to have half of your group role-play a grantor and the other half role-play a prospective grantee. Review one of the problems or needs your organization is planning to address and your organization's proposed solution. Then have the individuals playing the grantor ask those playing the prospective grantee why the grantseeker's organization should be the one selected to implement the proposed solution. Have the grantee group start by saying, "Our organization is uniquely suited to implement this solution because..."

USING YOUR ORGANIZATION'S CASE/MISSION STATEMENT TO SUPPORT YOUR PROPOSAL

Your case or mission statement is another key ingredient in convincing the grantor that your organization should be selected for funding. When you submit your application for funding, your approach should be based on the following three important factors:

1. There is a compelling need for the project.
2. Your organization is uniquely suited to carry out the project.
3. The project supports your organization's stated purpose or mission and fits with what you are currently doing or planning to do.

The third factor is especially important. Your case/mission statement should demonstrate your organization's predetermined concern for the project area. If

Federal and state proposal applications will require information on your organization's ability to perform the tasks you outline in your proposal. Your unique qualities or attributes are what enable you to perform these tasks. The sections of government applications that require this information are sometimes referred to as Adequacy of Institutional Resources, and Quality of Project Personnel.

On government applications, these sections may be assigned a point value. While these components may not be mandatory on foundation and corporate proposals, the information they contain is equally important in convincing private funding sources that your organization is the right grantee for them.

What makes your organization uniquely suited to carry out the work outlined in your proposal, and provide the grantor with the assurance it will receive a job well done?

1. **Adequacy of Institutional Resources**: Please list the positive qualities and uniquenesses that your organization/institution possesses that will insure a grantor you are the best place to do the job. When applicable, include factors such as:

   - relevance of purpose and mission,
   - geographic location,
   - relationship and availability to subject population,
   - presence of animal laboratories, and
   - data analysis capabilities.

   _____
   _____
   _____
   _____

2. **Quality of Project Personnel**: Please list the unique qualifications of your project personnel. Take into consideration factors such as:

   - Years of related experience,
   - Number of publications and presentations
   - Awards and special recognition
   - Number and dollar amount of grants and contracts successfully carried out

   _____
   _____
   _____
   _____

UNIQUENESS WORKSHEET

EXHIBIT 6.3

yours is a joint or consortia proposal, the mission or case statements of all the participating organizations should provide a documentable concern for the problem you will address. In short, this statement should give the funding source written documentation that the purpose of your organization (its reasons for existing), your project, and the grantor's values and concerns are a perfect match.

USING YOUR EXISTING CASE/MISSION STATEMENT

Most nonprofit organizations have an existing case or mission statement. Educational organizations use it to provide the foundation for accreditation, and in faculty and staff recruitment. While an institution's case/mission statement can provide the framework for a college, division, department, institute, or center, even the lowest level of the organization should be able to state its case for existence and inclusion in the future of the organization.

Grantors do not want their grant funding to influence what your organization becomes. Instead, they want you to tell them where your organization wants to go, and how your proposal will help move it toward that goal.

If you have a case/mission statement, use it to convince the grantor of your purpose. If you do not have a case/mission statement, or if the one you have is no longer accurate or too long, consider updating it, editing it to one concise page, or developing a new one tailored to the grants marketplace.

ELEMENTS OF A CASE/MISSION STATEMENT

Your case/mission statement should consist of how and why your organization got started, what your organization is doing today, and where your organization is going in the future.

How and Why Your Organization Got Started. Explain the original societal problems or needs that resulted in the formation of your organization. Most funding sources will find societal need today more important than the number of years your organization has been in existence. In fact, some funding sources actually have the greatest doubts about those nonprofit organizations that have been around the longest. These funders believe that such organizations generally are bureaucratic, have a tendency to lose sight of their mission, and have more so-called dead wood on their payrolls than younger nonprofit organizations.

What Your Organization Is Doing Today. Describe your organization's activities. What are its current priorities, programs, resources, and uniquenesses? Who are its clients? How has the passage of time affected its original mission and reason for being?

Where Your Organization Is Going in the Future. Because funding sources look at their support as an investment, they want to be sure they invest in organizations that will be around when their funding runs out. In other words, they want the organizations they invest in to have a five-year, ten-year, or even longer plan for operation. By demonstrating to funding sources that your organization has a long-range plan and the ability to secure future funding, you will show grantors that you are worthy of their funding and that the project they invest in will continue to benefit people for many years to come.

Use the case/mission statement worksheet (see exhibit 6.4) to determine what should be included in your case statement.

Remember, most potential grantors are more interested in how funding your proposal will move both of your organizations (theirs and yours) toward each of your missions than in your actual project methods. Funding sources consistently work to separate applicants who sought them out simply as a source of money from ap-

(Note: This worksheet can be completed based on the broad definition of your organization, college or university, as well as a smaller sub unit such as your center, school, department or program.)

1. How and Why Your Organization Got Started: _____
   Year: _____ Primary Movers/Founders: _____
   Original Mission: _____

2. *Today* - Where Your Organization Is Now:

   Changes from the Original Mission: _____
   _____

   Societal Need - Changes in Clients/Students: _____
   _____

   Current Priorities: _____
   _____

   Clients: _____
   Staff: _____
   Buildings: _____

3. *Future* - Where Your Organization Will Be Five Years from Now:

   Anticipated Changes in Mission: _____
   _____

   Anticipated Changes in Need: _____
   _____

   Resulting Alterations in Facilities and Staff: _____
   _____

4. Opportunities that Exist or New Opportunities that Will Exist to Move Your Organization Toward Its Plans/Goals: _____
   _____

CASE/MISSION STATEMENT WORKSHEET

EXHIBIT 6.4

plicants who can demonstrate that the direction outlined in their proposal is predetermined and an important component of their organization's overall mission.

In a funded proposal to the Bell South Foundation for over $250,000, the successful grantee told Bell South that it was their organization's goal and priority to approach the very same problem that the Bell South funding was designed to impact. In fact, the successful grantee told Bell South it could show them over five years of meeting minutes and budget expenditures that demonstrated its commitment to dealing with the problem. The grantee also went so far as to suggest that it would be committed to the same course of action even without Bell South's grant. Yes, the grantee told Bell South that it was so much a part of their goals, priorities, and case that the organization would move ahead with the project anyway! Naturally they also let Bell South know it would take 10 years without their money instead of three years with it. The Bell South money would be the catalyst in the equation for change. It would hasten the result.

The importance of relating your proposal to your organization's mission cannot be overemphasized. Before soliciting a potential grantor, be sure to ask yourself whether you are going to the funder just because you heard it had money and you want some, or because your proposal can serve the missions you both value.

CHAPTER 7

Creating Grant-Winning Teams and Consortia

Involving Volunteers through Advisory Committees and Advocacy Groups

The success of a proposal and the completion of a project rely on the incorporation of a complex mixture of supporting partners and expertise. How this combined effort is created and maintained is fast becoming one of the critical elements in attracting grant and contract support from government sources as well as private foundations and corporations. In most cases the creation of these critically important relationships has been left to chance and luck. However, by employing the science of group dynamics and team interaction, you can move your grant related groups away from relying on chance and toward increased efficiency and accountability.

The following suggestions for improving your grants success by increasing the effectiveness of your grant related groups come from my work and experience with grants professionals who have taken part in my effective grant team-building workshop. Participants of this workshop have been eager to evaluate how they function in groups and to work on developing more productive approaches to increase their group's effectiveness. I believe their positive responses to increasing personal and group effectiveness is a function of the difficulties they have encountered when attempting to work on proposal development with experts from multiple fields—something they are asked to do more and more frequently.

In today's grants marketplace, it is rare to find a project director or principle investigator who possesses *all* the expertise needed to complete a grant-funded project in any area; and research projects frequently depend on expertise in several disciplines that may have previously been thought to be unrelated. These interdisciplinary projects must now be completed by cooperating professionals who may think about and approach problems from radically different viewpoints. Even

46

demonstration grants and model projects require community integration and support from partners who just a few years ago would not have been approached but now must provide board resolutions and letters of support and endorsement.

An informal survey of 200 of my proposal development seminar participants revealed that very few had received formal training in group/team functioning or leadership skills. Except for those in technology areas such as software development, team functioning was not a part of their undergraduate or graduate education. However, from volunteers on your advisory committees and advocacy groups, to colleagues who must commit to be part of your project, the ability to organize and coordinate an effective group or team is *now* a necessary skill.

Consider the following suggestions for evaluating and improving your own personal group skills and the team skills of your grant related groups such as advisory committees, advocacy groups, proposal development teams, centers of excellence, multidisciplinary groups, consortia partners, and so on.

RECOGNIZING THE ROLES THAT COMPRISE AN EFFECTIVE TEAM

There are many theories and much research on effective team formation and development. However, after helping several universities develop more effective grant-related volunteer groups and development teams, I believe the basic element to group success is the role that individuals take in a group and how well the varying roles interact with one another to maximize strengths.

As you select the members for your grant-related group or analyze the makeup of your existing group or proposal development team, take into consideration the roles that must be assumed to assure effective group functioning. While there are a variety of techniques and materials that can be used to assist team members in developing awareness of the roles involved in a productive team, one simple and easy to use system is the *Team Dimension Profile* by Inscape Publishing (order through David G. Bauer Associates, Inc. at $15.50 each). This profile or survey helps individuals understand and value the contribution they make to successful innovation teams or groups by allowing them to determine their personal approach to thinking and behavior (conceptual, spontaneous, normative, or methodical) and their role on the team/group (creator, advancer, facilitator, refiner, or executor).

As you review the four basic approaches to thinking and behavior, consider which one best describes the approach you use in the team innovation process and the approaches taken by those you work with. Keep in mind that many individuals use more than one approach and, in essence, develop their own unique team and task orientation.

- Conceptual Approach—The individual who takes a conceptual approach is the idea developer who likes to brainstorm alternatives, focus on the future, and develop new theories.

- Spontaneous Approach—Those that take a spontaneous approach are free thinkers with little respect for tradition or rules. They move from one subject to another, focus on many things at once, and are sometimes impatient.
- Normative Approach—The individuals that take this approach want to see consequences before acting, prefer the norm or the familiar, and rely on past experiences and expectations.
- Methodical Approach—Those who takes a methodical approach like order in the universe. They are rational, follow scientific methods and step-by-step processes, and prefer to focus on details that make everything fit together.

Research by Fahden and Namakkal on these four approaches to innovation focuses on how the individual approaches work together in a group and how the various combinations of these approaches affect the completion of the work inherent in successful group/team projects. Their research resulted in their identification of five roles that must present in a team or group to achieve project success—the creator, the advancer, the facilitator, the refiner, and the executor. The four basic approaches to innovation naturally predispose individuals to accepting some of these roles with relative ease. The key to group success is to determine who prefers to take on the needed roles, who has certain of the skills inherent in the roles, and/or who will take on the role simply for the good of the group.

The theory is that in a well-functioning team all of the five roles are present and that the individual team members can hand tasks back and forth, utilizing the strengths that each role provides. Subgroups are developed when the team has more than one member who can function in each role and, therefore, can share tasks.

- Creator—Grant winning solutions must be innovative and fresh, and often require team members to think outside the box. The creator does just that. This individual helps generate new and unusual concepts, ideas, and solutions to the problem, and then passes them on to the advancer. Creators become bored discussing and explaining their new ideas (which to them are getting old) and can upset the group by coming up with newer and greater ideas before the team has completed working through the previous task. Creators will create grant proposal idea number 2 before number 1 is written. If not thoughtfully enjoined with the challenges and creativity of making idea number 1 work, they have a tendency to lose interest and skip group meetings.
- Advancer—In this role, the individual sees great ideas, solutions, or approaches and develops ways to promote them. The advancer develops objectives and plans by the most direct and efficient means. On grants teams they talk others through a new idea or concept, get the other team members on board, and keep them excited about the project. In addition, they are usually good at making preproposal contact with potential grantors.

- Facilitator—This is the group manager's role. This person monitors the proposal development process and work task distribution. This is a critical role for efficient proposal preparation and group productivity. When problems occur with the proposed protocol or solution, the facilitator hands tasks back to the responsible parties for their input and clarification.
- Refiner—This is the group's "devil's advocate." Refiners challenge, analyze, and follow a methodical process to detect process flaws or leaps in logic or process that creators sometimes make in brainstorming new approaches. They pass ideas and plans back to the facilitator to take to the creator and advancer.
- Executor—These are the workhorses of the group. They may not enjoy the more visible leadership roles. Their fun is in making the process an orderly and efficient one. Not only are they critical for developing the solution and proposal implementation plan, they are also essential in carrying out the proposal after it is funded. They pay attention to details and insist on quality.

On a successful team, the facilitator insures that tasks are handed off from the creator to the advancer, from the advancer to the refiner, and from the refiner to the executor.

You can probably see yourself in one or more of these roles, and now understand why some of your group efforts have failed—one or more of the five team roles—creator, advancer, refiner, executor, and/or facilitator—was missing and no one recognized this, or was willing to assume the missing role(s).

While working with an innovative interdisciplinary team seeking to develop federal proposals I discovered that five out of the seven-team members were creators. The group had been meeting together for one year, had brainstormed several unique approaches to problems, and were enjoying each other's company. The problem was that they never developed one completed proposal. The two non-creator types expressed exasperation with the group's inability to come to a consensus and develop a plan. The group's main problem was that the majority of its members assumed the role of creator—always generating new concepts and ideas. Unfortunately, they also needed individuals in the group who could:

- give some structure toward the implementation of these new concepts and ideas (advancers)
- work through the concept's/idea's problems (refiners)
- assume the responsibility of final implementation (executors)

They immediately started looking at each other to assume the missing roles, and the first role they chose to fill was that of the facilitator.

Poor team performance will result when there is an excess of team members assuming similar roles or coming from comparable orientations. A solid functioning group or team identifies the approaches and roles of its members, defines tasks, and hands them off from one role to another, allowing group members to focus on their strengths in the process. It also recognizes what roles are missing from the group. With awareness, the group can either add additional team members with the necessary orientation and skills, or the existing members can consciously take on the roles that are lacking and assume the subsequent tasks.

Higher education and nonprofit organizations are plagued by poorly functioning groups. From the dreaded committee assignments to proposal development teams, we have witnessed legendary failures.

The for-profit world has assumed the lead in seeking to develop highly successful teams at all levels, from the shop floor to top management. In his book *Teamwork is an Individual Skill—Getting Your Work Done When Sharing Responsibility*, Christopher Avery suggests that the first step to developing successful teams is to rid ourselves of the misconceptions we have about teamwork. One misconception we need to discard is that team members need to love each other. Believe it or not, we do not necessarily need to appreciate each other's personality to operate successfully. What we need to do is appreciate each group member's specific approach and to understand how it helps to get the job done. The second misconception we must eliminate is that our own personalities and individual orientation do not count, and that we should leave our personal needs at the door of each group meeting. In actuality, being a team player does not mean that you cannot be yourself, or that you cannot expect something back from the group for your time. The key to group success is to be yourself, act normally but responsibly, and recognize and appreciate what each group member naturally brings to the table. This knowledge will help you develop teams comprised of individuals with the mix of approaches and orientations necessary to achieve success.

INVOLVING VOLUNTEERS

One of the most important resources in a successful grants effort is the involvement of volunteers. When grantors are faced with volunteers who believe so strongly in a project that they are willing to work to further it with no personal benefit, the parent organization's credibility is greatly enhanced.

Involving others in increasing your potential to attract funding suggests that *who* you know may be more valuable than *what* you know and how you write your proposal. But a poorly developed idea and proposal will need much more than just friends and the suggestions presented here. If you have a great idea or proposal, however, you owe it to yourself to take advantage of every possible edge in your quest for funding. This includes involving individuals who can help ensure that your proposal receives the attention it deserves. One foundation director told me that approximately one-third of her foundation's grants went to the board members' favorite organizations and projects, one-third to the board members' friends' favorite projects, and the remaining one-third to the most skilled grantseekers.

While this may sound like politics, hold your condemnation just one more minute. The politics of grantseeking is a fascinating area that spells M-O-N-E-Y for those who master the art. Do not be frightened or disgusted by the word *politics*. The politics of grantseeking is a very understandable process that enables individuals to become advocates for what they value and believe in.

Those people who know your organization and identify with your cause or mission deserve to know how they can be of service to you and the cause or field you represent. When asked to become advocates for your project, individuals are free to say no or that they are too busy, but you should not make this decision for them by assuming that they would not want to be involved. There is no harm in asking, and you will be surprised by how many individuals welcome your invitation.

Consider exploring the area of advocacy and how you can help others help you. The worksheets in this chapter will assist you in determining who your advocates are and how they can best serve you. You will probably discover that there are more supporters for your project than you realized.

GRANTS ADVISORY COMMITTEES

One highly effective method for involving volunteers in your grants quest is to develop a grants advisory committee focused on the need or problem your grant proposal will address. For example, while working for a university-affiliated hospital, I initiated one grants advisory committee on health promotion and wellness for children and another on research for children's diseases with different individuals on each committee. Think of your grants advisory committee as an informal affiliation of individuals you invite to take part in attracting grant funds to the problem area you have chosen. These individuals will be surveyed to determine their willingness to supply resources, as well as play an advocacy role.

Invite fellow professionals, individuals from other organizations and the community, and corporate members who are interested in the area you have identified. By inviting a cross-section of individuals to join your committee, you develop a wider base from which to draw support. Ask yourself who would care if you developed grants resources to solve a particular problem. The one common denominator for all the committee members should be their concern for positive change in the identified area of need. Develop a list of individuals, groups, and organizations you think would volunteer a little of their time to be instrumental in making progress in the problem area. Be sure to include

- individuals who might know foundation, government, or corporate grantors

Please indicate the resource areas you would be willing to help with. At the end of the list, provide more detailed information. In addition, if you are willing to meet with funding sources, please list the geographic areas you travel to frequently.

___   Evaluation of Projects
___   Computer Equipment
___   Computer Programming
___   Layout and Design Work
___   Printing
___   Budgeting, Accounting, Developing Cash Flow, Auditing
___   Audiovisual Assistance (equipment, videotaping, etc.)
___   Purchasing Assistance
___   Long Distance Telephone Calls
___   Travel
___   Writing/Editing
___   Searching for Funding Sources
___   Other Equipment/Materials
___   Other

Description of Resources: _____
_____
_____
_____
_____

Areas Frequently Visited: _____
_____
_____
_____
_____

GRANT RESOURCES INVENTORY

EXHIBIT 7.1

- colleagues who may have previously prepared a proposal for the grantor you will be approaching or who may have acted as grant reviewers

Also consider current and past employees, board of trustee members, and former clients.

GRANT RESOURCES

After you have identified individuals or groups who would be interested in seeing change in the area identified, make a list of skills and resources that would be helpful in developing your proposal. Match these with the types of individuals who might possess them. Your list of skills and resources may give you some ideas about who you should recruit for your grants advisory committee. Consider the skills and resources and the types of individuals that could be useful in

- preparing your proposal (writers, experts in evaluation design or statistics, individuals with skills in the areas of computer programming, printing, graphics, or photocopying)

- making preproposal contact (individuals with sales and marketing skills, people who travel frequently, volunteers who could provide long-distance phone support)
- developing consortia or cooperative relationships and subcontracts (individuals who belong to other nonprofit groups with similar concerns)

Review the grant resources inventory (see exhibit 7.1) for those resources and skills your volunteers may be able to provide.

HOW TO INCORPORATE ADVOCATES TO INCREASE GRANTS SUCCESS

Specific activities to consider in relation to advocacy roles of individuals on your list are

- writing endorsement letters
- talking to funding sources for you and setting up appointments
- providing expertise in particular areas (finance, marketing, and so on)
- accompanying you to meetings with potential funders or even visiting a funding source with you

Use the advocacy planning sheet (see exhibit 7.2) to organize your approach.

Endorsement Letters

One very effective way to use advocates is to request that they write endorsement letters related to your organization's credibility and accomplishments. Without guidance, however, many advocates will develop endorsement letters that focus on inappropriate aspects of your project or organization. To prevent this, spell out what you are looking for. Provide advocates with a draft endorsement letter that suggests what you would like them to consider including in their letters, such as:

- pertinent facts or statistics that you may then quote or use in your proposal
- the length of time they have worked with you and/or your organization (e.g., number of hours, consortia, or cooperative work relationships)
- a summary of their committee work and their major accomplishments

Advocates should almost be able to retype your draft on their stationery and sign it. If the grantor has any special requirements concerning endorsement letters, make sure they are followed.

Contacts

Another way to involve your advocates is to present them with the names of potential grantors and their board members, and to ask whether they know any of

Project Title: _____   Project Director: _____

Select from the following list the techniques you can suggest your advocates employ to advance your project.

- Endorsement letters
- Testimonials
- Letters of introduction to grantors
- Set appointments with granting officials
- Accompany you to see funding sources
- Go see grantors for you

Techniques for This Project	Advocate to Be Used	Who Will Contact Advocate and When	Desired Outcome	Date Completed

ADVOCACY PLANNING SHEET

EXHIBIT 7.2

the grantors' key individuals. This approach is particularly useful if your advocates are reluctant to reveal all of their contacts and are holding back to see how serious you are in researching potential grantors.

If your advocates are trusting, you can ask them outright for a comprehensive list of their contacts. This includes asking your grants advisory committee members to reflect on their ability to contact a variety of potential grantors that may be helpful in your grants effort. To take this proactive approach, follow these steps:

1. Explain the advocacy concept to the individuals you have identified and how the information they provide will be used. Ask each participant to complete an advocacy/webbing worksheet (see exhibit 7.3) and return it to you. Some organizations find they have better results in introducing the advocacy concept when they relate the concept to a major project of the organization that has widespread support.

Our organization's ability to attract grant funds is increased substantially if we can talk informally with a funding official (or board member) before we submit our formal proposal. However, it is sometimes difficult to make pre-proposal contact without having a link to the funding source. We need your help. By completing this worksheet, you will identify any links that you may have with potential grantors and possibly open up an oasis of opportunities for our organization.

If you have a link with a funding source that our research indicates may be interested in supporting one of our projects, we will contact you to explain the project and discuss possible ways you could help us. For example, you could write an endorsement letter, arrange an appointment, or accompany us to see the funding source. Even a simple phone call could result in our proposal actually being read and not just being left in a pile. No matter what the case may be, you can rest assured that we will obtain your complete approval before any action is taken and that we will never use your name or link without your consent.

Links to foundations, corporations, and government funding sources are worth hundreds of thousands of dollars per year and your assistance can ultimately help us continue our vital mission. Thank you for your cooperation.

Your Name: _____   Phone No.: _____

Address: _____

1.   What foundation or corporate boards are you, your spouse, or close friends on?

2.   Do you know anyone who is on a foundation or corporate board? If so, whom and what board?

3.   Does your spouse know anyone on a foundation or corporate board? If so, whom and what board?

4.   Have you served on any government committees? If so, please list.

5.   Do you know any government funding contacts? If so, please list.

6.   Please list any fraternal groups, social clubs, and/or service organizations to which you or your spouse belong.

ADVOCACY/WEBBING WORKSHEET

EXHIBIT 7.3

2. Distribute the advocacy/webbing worksheet to the individuals you have identified as possible advocates. This may be done in a group or individually.
3. Input the advocacy information you collect from the completed worksheets
in your computer, or file it.
4. When a match between a potential funder and advocate is made, call your
advocate and discuss the possibility of having him or her arrange a meeting

for you with the funding source. Ask the advocate to attend the meeting with you to add credibility to your presentation.

Keep all completed advocacy/webbing worksheets on file and update them periodically. This is a good activity for volunteers. Be aware, however, that care should be taken to safeguard advocacy data. Advocacy data should be considered personal information that is privileged; you must not allow open access to the data or you will be violating your advocates' trust. Using a large central computing facility to store this information greatly reduces security. Instead, use a small personal computer system, and store a copy of your program in a safe place. This approach will ensure the privacy of this confidential information. An inexpensive software program designed especially for storing and using advocacy information entitled *Winning Links* is available from Bauer Associates. (For ordering information, see the list of resources available from Bauer Associates at the end of the book.)

If possible, computerize your advocacy information using *Winning Links* or other software. When a potential funding source is identified, search your advocacy database to determine whether any of your advocates have a relationship to the potential funding source.

You may have an advocate who:

- is a member of both your organization and the funding source's board
- can arrange an appointment to get you in to talk to the funder
- can write a letter to a friend on the funding source's board
- has worked for the grantor or been a reviewer for the funder's grant program.

Community Support

Advocacy can also play a valuable role in developing and documenting community support for your project. Some funding sources require that you demonstrate community support in the form of advisory committee resolutions and copies of the minutes of meetings, and more grantors are encouraging the development of consortia when applying for funding. Whether you are looking at a joint submittal for your proposal or just endorsement and support, it is important to start the process of applying for a grant early so that deadlines do not interfere with your ability to document your advisory committee's involvement and valuable work. To deal creatively with the area of community support:

- put together a proposal development workbook (see chapter 3) to focus on your problem area
- organize an advisory committee to examine the problem area

#	Techniques	Applicability Techniques to this Project	Who Will Call Meeting	Members of Committee	Dates
1	Use advisory committees to brainstorm uniquenesses of your organization (chapter 6).				
2	Use advisory committee to work on setting up needs assessment.				
3	Use advisory committee to brainstorm project ideas.				
4	Use your committee to develop a public relations package and produce it (printers, media reps.), including newspaper coverage for your organization (press releases, interviews) and television coverage (public service announcements, talk shows).				
5	Have an artist perform or have an open house for key people* in the community.				

HOW TO DEVELOP COMMUNITY SUPPORT WORKSHEET

EXHIBIT 7.4

- involve the advisory committee in brainstorming project ideas, examining needs assessment techniques, writing letters of endorsement, and providing links to funders.

Review the worksheet on developing community support (see exhibit 7.4) to help you determine how to use community support to increase your fundability.

Organize your supporters and maximize your chances for success by working through and with your volunteers. Involve those individuals who can be of service to your cause, from enhancing your resources to helping identify links to funders.

INVOLVING EXISTING BOARDS, ADVISORY GROUPS, VOLUNTEERS, AND STAFF

Do not overlook the advantages of using the linkages that your existing organizational groups may have. These groups have already demonstrated an affinity for your organization and your programs. Participation in this opportunity should be voluntary, and while some administrators may express concern over asking paid staff to contribute names of friends and relatives who have connections to funding sources, they will be surprised over the voluntary response they receive. Involve your employee associations and unions, and initiate the idea by relating it to strong needs and well-accepted programs and projects that many people want to see developed or expanded.

Many nonprofit organizations already have boards and standing committees that can be invited to become involved in this webbing and linkage process. Most corporate people will be happy that they have been asked to participate in a game that the corporate world plays all the time. From my experience at universities, I also have found that department chairs, deans, and members of boards of institutes and centers usually respond favorably to the concept.

The key to acceptance of the webbing and linkage process is to assure those participating that linkages will not be contacted without their knowledge or approval and in most cases, their assistance.

HOW TO USE WEBBING AND LINKAGE INFORMATION

To help you get the most out of your newly discovered linkages list them by linkage type, for example, foundation, corporate, federal, state, and so on. Then use the funding source research tools described in chapters 9 and 19 to look up the interest areas of the grantors you have a link to. Review your organization's needs and projects and look for potential matches with the grantors. When a match is found, make preproposal contact through your linkage.

CHAPTER

Choosing the Correct Grants
Marketplace

Proactive grantseeking involves assessing your grants potential, selecting the basic marketplace (government, foundation, or corporate) for your proposal idea, researching the best prospects within the chosen marketplace, and preparing a grant-winning proposal.

Many prospective and oftentimes overzealous grantseekers launch their efforts to research possible grantors too quickly. To maximize your grants potential, you must do the kind of planning described in the preceding chapters. Developing a proposal effort that will promote a professional image of your organization requires an approach to research that has the following characteristics:

- Reflects a win-win-win attitude. Your research must be in-depth enough to ensure that your project will meet the funding source's interests, needs, and values while moving your organization toward its mission and providing benefits to your clients or field of interest. In this case the funder wins, your organization wins, and your clients win.

- Provides you with the confidence to present yourself as worthy of funding because you have documented why you are the best grantee, and have uncovered through your research why they are the right grantor for your project. You have taken the time to find the right funder by doing your research, and this will become apparent to the prospective grantor. The funder will hear the confidence in your voice and see it in your proposal.

After you have redefined your project and developed your key search terms, you will begin to narrow down your search for the correct funding source. How do you know which funding marketplace is the right one for your project? Each marketplace has different types of funding sources and distinct funding characteristics. Certain factors predetermine how a funding source will "view the world," so you must match your proposal idea with those grantors most likely to find your proposal appealing.

Start by reviewing the distinct characteristics of each marketplace. After you select the right marketplace for your project, you may start researching individual funding sources within that marketplace.

GENERAL GRANTS MARKETPLACE INFORMATION

I have administered a grants marketplace quiz as a pretest assessment instrument to over 30,000 grantseekers since 1975. These grantseekers attended one of my training seminars and, therefore, were not randomly selected and may not represent all grantseekers. However, they do vary widely in grants expertise and background. What is interesting and surprising is that more incorrect answers are given to the quiz today than 25 years ago. Why is this, when today's grantseekers are exposed to an abundance of information about grants and funding sources through the general media, professional journals, newsletters, conferences, grants databases, and e-mail alerts? I believe that improved grants information may in fact contribute to current misconceptions about the grants marketplace and, consequently, to faulty grant strategies.

Grantseekers, and the administrators they work for, read announcements about nonprofit groups that attract large, above-average grant awards, but these awards that make the news are usually exceptions to the rule. These awards unfortunately are often interpreted by well-meaning, motivated grantseekers and their administrators as the norm or average. Nonprofit leaders use these large awards to shape their view of the marketplace. Judging the marketplace by what makes headlines thus creates and reinforces misconceptions about grant making and influences unrealistic expectations about the level of grant support from each sector of the marketplace. As a result, many grantseekers end up basing their strategic decision making on fantasy rather than fact.

To choose the correct marketplace for your proposal, you need to base your choice on knowledge. The two main sources of support for nonprofit organizations and their grant requests are government and private philanthropy.

In the public arena, the decrease in government grant funding in the mid-1980s created an initial overreaction on the part of nonprofit organizations. Because many grantseekers knew that government funding was cut, they did not even bother to apply for government funds, and the applications for government grants declined substantially. (Therefore, those that did apply were rewarded.) The same phenomenon reoccurred in the mid-1990s. Well-publicized cuts in a few government programs resulted in minimal increases in applications to federal sources and large increases in requests to foundations and corporations. The astute grantseeker will not make false and potentially costly assumptions but will look beyond the latest news and inquire into how changes in appropriations will affect specific federal grant programs.

The late 1990s saw a historic event—the balance of the federal budget. In previous years, when budget cuts had to be made, the only place to cut was the grants area. This is partly because most budget allocations are for fixed areas of expenditures such as social security and Medicaid with yearly cost of living raises, and no politician or federal bureaucrat wants to be associated with cuts to these programs. The grants area is one that does not have a political action committee or strong lobby. The grants area experienced cuts or no increases for many years, and only a few professional organizations appealed for no cuts or more funding. But with the balancing of the budget and then the actual 1998 budget surplus, politicians increased grant dollars to popular programs. However, because of the federal deficit at the beginning of the twenty-first century, this has all changed and grant appropriations will be negatively affected.

To help you choose the correct grants marketplace, you need to know your competition and where the money is. Answer the following questions to help develop your insight into these critical areas.

1. In the United States, approximately how many nonprofit organizations are eligible to receive gifts and grants?
   a. 50,000
   b. 500,000
   c. 1,500,000
   d. 900,000

2. What was the total amount of private money (nongovernment) donated to these nonprofit organizations (see question 1) as tax-deductible gifts in 2002?
   a. $10 billion
   b. $26 billion
   c. $133 billion
   d. $241 billion

3. The total amount of private money donated to nonprofit organizations came from the following four basic sources. Indicate the percentage attributed to each source.
   Foundation grants   _____%
   Corporate grants   _____%
   Bequests   _____%
   Individual giving   _____%

4. How much grant funding came from the federal marketplace in 2002?

   a. $50 billion
   b. $100 billion
   c. $150 billion
   d. $200 billion

Turn to the end of this chapter for the correct answers.

If taking this quiz reaffirmed what you already knew to be true, that's great. If your guesses were incorrect, be thankful that you now know the correct answers and can avoid approaching the wrong marketplace and experiencing unnecessary rejection.

Most of my seminar participants guess that foundation grants account for 40 to 50 percent of the $241 billion donated in private money, with corporate grants at 30 to 35 percent, and bequests and individuals representing the balance of 15 to 30 percent.

I wish these misconceptions were correct. That would mean that foundations and corporations would have more grant funding than the federal government! However, wishful thinking won't get you a grant. Knowledge and a sound grants strategy will pay off in the end with a funded project.

The fact is that the foundation and corporate marketplace provides over $39 billion in grants, and that their funding of projects can provide a catalyst in attracting the more plentiful government grant funds. However, these private grantors complain about the wild ideas and inappropriate monetary requests presented to them by grantseekers who have not done their homework and know little about the grants marketplace. To avoid this, I suggest you approach the marketplace in the following manner.

First, research the sector of the grants marketplace with the greatest amount of funds—the government marketplace (federal and state)—from the government. In order to approach these potentially valuable partners with knowledge and conviction, read through the government funding section (part 2) that follows. Take time to log on to the appropriate Web sites and do a search. Talking to a federal program official will often provide you with valuable insights into what you need to do to make your project competitive and fundable.

Then, approach the smaller marketplaces after you can demonstrate that you have searched the government grants area and can show why the private marketplace (foundation and corporate grants) is the most appropriate for your request. (Researching the government marketplace first will also provide you with the confidence to approach foundation and corporate grantors.) Keep in mind that foundations and corporations may provide valuable startup funding to develop preliminary data, test hypotheses, and develop your consortia that will eventually result in larger grants from the government. See parts 3 and 4 of this book for a more detailed discussion of private funding opportunities.

Remember, if you can recognize when you have identified an inappropriate grantor for your proposal, and/or when you are requesting an inordinate amount of funding and you do not apply, you avoid positioning your institution and yourself negatively, and you keep your grants success rate up. Learning about each of the marketplaces and developing your strategies from the information provided in this book is bound to pay off for you.

Question	Correct Answer
1. In the United States, approximately how many nonprofit organizations are eligible to receive gifts and grants?	1d. 900,000
2. What was the total amount of private money (nongovernment) donated to these nonprofit organizations (see question 1) as tax-deductible gifts in 2002?	2d. $241 billion
3. The total amount of private money donated to nonprofit organizations came from the following four basic sources. Indicate the percentage attributed to each source.	Foundation grants 11.2% Corporate grants 5.1% Bequests 7.5% Individual giving 76.3%
4. How much grant funding came from the federal marketplace in 2002?	4b. $150 billion

PART TWO

....

Public/Government
Funding Opportunities

CHAPTER 9

Understanding the
Government Marketplace

THE HISTORY OF GOVERNMENT GRANTS

The origin of public grants traces back to the granting of lands by state and federal governments for specific purposes. For example, at one time the government granted land to states for education purposes, hence the creation of land grant colleges and many state university systems. Both state and federal governments have used the granting system to create change, and affect our education, health, community development, and so on. Almost every facet of life in the United States has been, is, or will be influenced by the grants mechanism. For instance, the September 11 terrorist attack against the United States resulted in a variety of grant programs from federal and state governments to deal with public health and safety issues.

Using a competitive grant process to encourage the best and brightest minds to develop innovative and creative ways to deal with a specific problem or area of interest is a very efficient technique. When the grant concept is coupled with a peer review system that calls on individuals knowledgeable in their respective fields to evaluate and judge proposals, the grants process is fair as well as efficient.

The grants mechanism we twenty-first-century grantseekers know really took off in the late 1940s. Prior to that time, even research related to defense was funded primarily by foundations and corporations. However, after World War II, the government stepped up grants primarily to deal with medical and scientific problems. Federal agencies were then, and are now, appropriated tax dollars by Congress with specific objectives and goals in mind. For example, one such goal was to use the grants mechanism to close the scientific gap between the Soviets and the United States made evident by the Soviets' launch of *Sputnik*.

In the same way, President Kennedy used the grants mechanism in the New Frontier Initiative and President Johnson used it in the Great Society Initiative to improve education, health, and social programs. While both of these happen to be Democratic initiatives, the Republicans have also used grant-related initiatives to create change, and make a direct and often immediate impact on our cultural, social, health, education, and scientific/research infrastructures. A recent example is President George W. Bush's Faith Based Initiative that allows nonprofit groups who proselytize a particular religious ideology to be eligible for grants. Prior to this initiative, these groups were ineligible for grants because of concerns over the separation between church and state.

Grantseekers must understand how a specific program's or initiative's rules and guidelines for eligibility, review, and selection impact their chances of success. For example, the executive order by President Bush allowing faith-based groups to receive federal grants will increase the number of potential grantees competing for existing funds. Depending on how many and how fervently faith-based groups avail themselves of this new opportunity, non-faith-based organizations, when appropriate, may want to include faith-based groups in their grant proposals as subcontractors so that their proposals appeal to federal bureaucrats and to the reviewers charged with implementing this initiative.

In the 1970s, a growing trend began toward local, regional, and state distribution of federal government grant dollars. This trend was based on federalism, or the belief that local and state governments know best what they need. This "New Federalism," or revenue-sharing perspective, moved the grants marketplace from categorical grants, in which the federal government allocated funds to selected categories, problems, or areas, to formula and block grants, which allowed the state and local governments to combine categorical funding and pool federal funds to address problems. The Reagan administration encouraged this trend by signaling a decline in the government's use of the grants mechanism to initiate, direct, and sustain change in American society.

First, the Reagan administration called for a reduction of $40 billion in domestic grants. Although there were repeated attempts to virtually eliminate grants altogether, Congress did not allow cuts below the $20 billion to $22 billion level. However, grant funds were cut almost in half.

Second, the Reagan administration attacked the categorical grants funding mechanism. The administration's philosophy of "the government governs best which governs least" could not support a categorical grants system controlled by Washington bureaucrats.

President George Bush continued this movement toward local control of federal grant funds. While the president may set the agenda, Congress controls the purse strings and thus, the federalism concept was furthered under the Clinton administration with the passing of grant-related bills that used a formula or a percentage to appropriate funds to the states and a portion to be administered at the federal level. Since there was a budget surplus during the late 1990s, both restricted grants to states and competitive grants at the federal level flourished. Yet still, the conservative ideal of federalism prevailed.

Today, the notion of letting states have the right to set their own agendas has supporters in both the democratic and republican parties. However, many believe that certain types of research need to fall under a national rather than a state agenda, including research that

- tests new theories and breaks into untried fields
- asks and answers why something happens (fundamental research also known as bench, lab, or basic research)
- challenges established practices and seeks new innovations

Allowing states to carry out their own research agendas often results in redundancy and the waste of taxpayer funds, and, because of this, many fiscal conservatives agree with their more liberal colleagues that we need the National Science Foundation to coordinate and direct a national research agenda. The same holds true for other federal agencies such as the National Institutes for Health. In fact, numerous proponents of state control of federal funding agree that many programs at the Department of Education, Health and Human Services, the Department of Labor, and the Department of Commerce need federal coordination to avoid duplication of efforts and to support a national agenda.

However, disagreements on state versus national agendas seems to proliferate when grant support moves from research, testing new theories, and creating and evaluating models to implementing what works. Each state and each governor wants federal funds allocated to them with the right to decide what is best for their state. This desire for control of federal program dollars has resulted in the development and growth of block and formula grants. Under these grant mechanisms, some or all of a federal appropriation is supplied to each state and each state is allowed to determine how the funds will be disseminated. There are federal guidelines and restrictions that must be followed, but there is much more control at the state or local level. Therefore, it is imperative that grantseekers develop their grant strategies accordingly and recognize when to shift their grants research away from federal agencies and to the state or local government agencies that control the monies they (the grantseekers) desire.

BLOCK GRANTS

The block grant concept was founded on the premise that it was not the purview of the federal government to force the states to follow categorical grant program priorities. Similar categorical grant programs were blocked, or synthesized into groups of related programs, and the federal funds were sent directly to the states. The states could set their priorities and grant the federal funds to the high-priority areas and projects they saw fit.

The block grant movement caused mass confusion in the grants world because, when first introduced in the late 1970s and 1980s, the current recipients of these grants had to figure out who in their states now had the funds and what would be funded. In most cases the states received more decision-making power but less money than they did under categorical grants. The block grant mechanism allowed the federal government to reduce staff formerly used to administer categorical grant programs. Decreases in staff were limited, however, because the federal government still had to direct the research component of categorical programs to avoid duplication and to coordinate research efforts.

Because of the federal government's continued involvement in the administration of grants (especially research grants), and Congress's desire to deal with problems in education, employment, and crime, the late 1980s marked the decline of the block grant mania of the early Reagan years, and the use of categorical funding mechanisms increased. Virtually all of the new grant programs introduced in the late 1990s were categorical grant programs designed to impact long existing or new problems. The conservative agenda of the early 2000s and its current and projected tax cuts could result in more budget reductions, the blocking of more federal grant programs and, in general, fewer grant dollars.

FORMULA GRANTS

The term *formula grants* refers to granting programs under which funds are allocated according to a set of criteria (or a formula). The criteria for allocation of these grant funds may be census data, unemployment figures, number of individuals below the poverty level, number of people with disabilities, and the like, for a state, city, or region. Formula grant programs are generally specific to a problem area or geographic region and historically have been used to support training programs in the fields of health, criminal justice, and employment.

The formula grant funds must pass through an intermediary, such as a state, city, or county government, or a commission, before reaching the grantee. The formula grants mechanism is another example of the New Federalism that started developing in the early 1970s. While the general guidelines for formula grants are developed at the federal level, the rules are open to interpretation, and local input can significantly alter the intent of the original federal program. To encourage local control and input into how federal funds are spent, the formula grants mechanism requires a mandated review by local officials but usually very little accountability or evaluation of the actual impact of the funds. Because of this, it is difficult to substantiate the results of these programs at subsequent congressional appropriation hearings, which means that they (the programs placed in formula and block grant formats) are often easy targets for elimination.

CATEGORICAL GRANTS

As previously mentioned, categorical grants are designed to promote proposals within very specific, well-defined areas of interest. These grant opportunities address a specific area with which a federal program is concerned, such as arts, humanities, drug abuse, dropout prevention, nutrition for the elderly, or research on certain types of diseases and scientific advances. The government, through hearings selects the problem to be corrected, appropriates funds, and prospective grantees design approaches to solve or reduce the problem, or to increase knowledge in the area through research.

Project and research grants are awarded by various agencies under these congressionally authorized programs. Ideally, grants are awarded to the organizations (and individuals) whose proposals most clearly match the announced program guidelines. Most federal grant programs use nongovernment review panels (often referred to as peer review panels) to evaluate the projects. Peer review helps ensure that the best proposals are selected for funding. Because project design is left to the grantseekers, there is room for a wide variety of creative solutions, making the project and research grants approach very popular among grantseekers.

Government granting agencies usually require grantseekers to complete detailed applications. As categorical grants have increased, each federal agency that controls funds has developed its own grants system. Grants applications and the administration of grants differ in format from agency to agency, and sometimes from program to program within the same agency. Even with the use of online creation and submittal, the applications are tedious, complicated, and time-consuming to complete. It is a challenge to tailor your proposal content to meet the requirement of the granting agency as well as your own needs. There is usually a three- to six-month review process, which may include a staff review by federal agency personnel and a peer review. Successful grantees are required to submit frequent reports, maintain accurate project records, and agree to possible federal audits and site visits by government staff.

To be successful in research and project grants, grantseekers must be mindful of the constant changes in emphasis and appropriations. Hidden agendas and shifts in focus result from the funding agency's prerogative to interpret and be sensitive to changes in the field of interest, and to what Congress expects from each year's appropriations.

CONTRACTS

No discussion of federal support would be complete without a discussion of government contracts. In recent years, the differences between a grant and a contract have become harder to discern. Indeed, after hours of negotiation with a federal agency on your grant, you may end up having to finalize your budget with a contract officer.

While there are several types of contracts, including fixed cost, cost reimbursable, and those that allow the contractor to add additional costs incurred during the contract, the basic difference between a grant and a contract is that a contract outlines precisely what the government wants done. You are supplied with detailed specifications, you propose a procedure to produce what the government agency has specified, and the contract is awarded on a lowest-bid basis. With a contract, there is decidedly less flexibility in creating the approach to the problem. To be successful in this arena, you must be able to convince the federal contracting agency that you can perform the contract at an acceptable level of competency and at the lowest bid. Contracts are also publicized or advertised in different ways than grants. Grant opportunities are published in the *Catalog of Federal Domestic Assistance*, while contracts are advertised in Federal Business Opportunities (FedBizOpps). Both of these publications will be explained in chapter 10.

The $150 billion in federal grants quoted in question 4 of the quiz in chapter 8 does not include government *contract* monies. One reason that contract monies are not included in federal grant statistics has to do with rollovers. Grant funds are appropriated and spent in the federal budget or fiscal year, which runs from October 1 to September 30. Even multiyear grants contain a caveat that future funding is dependent on yearly federal budget allocations. While a grantee can usually obtain an extension on expending their awarded grant funds beyond the end of their grant period, rollovers of unexpended federal agency funds are prohibited. Unexpended grant funds revert back to the federal treasury, except for federal contracts. For example, the Department of Defense may accrue rollover funds in certain contract areas for several years. This rollover variable makes it virtually impossible to estimate how much total contract funding is available from all of the federal agencies in any one year. However, it is safe to say that the variety, number, and dollar value of government contracts are staggering and go far beyond the $150 billion in government grants cited in chapter 8, and could be in the trillions of dollars.

Contracts have been increasingly pursued by nonprofit groups in recent years. For example, shifts away from domestic grant program funds have led some nonprofit organizations to look at Defense Department contract opportunities for implementation of their programs and research. However, the contracts game, requires a successful track record and documentable expertise. The best way to break into this marketplace is to identify a successful bidder and inquire as to whether you can work for them as a subcontractor. This way, you gain experience, confidence, and contacts with the contractor.

Many nonprofit groups have found that they can reduce the problems they routinely encounter in bidding on contracts by developing separate profit and nonprofit entities for dealing with such issues as security agreements, academic freedom, patents, and copyrights. In addition, changes in the contracts area have been made to simplify government purchasing and to reduce paperwork. These changes, brought on by scandals over inflated prices for parts, have alleviated some of the problems associated with the administration of contract bids. Still, bidding on government contracts is a task for the experienced grantseeker only.

STATE GOVERNMENT GRANTS

The astute grantseeker will be ready to act when discovering a federal grant opportunity in which the eligible recipient must be a state agency. In these cases, federal funds have been passed on for dissemination to the state agency that the state designates as best suited to do so. The federal program officers will know where the funds were directed in each state. States also place their own funds into state grant programs other than federal formula and block grants. Locating state grant funds is much more difficult than locating federal grant opportunities. Information on all federal funding opportunities must be accessible to the public and therefore, are listed in a public grants database known as the Catalog of Federal Domestic Assistance (to be explained in detail in chapter 10). Most states do not have a similar public database. To discover state grant opportunities you will need to look at state agency Web sites and talk to state officials. Many states appropriate grant funds to programs and projects that their elected officials value. For example, states that have secured funding from the recent tobacco company settlement can use these funds as their legislature and executives see fit. One state used the funds for grant opportunities related to the expansion of opportunities and employment in the technology sector; while a number of other states have used the funds to develop antismoking programs.

It is difficult to estimate how many grant dollars are awarded through individual state program initiatives. Many states develop their own initiatives in the social welfare and health areas, while few states deal in research funding. In most states, the majority of state grant funds are federal funds that must pass through the state to you, the grantseeker.

There are some grantseeker advantages to state control of grants. Because states distribute federal block and formula grants, these grants are easier to access. They require less long-distance travel and allow you to use your state and local politicians to make your case heard. These advantages are counterbalanced, however, by the fact that some states develop their own priorities for federal funds. States may add additional restrictions and use a review system similar to the federal peer review system, or use a system made up of state bureaucrats and political appointees. Although states have their own monies, granting programs, and rules, if they distribute grant monies obtained from the federal government, they must guarantee that the eventual recipient of those funds will follow all federal rules and circulars.

Many of the federal government grantseeking techniques found in the preceding chapters of this book also apply to accessing state grant funds. However, to determine which of the government sectors (federal or state) is best for your proposal, you must first learn how to research the marketplace.

CHAPTER 10

Researching the Government Marketplace

THE FEDERAL GRANTS SYSTEM

Federal granting programs are created by Congress though the enactment of public laws and the appropriation of funds. The actual disbursement of these funds follows a systematic progression based on publicly announced rules. Many grantseekers are unaware of how this federal funding system works and, therefore, are unable to take advantage of grant-related announcements and rules published early in the funding process.

When you do not know the system, you are forced to react to a Request for Proposals (RFP) announcement and develop your proposal in a few short weeks. Grantseekers who know the system, however, can develop a proactive approach to seeking funds that alerts them to a deadline four to six months or more in advance.

Since many federal grants have matching funds and other requirements, use the preproposal summary and approval form in chapter 4 (see exhibit 4.2) to insure you will have the support of your administration before you invest your time. Almost all federal funding documents use key words and subject areas to categorize granting programs. Therefore, your redefinition/key search terms worksheet (see chapter 5, exhibit 5.1) will be useful in your research.

FEDERAL GRANTS RESEARCH FORM

Gathering the information necessary to choose your best federal grant prospect requires persistence. You must make personal contacts, gather data, and analyze the data. Without careful attention to detail, the information you were sure you would remember can easily get lost. As one grantseeker reported in a grants sem-

For *(Your Project Reference or Title)*: _____
CFDA No. _____ Deadline Date(s): _____
Program Title: _____ Gov't Agency: _____

Create a file for each program you are researching and place all information you gather on this program in the file. Use this Federal Grants Research Form to

- keep a record of the information you have gathered
- maintain a log of all telephone and face-to-face contacts made with the government agency
- log all correspondence sent to and received from the agency

Agency Address: _____ Agency Director: _____
Telephone Number: _____ Program Director: _____
Fax Number: _____ Name /Title of Contact Person: _____
E-mail: _____

Place a check mark next to the information you have gathered and placed in the file.

___ Program description from **CFDA**
___ Letter requesting to be put on mailing list
___ List of last year's grantees ___ Sent for ___ Received
___ List of last year's reviewers ___ Sent for ___ Received
___ Application package ___ Sent for ___ Received
        Expected Availability Date _____
___ Comments on rules/final rules from *Federal Register*
___ Notices of rules for evaluation from *Federal Register*
___ Grant Scoring System - Point allocation for each section
     Source _____
___ Sample funded proposal
___ Federal Funding Source Staff Profile (exhibit 10.5)
     Written summary of each contact made

FEDERAL GRANTS RESEARCH FORM

EXHIBIT 10.1

inar, "The only way I can extort my unusually high salary from my boss is to keep all my grants research and contacts in my head. Nothing is written down, and my board prays that nothing will ever happen to me!" This is not a good idea because all those contacts and bits of information could be lost.

The key to providing your organization with federal funding is a combination of determination, hard work, and homework. The homework consists of systematic research, record keeping, and follow-up. The federal grants research form (see exhibit 10.1) will allow you to keep track of the grant programs you investigate (i.e., those that seem like your most logical grant sources) and will prevent your contacts and projects from being lost if anything happens to you. Copy this form and pass out a sufficient number of copies to your grants researchers so that your data gathering will be consistent and complete.

As you look at examples of the resources available on funding opportunities, you will see that information necessary to complete the federal grants research form is readily available. Do not stop with the first few funding sources that sound or look good. Remember, your goal is to locate the best funding sources for your project. Complete your research, then review and rate those funding sources you have identified using the past grantees analysis worksheet in chapter 11 (see exhibit 11.2).

FEDERAL RESEARCH TOOLS

How do you research and track federal grants? The federal research tools worksheet (see table 10.1) outlines some of the more useful resources for locating government funds.

Catalog of Federal Domestic Assistance

The Catalog of Federal Domestic Assistance (CFDA), which is published by the federal government, lists over 1,499 granting programs that disseminate over $100 billion in grants annually. The *Catalog* is provided free of charge on the Internet at <http://www.cfda.gov/> and is available in hard copy in at least two of the federal depository libraries in every congressional district. If you prefer to work with a hard copy, contact your congressperson's office to locate the copy nearest you.

In addition to the hard copy *Catalog* data, program information is also available on CD-ROM. The CD-ROM, which can be purchased from the Superintendent of Documents, Government Printing Office, includes the complete *Catalog*, a powerful search engine with an online tutorial, and the Federal Assistance Award Data System (FAADS) database, which lists who received financial awards by program number, geographical distribution, and organization (see table 10.1).

The basic edition of the *Catalog* is published annually in June, and is revised periodically online to reflect completed congressional action on the president's budget proposals and on substantive legislation as of the date of compilation, and includes information on Federal programs not available at the time the latest edition of the *Catalog* was published.

In addition to accessing the *CFDA* for free on the Internet, many colleges, universities, and large nonprofit organizations also subscribe to other grants databases to research federal grants opportunities. Subscribers pay a fee for access as opposed to the free access on the Internet, but these databases often offer more user friendly, faster ways to get to the best federal sources. Many have an auto-

TABLE 10.1

FEDERAL RESEARCH TOOLS WORKSHEET

Name	Description	Where to Get it	Cost
Catalog of Federal Domestic Assistance (866)512-1800 or (202)512-1800 in DC metro area Fax (202)512-2250	A database of all federal programs created by law (see sample entry)	Published in hard copy annually in June, updated twice a year June and December in CD-ROM and diskette format Mail Orders: Supt. Of Documents P.O. Box 371954 Pittsburgh, PA 15250-7954 Online at http://www.cfda.gov/	Printed Copy $63/year Online: Free access
Federal Register (866)512-1800 or (202)512-1800 in DC metro area Fax (202)512-2250	Official news publication for the federal government; makes public all meetings, announcements of granting programs, regulations, and deadlines (see sample entry).	Mail Orders: Supt. Of Documents P.O. Box 371954 Pittsburgh, PA 15250-7954 Online at http://www.nara.gov/fedreg/	Printed Copy: One year subscription including subject index and Code of Federal Regulation $764.00 Online: Free access
Federal Directory (800)336-4240 Fax (301)263-9801	Directory providing nearly 46,000 names, titles, telephone numbers, and e-mail addresses of senior and mid-level government officials in the executive office of the president, all 14 cabinet level federal departments, quasi-governmental agencies, US Congress, and the federal court system	Carroll Publishing 4701 Sangamore Road, Suite S-155 Bethesda, MD 20816	Print Version: $375.00 (6 issues) Also available online; online version also includes federal regional Information Call for online subscription price

matic searching function that periodically scans the database for sources related to the grantseeker's key search terms and alerts the grantseeker by e-mail of the most current opportunities. More information on these databases will follow. However, be aware that most of these databases provide an abbreviated description of the federal grant programs. Therefore, you will still need to access the *CFDA* to develop a full description of a prospective grantor's program.

TABLE 10.1			
FEDERAL RESEARCH TOOLS WORKSHEET *(continued)*			
Federal Business Opportunities FedBizOpps (877)472-3779	This government database list notices of proposed government procurement actions, contract awards, sales of government property,and other procurement information over $25,000	Issued by the U.S. Government Printing Office (GPO) and published on the Web by Community of Science, FedBizOpps is available online at http://www.fedbizopps.gov/	Online: Free access
Congressional Record (866)512-1800 or (202) 512-1800 in DC metro area, Fax (202)512-2250	Day-to-day proceedings and debates of the Senate and House of Representatives, includes all grant program money appropriated by Congress	Mail Orders: Supt. of Documents P.O. Box 371954 Pittsburgh, PA 15250-7954 Online at http://www.access.gpo.gov/su_docs /aces/aces150.html	Subscription $434/year Online: Free access
Listing of Federal Depository Libraries (866)512-1800 or (202) 512-1800 in DC metro Area, Fax (202) 512-2250	Locations of public and university libraries that allow free access to government publications like the CFDA	Mail Orders: Supt. Of Documents P.O. Box 371954 Pittsburgh, PA 15250-7954 Online at http://www.access.gpo.gov/su_docs/ locators/findlibs/index.html	Free
Agency Newsletters and Publications, RFPs, and Guidelines	Many federal agencies publish newsletters to inform you about the availablility of funds and program accomplishments. You may also request application materials, guidelines, and so on.	From agency. See "Regulations, Guidelines, and Literature" in CFDA entry.	Usually Free

The *Catalog* contains five indexes that can be used to help you identify your specific areas of program interest more efficiently. They include:

- Functional Index: Groups programs into 20 broad categories, such as agriculture, education, health, and so on, and 176 subcategories that identify specific areas of interest.
- Subject Index: The most commonly used index, since most people express their interests according to subject.
- Applicant Index: Allows you to look up a program to see whether you are eligible to apply. Because you must already know of the program to use this index, it is not a great help in identifying sources.
- Deadlines Index: Enables you to look up the deadline dates for programs to see whether the programs have a single or multiple deadline system.
- Authorization Index: Indexes the laws creating the funding.

Users should also be aware of the other sections of the *Catalog* that provide valuable information, such as:

- Programs added and deleted since the last edition of the *Catalog*
- A crosswalk of program numbers and title changes
- Regional and local offices
- Intergovernmental review requirements
- Definitions of the types of assistance under which programs are administered
- Proposal writing
- Grant application procedures

Accessing and Using the CFDA on the Internet: The *CFDA* can most easily be accessed on the Internet at <http://www.cfda.gov/>. Once you have gained access to the Web site, click "Find Assistance Programs" to perform a search. Then follow the instructions on screen. In the sample search (exhibit 10.2), the grantseeker performed a keyword search for programs related to teacher recruitment. Search results are shown in exhibit 10.3. By clicking one of the programs listed on the search results, the grantseeker can retrieve a *CFDA* entry describing the program.

Reading the CFDA: A sample *CFDA* entry (see exhibit 10.4) has been included to show the information provided in this valuable resource. All program descriptions/entries contain the following basic information.

Program Number and Title

Federal Agency: This is the branch of government administering the program, which is not much help to you except as general knowledge or for looking up programs and agencies in the *United States Government Manual*.

CFDA

The Catalog of Federal
Domestic Assistance

Skip Navigation

Home | FAQ | Privacy | Feedback | Tips on Searching for Programs

Browse The Catalog

By Functional Area

By Agency

By Sub-Agency

Alphabetically by Program Title

By Applicant Eligibility

By Beneficiary

By Program Deadline

By Type of Assistance

By Programs Requiring Executive
Order 12372 Review

By Budget Function Code (App. III)

By Programs Having Assistance
Formulas

Order Your Own Copy of the Catalog

Lookup Programs

Go Directly to a Program Number
If you know the program number you wish to view, enter it here.

Program Number:

[   ]   View Program

Keyword Search
Search for words or phrases in program text. (Search Tips)

Keyword:

["teacher recruitment"   ]   Search

Find a Grant
Search the Catalog for only grant programs.

Advanced Search
Run your own SQL-like queries against the CFDA database.

All Programs Listed Numerically
Shows a complete listing of all programs (BIG page).

Top 10 Percent of Programs
A list of the top 10% by number of viewings.

General Services Administration
Office of Governmentwide Policy
Office of Acquisition Policy
Regulatory and Federal Assistance Publication Division (MVA)

SEARCHING THE CATALOG OF FEDERAL DOMESTIC ASSISTANCE ONLINE

EXHIBIT 10.2

Authorization: You need this information to fill out some program applications and/or to look up the testimony and laws creating the funding (for the hardcore researcher and grantseeker only).

Objectives: Compare these general program objectives to your project. Do not give up if you are off the mark slightly; contact with the funding source may uncover new programs, changes, or hidden agendas.

Types of Assistance: Review and record the general type of support from this source, and then compare the information to your project definition.

Uses and Use Restrictions: Compare your project to this description of eligible projects.

Eligibility Requirements: Be sure your organization is designated as a legal recipient. If it is not, find an organization of the type designated and apply as a consortium or under a cooperative arrangement. Determine whether your project can benefit those that the program is intended to benefit.

The Catalog of Federal
Domestic Assistance

Home | FAQ | Privacy | Feedback | About The CFDA Web Site

Search Results

Documents 1 to 6 of 6 matching the query " "teacher recruitment" ".

New query

1. 84.320 - Alaska Native Educational Planning, Curriculum Development, Teacher Training, and Recruitment Program

Abstract: Home. FAQ. Privacy. Printer Friendly Version of 84.320. 84.320 Alaska Native Educational Planning, Curriculum Development, Teacher Training, and Recruitment ProgramAlaska Native Education). FEDERAL AGENCY: OFFICE OF ELEMENTARY AND SECONDARY EDUCATION, DEPARTMENT OF EDUCATION.

http://cfda.gov/static/p84320.htm
size 8,104 bytes - 11/30/2001 6:19:16 PM GMT

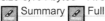 Summary Full

2. 84.336 - Teacher Quality Enhancement Grants

Abstract: Home. FAQ. Privacy. Printer Friendly Version of 84.336. 84.336 Teacher Quality Enhancement Grants. FEDERAL AGENCY: OFFICE OF THE ASSISTANT SECRETARY FOR POSTSECONDARY EDUCATION, HIGHER EDUCATION PROGRAMS, DEPARTMENT OF EDUCATIONAUTHORIZATION: Higher Education Act of 1965, Title II, Public Law 105-244.. OBJECTIVES: To improve st

http://cfda.gov/static/p84336.htm
size 10,818 bytes - 11/30/2001 6:19:21 PM GMT

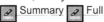 Summary Full

3. 84.297 - Native Hawaiian Curriculum Development, Teacher Training and Recruitment

Abstract: Home. FAQ. Privacy. Printer Friendly Version of 84.297. 84.297 Native Hawaiian Curriculum Development, Teacher Training and Recruitment. FEDERAL AGENCY: OFFICE OF ELEMENTARY AND SECONDARY EDUCATION, DEPARTMENT OF EDUCATION. AUTHORIZATION: Elementary and Secondary Education Act of 1965, Title IX, Part B, as amended, 20 U.S.C. 7909.

http://cfda.gov/static/p84297.htm
size 8,211 bytes - 11/30/2001 6:19:13 PM GMT

 Summary Full

CFDA SEARCH RESULTS

EXHIBIT 10.3

Application and Award Process: Review this information and record it on your federal grants research form. Do not let the deadline data bother you. If the award cycle has passed, you should still contact the agency and position yourself for the following year by asking for copies of old applications and a list of current grantees and by requesting to be a reviewer.

Assistance Considerations: Record any information on any match you are required to provide. This will be useful in evaluating funding sources. Matching requirements may eliminate some funding sources from your consideration.

The Catalog of Federal
Domestic Assistance   Home | FAQ | Privacy | Printer Friendly Version of 84.336

84.336 Teacher Quality Enhancement Grants

FEDERAL AGENCY:

OFFICE OF THE ASSISTANT SECRETARY FOR POSTSECONDARY EDUCATION,
HIGHER EDUCATION PROGRAMS, DEPARTMENT OF EDUCATION

AUTHORIZATION:

Higher Education Act of 1965, Title II, Public Law 105-244.

OBJECTIVES:

To improve student achievement; improve the quality of the current and future teaching
force by improving the preparation of prospective teachers and enhancing professional
development activities; hold institutions of higher education accountable for preparing
teachers who have the necessary teaching skills and are highly competent in the academic
content areas in which the teachers plan to teach, such as mathematics, science, English,
foreign language, history, economics, art, civics, Government, and geography, including
training in the effective uses of technology in the classroom; and recruit highly qualified
individuals, including individuals from other occupations, into the teaching force.

TYPES OF ASSISTANCE:

Project Grants.

USES AND USE RESTRICTIONS:

Awards may be used to reform teacher preparation programs, reform certification and
licensure requirements, provide alternatives to traditional preparation for teaching, create
alternative routes to State certification, develop and implement effective mechanisms for
recruitment, pay, and removal of teachers, address the problem of social promotion, and to
recruit teachers.

ELIGIBILITY REQUIREMENTS:

Applicant Eligibility: Eligible States and partnerships consist of high-need local
educational agencies; this refers to an agency that serves an elementary school or
secondary school located in an area containing: 1) A high percentage of individuals or
families with incomes below the poverty line, 2) a high percentage of secondary teachers
not teaching in the content area that they were trained to teach, or 3) a high teacher
turnover rate. An accredited institution of higher education, with a teacher training program
must demonstrate the following: (A) A graduate from the teacher training program exhibits
strong performance on State-determined qualifying assessments for new teachers
demonstrating that 80 percent or more of the graduates of the program intending to enter
the field of teaching have passed all of the applicable State qualification assessments for
new teachers including an assessment of each prospective teacher's subject matter
knowledge in the content area or areas in which the teacher intends to teach; (B) be ranked
among the highest-performing teacher preparation programs in the State as determined by
the State; (C) the teacher training program requires all the students of the program to
participate in intensive clinical experience that meets high academic standards in the case
of secondary candidates to successfully complete an academic major in the subject area in
which the candidate intends to teach; (D) competence through a high level of performance
in relevant content area; (F) successful completion of an academic major in the arts and
sciences in the case of elementary school candidates, or (G) competence through a high
level of performance in core academic subjects areas. (Note: Entities that may constitute a
partnership are specifically listed in the Law.)

SAMPLE *CFDA* ENTRY

EXHIBIT 10.4

Beneficiary Eligibility: Benefiting are students and communities within the high-need area.

Credentials/Documentation: None.

APPLICATION AND AWARD PROCESS:

Preapplication Coordination: This program is eligible under Executive Order 12372, "Intergovernmental Review of Federal Programs." An applicant should consult the office or official designated as the single point of contact their State for more information on the process the State requires to be followed in applying for assistance, if the State has selected the program for review.

Application Procedure: In any fiscal year in which funds are available for new awards, the Department of Education publishes a notice in the Federal Register inviting applications and establishing a deadline date. An application package is available from the Office of Higher Education Programs. Copies are available on the web page and will also be mailed upon request. This program is subject to the provisions of OMB Circular No. A-110.

Award Procedure: Peer review panels composed of representatives from public and private higher education, State and local educational agencies with expertise in teacher education are designated to review applications.

Deadlines: The deadline date is published in the Federal Register.

Range of Approval/Disapproval Time: Notification usually is made with 4 months of the deadline for submission of applicants.

Appeals: None.

Renewals: Applications for renewal of multi-year projects are processed and funded before those for new projects. Renewals are subject to the availability of funds.

ASSISTANCE CONSIDERATIONS:

Formula and Matching Requirements: This program has statutory requirements as follows: State applicants are required to match 50 percent of the grant. Partnership applicants are required to match at 25 percent the first year of the grants, 35 percent in the second year of grant, and 50 percent in the third through fifth years of the grant.

Length and Time Phasing of Assistance: Grants may be awarded for up to 3 years for State applicants and for up to 5 years for partnership applicants, subject to the availability of funds.

POST ASSISTANCE REQUIREMENTS:

Reports: A final performance report is required.

Audits: In accordance with the provisions of OMB Circular No. A- 133 (Revised, June 24, 1997), "Audits of States, Local Governments, and Non-Profit Organizations," nonfederal entities that expend financial assistance of $300,000 or more in Federal awards will have a single or a program-specific audit conducted for that year. Nonfederal entities that expend less than $300,000 a year in Federal awards are exempt from Federal Audit requirements for that year, except as noted in circular No. A-133.

Records: Records supporting claims under a grant must be maintained for 5 years after termination of the awards.

FINANCIAL INFORMATION:

SAMPLE *CFDA* ENTRY *(continued)*

EXHIBIT 10.4

Account Identification: 91-0201-0-1-502.

Obligations: (Grants) FY 00 $98,000,000; FY 01 est $98,000,000; and FY 02 est $54,000,000.

Range and Average of Financial Assistance: The fiscal year 2000 average continuation award for State grants is $1,612,000, new was $732,000; for continuation partnership grants $1,515,000, new $743,000; and for teacher recruitment continuation grants $361,000.

PROGRAM ACCOMPLISHMENTS:

In fiscal year 2000, approximately 91 awards are expected to be made. Thirty one State grants, 33 partnerships, and 27 teacher recruitment grants.

REGULATIONS, GUIDELINES, AND LITERATURE:

Contact the Program Office for additional information.

INFORMATION CONTACTS:

Regional or Local Office: Not applicable.

Headquarters Office: Department of Education, Office of Postsecondary Education, Higher Education Programs, Office of the Deputy Assistant Secretary, 400 Maryland Avenue, SW., Washington, DC 20202. Contact: Ed Crowe. Telephone: (202) 502-7878.

Web Site Address: http://www.ed.gov/offices/OPE/OHEP

RELATED PROGRAMS:

None.

EXAMPLES OF FUNDED PROJECTS:

This is a new program; examples are not yet available.

CRITERIA FOR SELECTING PROPOSALS:

Contact the Program Office for this information.

General Services Administration
Office of Governmentwide Policy (M)
Office of Acquisition Policy (MV)
Governmentwide Information Systems Division (MVS)
Federal Domestic Assistance Catalog Staff

SAMPLE *CFDA* ENTRY *(continued)*

EXHIBIT 10.4

In addition, assistance considerations will help you develop your project planner (see chapter 12). When you know about matching requirements in advance, you can identify what resources your organization will be required to provide. Watch for confusing comments such as, "a match is not required, but is advised."

Post Assistance Requirements: This section provides you with report, audit, and record requirements.

Financial Information: This section gives you an idea of what funds the agency program may have received, but do not take the information here as the last word. One entry I reviewed said the funding agency had $3 million for research. When contacted, the agency had over $30 million to disseminate under the program described and similar ones in the CFDA. Refer to the entry, but investigate it further.

Program Accomplishments: This section provides you with information on how many and what types of projects were funded in the previous fiscal year.

Regulations, Guidelines, and Literature: Record and send for any information you can get on the funder.

Information Contacts: Record and use to begin contacting funders as outlined in this book. If provided, note the name and phone number of the contact person. While the contact person or phone number may have changed, you at least will have a place to start.

Related Programs: Some CFDA entries include suggestions of other programs that are similar or related to your area of interest. While these suggestions are usually obvious and you may have already uncovered the programs in your research, review this section for leads.

Examples of Funded Projects: Compare your project with those listed and asked yourself how it fits in.

Criteria for Selecting Proposals: Review and record the information here. Criteria are frequently listed with no regard to their order of importance and lack any reference to the point values that they will be given in the review. Therefore, you should also obtain the rules from the *Federal Register,* the agency publication, or a past reviewer.

After reviewing the CFDA entries, select the best government funding program for your project. Contact the federal agency by using the information listed under "Information Contacts."

Federal Register

The *Federal Register* is the newspaper of the federal government. To make legal notices on a great variety of federal issues official, the government must publish notices in the *Federal Register*. The creation of new government granting programs must be published in the *Federal Register*. Rules to evaluate proposals are also printed in the *Federal Register*. The hard copy of this government publication is provided free of charge at federal depository libraries in your congressional district. Locate your nearest library by visiting <http://www.access.gpo.gov/su_docs/locators/findlib>. The *Register* can also be accessed for free through the Internet at <http://www.nara.gov/fedreg/>.

Once you have used the CFDA to select the best government funding program for your project, phone, fax, or e-mail the contact listed in the CFDA entry to find out the day(s) the *Federal Register* published notices, proposed rules, and/or final rules and regulations regarding the program you are interested in. Ask for the vol-

Federal Register
Online via *GPO Access*

Attention: New Federal Register Browse Feature ◀▬◀

Database for the 1995, 1996, 1997, 1998, 1999, 2000, 2001, 2002 and 2003 *Federal Register* (Volumes 60, 61, 62, 63, 64, 65, 66, 67 and 68)

The *Federal Register* is the official daily publication for Rules, Proposed Rules, and Notices of Federal agencies and organizations, as well as Executive Orders and other Presidential Documents. Helpful Hints provide instructions for searching the database. Documents may be retrieved in ASCII "TEXT" format (full text, graphics omitted), Adobe Portable Document Format, "PDF" (full text with graphics), and "SUMMARY" format (abbreviated text).

Live HTTP links in 2000 Federal Register documents.

The 1994 Federal Register (Volume 59) database is also available, however, it contains no fields or section identifiers.

Federal Register **Volume:**

⬜ 2003 Federal Register, Vol. 68   ☑ 2002 Federal Register, Vol. 67

⬜ 2001 Federal Register, Vol. 66   ⬜ 2000 Federal Register, Vol. 65

⬜ 1999 Federal Register, Vol. 64   ⬜ 1998 Federal Register, Vol. 63

⬜ 1997 Federal Register, Vol. 62   ⬜ 1996 Federal Register, Vol. 61

⬜ 1995 Federal Register, Vol. 60

Federal Register **Sections (If you select none, all sections will be searched, but you may select one or more sections):**

⬜ Contents and Preliminary Pages   ⬜ Presidential Documents
⬜ Final Rules and Regulations   ⬜ Sunshine Act Meetings*
⬜ Proposed Rules   ⬜ Reader Aids
☑ Notices   ⬜ Corrections

* As of March 1, 1996, Sunshine Act Meetings were incorporated into the Notices section of the *Federal Register*.

Issue Date (Enter either a range of dates or a specific date in the format

Side navigation menu:
- **Federal Register**
- **Code of Federal Regulations**
- **Public and Private Laws**
- **Weekly Compilation of Presidential Documents**
- **Public Papers of the Presidents of the United States**
- **United States Government Manual**
- **Privacy Act Issuances**
- **Document Drafting Handbook & Information for Agencies**
- **U.S. Congress Information**
- **GPO Access Search Page**

SEARCHING THE *FEDERAL REGISTER* **ONLINE**

EXHIBIT 10.5

mm/dd/yyyy):

Date Range: From `06/20/2002` to `06/20/2002`

OR

⦿ ON ⦿ BEFORE ⦿ AFTER `_____`

Search Terms:

`"teacher recruitment"`

[SUBMIT] [CLEAR]

Maximum Records Returned: `40` Default is 40. Maximum is 200.

Enter search terms in the space above. Phrases must be in quotation marks
(" "). The operators **ADJ (adjacent)**, **AND**, **OR** and **NOT** can be used, but
must be in capital letters. For example: "environmental protection agency"
AND superfund. The page cited as 60 FR 12345 can be retrieved using the
search **"page 12345"**. CFR parts should also be searched as phrases; for
example: **"40 CFR part 55"**. Word roots can be searched using an asterisk
(*) following the word stem. For example: **regulat*** will retrieve both
regulation and regulate. Additional instructions and examples.

Browse the Table of Contents of the current issue of the *Federal Register*
HTML PDF ◄███

Browse back issues of the *Federal Register* Table of Contents 2003, 2002,
2001, 2000, 1999, 1998

History of Line Item Veto Notices (as published in the *Federal Register*)
prior to Supreme Court Opinion No. 97-1374 (Text) (PDF) (Argued April
27, 1998 -- Decided June 25, 1998).

About the *Unified Agenda*.

To search the *Unified Agenda,* return to the multidatabase search form.

Browse the *Unified Agenda* - December 2002.

───

This document is sponsored by the Office of the Federal Register, National
Archives and Records Administration on the United States Government
Printing Office Web site.

Questions or comments regarding this service? Contact the *GPO Access*
User Support Team by e-mail at gpoaccess@gpo.gov; by telephone at (202)
512-1530 or toll free at (888) 293-6498; by fax at (202) 512-1262.

SEARCHING THE *FEDERAL REGISTER* ONLINE *(continued)*

EXHIBIT 10.5

Federal Register Search Results

Search Database:

Federal Register, Volume 67 (2002)

***For: " "teacher recruitment"" ***

Total Hits: 2

[1]
fr20jn02N Teacher Quality Enhancement Grants Program--Teacher Recruitment
   Size: 11924 , **Score:** 1000 , HTML , PDF , SUMMARY

[2]
Query Report for Search of: 2002_register
   Size: 3156 , **Score:** 1 , TEXT

Questions or comments regarding this service? Contact the ***GPO Access*** **User Support Team** by Internet e-mail at *gpoaccess@gpo.gov*; by telephone at 202-512-1530; or by fax at 202-512-1262.

Page #ACES140.wrapper February 27, 1997

***FEDERAL REGISTER* SEARCH RESULTS**

EXHIBIT 10.6

ume(s), the number(s), the issue date(s), and the page(s). The more information you have, the easier it will be for you to locate the information you are looking for.

When accessing the Federal Register through the World Wide Web, you can search online for the information you need. In the sample search shown in exhibit 10.5, the grantseeker asked to search the June 20, 2002, *Federal Register* for notices related to teacher recruitment. Search results are shown in exhibit 10.6. By clicking on the first hit listed on the search results, the grantseeker retrieved the notice inviting applications for new awards for fiscal year 2002 under the Teacher Quality Enhancement Grants Program—Teacher Recruitment Competition CFDA No. 84.336C (see exhibit 10.7). This particular notice describes the purpose of the program, eligible applicants, project period, application regulations (such as page limit), and supplementary information. However, contents of notices do vary.

As you can see in exhibit 10.5, Notices is not the only section of the *Federal Register* that can be searched. Grantseekers can also look at Contents and Preliminary Pages, Final Rules and Regulations, Proposed Rules, Presidential Documents, Sunshine Act Meetings, Reader Aids, and Corrections.

[Federal Register: June 20, 2002 (Volume 67, Number 119)]
[**Notices**]
[Page 41968-41970]
From the Federal Register Online via GPO Access [wais.access.gpo.gov]
[DOCID:fr20jn02-57]

DEPARTMENT OF EDUCATION

[CFDA No. 84.336C]

Teacher Quality Enhancement Grants Program--**Teacher Recruitment**
Competition; Notice Inviting Applications for New Awards for Fiscal
Year (FY) 2002

    Purpose of Program: This program provides grants to States and to
partnerships to promote improvements in the quality of new teachers
with the ultimate goal of increasing student achievement in pre-K-12
classrooms.
    Eligible Applicants: States (including the District of Columbia,
Puerto Rico and the insular areas) and partnerships comprised, at a
minimum, of an institution of higher education with an eligible **teacher**
preparation program, a school of arts and sciences, and a high-need
local educational agency (LEA). These terms are defined in section 203
of the Higher Education Act and in regulations for this program in 34
CFR 611. States and partnerships that received an FY 1999 grant under
this program are not eligible for this competition.
    Applications Available: June 20, 2002.
    Deadline for Transmittal of Applications: July 25, 2002.
    Deadline for Intergovernmental Review: September 24, 2002.
    Estimated Available Funds: $8,920,000.
    Estimated Range of Awards: $195,000 -- $465,000.
    Estimated Average Size of Awards: $372,000.
    Estimated Number of Awards: 24.

    Note: The Department is not bound by any estimates in this
notice.

    Project Period: Up to 36 months.
    Page Limit: The application narrative is where you, the applicant,
address the selection criteria reviewers use to evaluate your
application. You must limit your narrative to the equivalent of no more
than 50 pages. In addition, you must limit your accompanying work plan
to the equivalent of no more than 10 pages, your budget narrative to
the

[[Page 41969]]

equivalent of no more than 10 pages and your evaluation plan to the
equivalent of no more than 5 pages, using the following standards:
    A ``page'' is 8.5[sec] x 11[sec], on one side only, with
1[sec] margins at the top, bottom, and both sides.
    Double space (no more than three lines per vertical inch)
all text in the application narrative, work plan, budget narrative, and
evaluation plan, including titles, headings, quotations, references,
and captions, as well as all text in charts, tables, figures, and
graphs.
    Use a font that is either 12-point or larger or no smaller
than 10 pitch (characters per inch).

SAMPLE *FEDERAL REGISTER* NOTICE

EXHIBIT 10.7

Our reviewers will not read any pages of your application that--
Exceed the page limit if you apply these standards; or
Exceed the equivalent of the page limit if you apply other standards.

Applicable Regulations: (a) The Education Department General Administrative Regulations (EDGAR) in 34 CFR parts 74, 75, 77, 79, 80, 82, 85, 86, 97, 98 and 99. (b) The regulations for this program appear in 34 CFR part 611.

SUPPLEMENTARY INFORMATION: The **Teacher Recruitment** Grants program, one of the three **Teacher** Quality Enhancement Grant programs contained in Title II, Part A of the Higher Education Act (HEA), is authorized in section 204 of the HEA. The program affords an opportunity for States and partnerships to address the challenge of America's **teacher** shortage by making significant and lasting systemic changes to the ways that teachers are recruited, prepared--either through postsecondary **teacher** preparation programs or alternative routes to teaching for those coming to the profession from other careers or educational backgrounds--and supported to teach in high-need schools. In administering the program, the Department of Education's goal is to support the efforts of the States and partnerships to ensure that all students, especially those in high-need school districts, have a highly qualified **teacher** to help them achieve to challenging State content and performance standards.

Through this notice the Secretary announces requirements and procedures to govern the competition for FY 2002 grant funds. In particular, the Department will implement only a single application review process and use the selection criteria identified in 34 CFR 611.32 rather than the two-step review process identified in 34 CFR 611.3(a)(iii). In all other respects the requirements and procedures for the upcoming FY 2002 competition are the same as those authorized in the **Teacher** Quality Enhancement Grant program regulations (34 CFR part 611) and the Education Department General Administrative Regulations (EDGAR).

Waiver of Proposed Rulemaking

Under the Administrative Procedure Act (5 U.S.C. 553) the Department generally offers interested parties the opportunity to comment on proposed regulations. However, these regulations make procedural changes only and do not establish new substantive policy. Therefore, under 5 U.S.C. 553(b)(a), the Secretary has determined that proposed rulemaking is not required. These requirements will apply to the FY 2002 grant competition only.

Because the Department did not receive from Congress a FY 2002 appropriation for this and other programs until January of 2002, the Department has had insufficient time to implement the two-stage application process otherwise required by 34 CFR 611.3(a)(3) and still make awards by September 30, 2002, the last day on which the Department may obligate these funds. The public is not prejudiced by eliminating the first of the two-stage review procedures in the upcoming competition because all potential applicants are eligible to apply for awards under the selection criteria identified in 34 CFR 611.32 and will be treated equally.

Pilot Project for Electronic Submission of This Application

In FY 2002, the U.S. Department of Education is continuing to expand its pilot project of electronic submission of applications to include additional formula grant programs and additional discretionary grant competitions. The Title II, **Teacher Recruitment** Program (CFDA No. 84.336C) is included in the pilot project. If you are an applicant under the Title II, **Teacher Recruitment** Program, you may submit your application to us in either electronic or paper format.

The pilot project involves the use of the Electronic Grant

SAMPLE *FEDERAL REGISTER* NOTICE *(continued)*

EXHIBIT 10.7

Application System (e-APPLICATION, formerly e-GAPS) portion of the
Grant Administration and Payment System (GAPS). We request your
participation in this pilot project. We shall continue to evaluate its
success and solicit suggestions for improvement.
    If you participate in this e-APPLICATION pilot, please note the
following:
    Your participation is strictly voluntary.
    You will not receive any additional point value or penalty
because you submit a grant application in electronic or paper format.
    You can submit all grant documents electronically,
including the Application for Federal Assistance (ED 424), Budget
Information-Non-Construction Programs (ED 524), and all necessary
assurances and certifications.
    Within three working days of submitting your electronic
application, fax a signed copy of the Application for Federal
Assistance (ED 424) to the Application Control Center after following
these steps:
    1. Print ED 424 from the e-APPLICATION system.
    2. Make sure that the institution's Authorizing Representative
signs this form.
    3. Before faxing this form, submit your electronic application via
the e-APPLICATION system. You will receive an automatic
acknowledgement, which will include a PR/Award number (an identifying
number unique to your application).
    4. Place the PR/Award number in the upper right hand corner of ED
424.
    5. Fax ED 424 to the Application Control Center at (202) 260-1349.
    We may request that you give us original signatures on all
other forms at a later date.
    You may access the electronic grant application for the Title II,
Teacher Recruitment Grants program at: http://e-grants.ed.gov.
    We have included additional information about the e-APPLICATION
pilot project (see Parity Guidelines between Paper and Electronic
Applications) in the application package.

For Applications Contact: Education Publications Center (ED Pubs), P.O.
Box 1398, Jessup, MD 20794-1398, Telephone (toll free): 1-877-433-7827.
FAX: (301) 470-1244.
    If you use a telecommunications device for the deaf (TDD), you may
call (toll free): 1-877-576-7734.
    You may also contact ED Pubs at its Web site: http://www.ed.gov/
pubs/edpubs.html.
    Or you may contact ED Pubs at its e-mail address:
edpubs@inet.ed.gov.
    If you request an application from ED Pubs, be sure to identify
this competition as follows: CFDA number 84.336C. You may also request
application forms by calling (202) 502-7878 or submitting the name of
the competition and your name and postal address to:
teacherquality@ed.gov.
    Applications are also available on the **Teacher** Quality Web Site:
http://www.ed.gov/offices/OPE/heatqp/.

[[Page 41970]]

FOR FURTHER INFORMATION CONTACT: Brenda Shade, U.S. Department of
Education, 1919 K Street, NW., Room 6148, Washington, DC 20006-8525.
Telephone: (202) 502-7878 or via Internet: Brenda.Shade@ed.gov.
    If you use a telecommunications device for the deaf (TDD), you may
call the Federal Information Relay Service (FIRS) at 1-800-877-8339.
    Individuals with disabilities may obtain this document in
alternative format, (e.g., Braille, large print, audiotape, or computer
diskette) on request to the program contact person listed under FOR
FURTHER INFORMATION CONTACT.

SAMPLE *FEDERAL REGISTER* NOTICE *(continued)*

EXHIBIT 10.7

```
        Individuals with disabilities may obtain a copy of the application
package in an alternative format by contacting that person. However,
the Department is not able to reproduce in an alternative format the
standard forms included in the application package.

Electronic Access to This Document

    You may view this document, as well as all other Department of
Education documents published in the Federal Register, in text or Adobe
Portable Document Format (PDF) on the Internet at the following site:
www.ed.gov/legislation/FedRegister.
    To use PDF you must have Adobe Acrobat Reader, which is available
free at this site. If you have questions about using PDF, call the U.S.
Government Printing Office (GPO), toll free, at 1-888-293-6498; or in
the Washington, DC, area at (202) 512-1530
```

SAMPLE *FEDERAL REGISTER* NOTICE *(continued)*

EXHIBIT 10.7

Federal Business Opportunities

Effective January 1, 2002, the *Commerce Business Daily* was replaced by the Fed-BizOpps (FBO) database. Issued by the U.S. Government Printing Office (GPO) and published on the Web by Community of Science, FBO lists notices of proposed government procurement actions, contract awards, sales of government property, contract awards, and other procurement information. Published daily Monday through Friday, FBO lists all available contracts in excess of $25,000. Thousands of separate contracting offices and countless grant programs advertise billions in government contracts each year in this publication. The successful bidders are listed in the back section of each issue.

Many successful nonprofit organizations have used the list of successful bidders to develop subcontracts and form consortia. Through subcontracts and consortia, these organizations are able to build a track record and gain familiarity with both the contracts process and federal contract offices. The FBO also advertises notices of meetings that assist bidders in developing insight into upcoming contracts. Fed-BizOpps is available online, free of charge, at <http://www.fedbizopps.gov/>.

GRANTS DATABASES

GrantSelect

Produced by Oryx Press, a division of Greenwood Publishing Group, *GrantSelect* is an online grants database that provides information on more than 10,000 funding programs available from state and federal governments, corporations, foundations, and associations. Grantseekers can subscribe to the entire research grants database or to any one of the seven special segments offered: arts and humanities, biomedical and health care, children and youth, community development, K-12 and adult basic education, international programs, and operating grants. For an additional fee, the database comes with e-mail alert service that notifies the grantseeker of any new funding opportunities within his or her area of interest. To try a trial version of GrantSelect, visit <http://www.grantselect.com>. For further information, you may call the Oryx Press/Greenwood Publishing at (800) 225–5800; or, for questions on registration, pricing, and information for consortia, you may also contact them at info@oryxpress.com. For questions about the content of GrantSelect, use grantsadmin@oryxpress.com.

Sponsored Programs Information Network (SPIN)

SPIN is a database produced by Infoed International, Inc. Originally developed by the Research Foundation of the State University of New York (SUNY), the database contains profiles on thousands of national and international government and private funding sources. It is a fee-based system used by over 800 institutions worldwide. *SPIN.PLUS* is also available. It is composed of three modules, including *SPIN*, the funding opportunities database; *GENIUS*, the searchable expertise profile system that currently contains faculty CVs and will eventually be expanded to contain facilities and institutional profiles; and *SMARTS*, a program that matches the profiles with the funding opportunities and delivers automatic daily updates. The *SMARTS* service is aimed at helping investigators keep current on new funding opportunities, new and approaching deadlines, and sponsor updates, and administrators on who is getting what "hits." You can reach InfoEd International by calling (800) 727–6427 or find out more about their products by visiting <http://infoed.is.mcgill.ca/Products.stm>.

Illinois Researcher Information Service (IRIS)

IRIS, a unit of the University of Illinois Library at Urbana-Champaign, offers colleges and universities three fee-based online funding and research services:

- the IRIS database, which is updated daily, available in World Wide Web and Telnet versions, and contains records on over 8,000 federal and private funding opportunities in the sciences, social sciences, arts, and humanities

- the IRIS Alert Service, which allows subscribers to create personal IRIS search profiles and select their preferred search frequency, delivery method (e-mail or Web), and keywords

- the IRIS Expertise Service, which enables researchers at subscribing institutions to create detailed electronic CVs that can be used in the electronic submission of grant proposals, and can also be posted to a Web-accessible database for viewing by colleagues at other institutions, program officers at federal and private funding agencies, and private companies.

The IRIS office does not sell subscriptions to individual researchers. However, you can arrange a free trial period for your community college, college, university, or nonprofit institution (research institutes, government departments, etc.) by contacting the IRIS office at (217) 333–0284 or visiting <http://www.library.uiuc.edu/iris/>.

Community of Science (COS)

Community of Science (COS) is a global registry of information about scientists and the funding of science, and is designed to meet the needs of the research and development community. The COS system includes:

- the COS Funding Opportunities database, which includes more than 23,000 records, representing over 400,000 funding opportunities, worth over $33 billion from government sources, foundations, corporations, and other organizations
- the COS Funding Alert, which provides the user with a weekly, customized, e-mailed list of funding opportunities based on his or her specified criteria
- the COS Expertise database, which connects academic and corporate researchers via the Internet and contains more than 480,000 profiles of researchers from over 1,300 institutions
- COS Funded Research, which enables members to research and track information on funding and award histories at leading research facilities around the world

COS Funding Opportunities is included as part of a full COS membership, but may also be purchased as a stand-alone information resource. There are two types of subscription plans—small business and institutional. Subscription plans for individuals are not available. For more information and subscription rates, call (410) 563–2595 ext. 302 or visit <http://www.cos.com>.

FEDERAL AGENCY INTERNET MAILING LISTS

Several federal agencies have established Internet mailing lists to electronically disseminate news about their activities and services. You can subscribe to these LISTSERVs to help keep up to date on federal funding opportunities. The following is a list of some of the federal agencies that provide this type of service.

- National Science Foundation (NSF)—NSF has created the Custom New Service to provide you with a weekly summary of all new documents posted on the NSF Web site. It also has a personal profile component and an e-mail funding alert service. You can subscribe to the Custom News Service at <http://www.nsf.gov/home/cns/start.htm>.

- National Institutes of Health (NIH)—National Institutes of Health will automatically e-mail subscribers the Table of Contents (TOC) information for each week's issue of the NIH Guide for Grants and Contracts. Associated with each TOC entry is the Web address (URL) for each Guide Article. To subscribe to the Guide TOC Notification LISTSERV, send an e-mail to listserv@list.nih.gov and, in the first line of the e-mail message, not the subject line, provide the following information: subscribeNIHTOC-L your name. Your e-mail address will be automatically obtained from the e-mail message you send to the LISTSERV.

- Centers for Disease Control and Prevention (CDC)—At the Centers for Disease Control and Prevention (CDC), you can subscribe to several mailing lists. For a list of available mailing lists, and to subscribe, go to <http://www.cdc.gov/subscribe.html>.

- U.S. Department of Justice (DOJ)—JustInfo, sponsored by the U.S. Department of Justice National Criminal Justice Reference Service (NCJRS), is an electronic newsletter sent to subscribers on the first and fifteenth of each month, highlighting agency initiatives, new publications, funding opportunities, conferences, and other news from NCJRS sponsoring agencies. Archived issues are available at <http://www.ncjrs.org/justinfo/dates.html>. To subscribe go to <http://puborder.ncjrs.org/listservs/subscribe_JUSTINFO.asp>.

- U.S. Department of Education (DOE)—The Department of Education has three mailing lists:

  - *EDInfo* is an information service that delivers two e-mail messages a week featuring new reports, funding opportunities, and other information from the U.S. Department of Education. A special monthly issue describes new teaching and learning resources on the Web. To subscribe address, an e-mail message to listproc@inet.ed.gov and write in the message this, and nothing else: subscribe Edinfo yourfirstname yourlastname

  - *No Child Left Behind* Electronic Newsletter updates you on information, events, and announcements about *No Child Left Behind*. To subscribe, go to <http://www.nclb.gov/subscribe.html>.

  - EDTV Mailing List is a free e-mail information service to provide details of the Department of Education's monthly television series entitled Education News Parents Can Use. To subscribe, address an e-mail message to listproc@inet.ed.gov. Write nothing in the subject line (leave blank). Write this in the message: subscribe edtv yourfirstname yourlastname

- National Institute for Standards and Technology (NIST) has three electronic newsletters. *NIST Update* is a bimonthly report that highlights NIST activities, research, and services. *NIST Tech Beat* is a monthly newsletter containing science and technology news briefs from NIST written for general audiences. *NIST News Releases* are only obtainable by e-mail, not print, and are available in a variety of categories. To subscribe to any or all of these materials, go to <http://www.nist.gov/public_affairs/mailform.htm>.

Accessing the information you need to locate available government funding is not difficult or expensive. While this chapter provides sufficient detail to satisfy the computer-literate grantseeker, such skills and equipment are not prerequisites for accessing information.

Whether you use the Internet, a commercial database, or hard copies of government publications, the key to locating federal grant funds and to commanding the respect of the bureaucrats you will interact with in your quest for grants is to do your homework and learn all you can about each program you are thinking about approaching.

CHAPTER 11

How to Contact Government Grant Sources

At this point, you have researched a potential federal grant opportunity, but you may not be convinced of the importance of preproposal contact with a federal program officer, especially if you have book marked the program's Web site and already have its application form and guidelines. Like many other prospective grantseekers, you probably do not want or see the need to talk to government bureaucrats. You just want to get your proposal submitted. However, you should remember that your goal is not to *apply* for a grant; it is to be *awarded* a grant. Therein lies the reason for making preproposal contact. In fact, after 30 years in the grants field, I can assure you that principal investigators and project directors who are consistently funded actually contact government grantors several times a year, and not just during the preproposal period.

Several years before the first edition of this book was created, a study of 10,000 federal grant applicants documented that those grantseekers who had made contact with federal program staff before submitting their applications, experienced a threefold increase in success over those who simply submitted the application. The key to their success was the opportunity to ask questions that may not have been covered in *CFDA* program descriptions or agency publications.

When asked what the successful grantees discussed with the federal program officers, many said they asked questions that help them to more closely meet the program guidelines. While this was the most frequent response, I believe they really asked questions aimed at uncovering what the program was really interested in funding.

When contacting a program officer make no mistake about your intention. It is to confirm your research and provide a more complete picture of what the grant

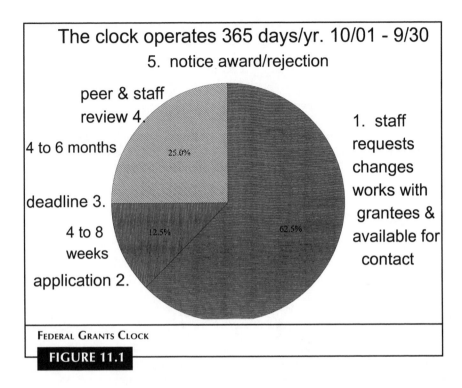

The clock operates 365 days/yr. 10/01 - 9/30
5. notice award/rejection

peer & staff
review 4.

4 to 6 months   25.0%

1. staff
requests
changes
works with
grantees &
available for
contact

deadline 3.

4 to 8   12.5%   62.5%
weeks

application 2.

FEDERAL GRANTS CLOCK

FIGURE 11.1

program seeks to create and fund in your field. Your contact is professional, not personal. Even if you have very limited resources and cannot get to Washington, DC, do not be frustrated. While the study of 10,000 federal grantees was done years before e-mail was possible, it revealed no differences between telephone and face-to-face contact. The crucial point is that while you have done your homework, you need to make preproposal contact to confirm what you do know, and to find out more about the projects funded, how the submitted proposals will be evaluated, and by whom in order to prepare a winning proposal.

WHEN TO MAKE PREPROPOSAL CONTACT

The timing of contact is critical. Each of the 1,499-plus federal programs has a unique sequence of events related to its granting cycle. Review the diagram of the federal grants clock to help you determine where a particular federal agency program is in the grants process (see figure 11.1).

The federal grants clock can be thought of as a five-step cycle or process.

1. The first step involves the dissemination of and comment on the rules and regulations governing each program to be reviewed, and comments are encouraged from any interested party. The comments are published, the final

rules are printed, and the announcements of deadlines are made in such publications as the *Federal Register, NIH Guide*, and *National Science Foundation E-Bulletin*.

2. The federal program officer then develops the actual application package
   and places it on the agency's Web site for public access. This package is referred to as the Request for Proposal (RFP) or the Request for Application
   (RFA).

3. The deadline for submission occurs.

4. Once proposals are submitted, they are sent by e-mail or hard copy to selected peer reviewers for evaluation. In some cases, the reviewers are required to go to a specified site to receive and review the proposals. The
   reviewers must follow the agency's evaluation system and score each proposal according to the published guidelines. There also may be a staff review. In these cases, the staff reviewers provide the head of the agency with
   a list of proposals they recommend for funding.

5. The notices of award and rejection are made and the cycle starts again.

Establishing preproposal contact for the next funding cycle is most productive
when initiated after the notices of award or rejection have been given (step 5) for
the previous cycle and before the application packages are made available (step
2) in the new cycle. Use the techniques outlined in this chapter to maximize the
benefits of preproposal contact and gain the insight you will need to prepare a
grant-winning proposal.

GETTING THE MOST FROM PAST GRANTEES

You will find it beneficial to discover who has previously received funding by the
program that interests you. In many cases you can locate a list of past grantees on
the agency's Web site, or you can use the sample e-mail in exhibit 11.1 to request
a list. E-mail the contact person identified in the CFDA entry or the program announcement. You may have to request the list of past grantees again by phoning
the contact person. If you get his or her voice mail, leave a message on what you
want and leave your phone and fax number as well as your e-mail address. Access
to this list and the valuable information it provides is your right. If you do not receive a response to your initial request, request the list again making sure to let
the funding source know why you want it, and also that you are aware that you
are entitled to this list under the Freedom of Information Act. If all else fails, you
may be able to get this information from the public information office of the
agency, or you can ask your congressperson to get the list for you. By law, federal
bureaucrats have to respond to a congressperson's request. He or she *will* get the
list. Be aware, though, that bureaucrats may react negatively to the intervention
of elected officials. Therefore, you should ask the elected official not to reveal for
whom they are getting the list.

From:	<grantseeker@proactive.edu>
To:	<contact person@feds.gov>
Cc:	
Sent:	date, time
Subject:	RE: Information Request

Dear [Contact Person]:

I am interested in receiving information on [CFDA #, Program Title]. Please e-mail all relevant web site information and Internet addresses for application forms, guidelines, etc.

In order to increase my understanding of your program, I would also appreciate a list of last year's grant recipients. If this list is available on the Internet please provide the address. If it is not, please e-mail the list to me as an attachment or fax it to me at [fax number].

Thank you for your assistance.

Name
Title
Organization/Institution
Address
Telephone Number

SAMPLE E-MAIL TO A FEDERAL AGENCY REQUESTING INFORMATION AND GUIDELINES

EXHIBIT 11.1

With your past grantee list in hand, you are now ready to begin the analysis of your chances for success. Complete the past grantee analysis worksheet (exhibit 11.2) and analyze the information contained in the list of grantees. When this worksheet is completed, you will be able to approach the grantor with knowledge and insight into its granting program.

Contacting a Past Grantee

Successful grant recipients can be approached and will generally share helpful information with you. Grantees will generally feel flattered that you called. They are usually not competing with you for funds because you will be seeking first-year funding and they will be seeking a continuation grant. Select a past grantee to call. Choose one outside of your geographic area and one who is less likely to view you as a competitor. Tell the grantee how you got his or her name, congratulate him or her on the award, and then ask to speak to the person who worked on the proposal.

Select questions from the following list to ask the person who worked on the proposal, or ask any other questions that will help you learn more about the funding source.

- Did you call or go to see the funding source before writing the proposal?

1.   Award Size

      •   What was the largest award granted? _____
           For what type of project?   _____

      •   What was the smallest award granted?   _____
           For what type of project?   _____

2.   Grantor Type

      •   What characteristics or similarities can be drawn from last year's list of grant
           recipients?

      •   What is the size or type of grantee organization (i.e., public, private, colleges)?

      •   What are the geographic preferences or concentrations?

3.   Project Director/Principle Investigator

      •   What title or degrees appear most frequently on the list of last year's recipients?

      •   Does there seem to be a relationship between award size and project director
           degree?

4.   From the list of last year's grantees, select two to contact for more information. Select
      grantees that you may have a link with and/or organizations that you are familiar with.

5.   Based on the information gathered in questions one through four, rate how well your
      proposal idea matches the prospective grantor's profile.

      ___ very well   ___   good   ___   fair   ___   not well

6.   What programs can you now ask the program officer/contact person as a result of your
      analysis?

PAST GRANTEE ANALYSIS WORKSHEET

EXHIBIT 11.2

• Whom did you find most helpful on the funding source's staff?

• Did you use your advocates or congressperson?

• Did the funding source review your idea or proposal before submission?

• Did you use consultants to help you on the proposal?

• Was there a hidden agenda to the program's guidelines?

• When did you begin the process of developing your application?

• When did you first contact the funding source?

• What materials did you find most helpful in developing your proposal?

- Did the funding source come to see you (site visit) before or after the proposal was awarded? Who came? What did they wear? How old were they? Would you characterize them as conservative, moderate, or liberal? Did anything surprise you during their visit?
- How close was your initial budget to the awarded amount?
- Who on the funding source's staff negotiated the budget?
- How did you handle matching or in-kind contributions?
- What would you do differently next time?

UNDERSTANDING THE PROPOSAL REVIEW PROCESS

To prepare the best possible proposal, you must know who will be reading it and how it will be reviewed. Request a list of last year's reviewers in writing, by phone, by e-mail, or in person. I suggest sending an e-mail and then following up with the other methods if necessary. Exhibit 11.3 provides a sample e-mail you may use.

You want a list of last year's reviewers or a profile of what the grantor looks for in a reviewer so you can write a proposal based on the reviewers' expertise, reading level, background, etc. Once you have the list, you can contact a reviewer to discuss the areas they look for when reviewing proposals. Preferably you can get the program official to identify who he or she believes to be the program's best reviewers from the list. Then you can contact them for more specific information like how much time they spend reading each proposal, how many proposals they have to read in one sitting, and so on. This information will help you perform a mock review of your proposal before submitting it.

Some federal programs use the same reviewers each year and may be reluctant to give you their names. If this is the case, tell the federal bureaucrat that you would like to know at least the general background and credentials of the reviewers so that you can prepare the best possible proposal by writing toward their level. You would ultimately like to know the types of organizations the reviewers come from, their titles and degrees, and, if possible, the selection criteria for choosing them. This may be a good opportunity to make your interest in becoming a reviewer known to the program officer. Whether the reviewers meet in Washington, DC, or review proposals at home, you would learn a great deal about the evaluation process and the grantor by being a member of a peer review committee.

If the system that the reviewers must adhere to has been published in the *Federal Register* or an agency publication, request a copy or the date of publication. Let the funding source know that you will be using a quality circle (see chapter 13) to perform a mock review of your proposal before submission and that you would like to mirror the actual review process as closely as possible. Request a copy of their reviewer training materials or the scoring system that was used.

From:	<grantseeker@proactive.edu>
To:	<contactperson@feds.gov>
Cc:	
Sent:	date, time
Subject:	RE: Request for List of Reviewers

Dear [Contact Person]:

I am presently developing a proposal under your _____ program. I would find it very helpful if you could e-mail or send me a list of last year's reviewers and information on the makeup of this year's review committee.

The list of last year's reviewers and information on the composition of this year's committee will help me prepare a quality proposal based upon the level, expertise, and diversity of the reviewers.

If you need to send me the information in hard copy, I have enclosed a self-addressed label for your convenience. I will use the materials you forward to me, and I thank you for your consideration in providing them.

Name
Title
Organization/Institution
Address
Phone Number
Fax Number

SAMPLE E-MAIL TO A FEDERAL AGENCY FOR A LIST OF REVIEWERS

EXHIBIT 11.3

Contacting a Past Reviewer

As you examine the list of reviewers, look for any links you could use in contacting them. If none is apparent, select any reviewer to call. When calling a past reviewer, explain that you understand he or she was a reviewer for the program you are interested in and that you would like to ask a few questions about his or her experience as a reviewer for the program. Select a few questions to ask from the following list, or make up your own.

- How did you get to be a reviewer?
- Did you review proposals at a funding source location or at home?
- What training or instruction did the funding source give you?

- Did you follow a point system? What system? How did you follow it? What were you told to look for?
- How would you write a proposal differently now that you have been a reviewer?
- What were the most common mistakes you saw?
- Did you meet other reviewers?
- How many proposals were you given to read?
- How much time did you have to read them?
- How did the funding source handle discrepancies in point assignments?
- What did the staff members of the funding source wear, say, and do during the review process?
- Did a staff review follow your review?

TELEPHONING, FAXING, AND E-MAILING FEDERAL AND STATE FUNDING SOURCES

Contacting public funding sources is an experience in itself. Your initial research should yield a contact name, e-mail address, phone number, and fax number. Because of personnel changes and reassignments, the contact listed may not be the best person to assist you. However, he or she should be able to tell you who at the agency or program could best answer your questions. You can also check the agency's/program's Web site to make sure your contact information is current. If your research does not yield the information you need, you could use the *United States Government Manual* (see list of resources) to track down the phone number and/or e-mail address of the office likely to handle the funds you are seeking.

After you have identified the appropriate program officer, my first choice is to go to see him or her in person. However, if this is not possible, I recommend a combination of phone, fax, and e-mail contact. The purpose of this contact is twofold.

1. You want to confirm the validity of the program information you have, and ask intelligent questions that demonstrate your understanding of the program's grants system while eliciting information that will assist you in developing your proposal.
2. You want to position yourself and your institution or organization as thorough and capable.

Try to demonstrate that you have done your homework (research) and know about the program, and then ask a question or make a request to further your knowledge of their grant opportunity. For example, if you are requesting information on matching funds, state what you know from your research and then, ask your question. Do not ask what the matching requirements are when you already discovered this information in the CFDA. Instead, let the program officer know that you know a match is not *required*, and then ask if past applicants that ultimately became grantees chose to provide one anyway and if so, what was the average size or range.

What really bothers federal program officers is when they get calls or e-mails from grantseekers asking what kinds of projects they're funding this year or what they're looking for this year. These are what I call flavor of the month questions, and are indicative of the types of questions asked by lazy grantseekers.

In addition, several federal and state program officers have told me that they are overwhelmed with questions and requests from grantseekers for information that is readily available from other sources such as the CFDA, *Federal Register*, program guidelines, and so on. One way they deal with these lazy grantseekers is to ignore their e-mail, telephone, and fax requests. One federal program officer told me that his simple solution is to never respond to a first request for information unless it is an intelligent question that demonstrates that the grantseeker has done his or her homework (research). He then went on to say that 80 percent of the prospective grantseekers he does not respond to initially do not call, fax, or e-mail a second time. His rationale for not responding initially is how critical could the information be if the grantseeker doesn't even call, fax, or e-mail back. On the up side, he stated that he always responds to a second request. So the moral of the story is, select intelligent questions to ask that demonstrate your knowledge of the program, be persistent, phone first, and then follow up with an e-mail.

Be careful not to ask too many questions or to make too many requests at one time. Determine which of your possible questions will be the most critical in helping you determine your proposal approach, and ask them. If you do not get a response the first time, try again. In your follow-up contact, reformat the questions, note the date of your initial request, and ask again. Let the program officer know that you respect his or her time and understand how busy they are, but that you need to know the answers to your questions and that you will recontact them another time if necessary.

Once contact is made with the program officer (whether it is by phone, fax, or e-mail), you should gather the same information as you would face-to-face. Since it may be difficult for the funding official to discuss your idea and approaches without seeing a written description of your project, ask whether you could mail, fax, or e-mail them a one-page concept paper, and then recontact them for the purpose of discussion.

Although it may be difficult for you to "read" what the funding source is really saying through phone or e-mail contact, you must at least try to uncover any hidden agenda so that you can meet the grantor's needs and increase your chances of success. Review the list of questions in the "Questions to Ask a Program Officer" section of this chapter.

Making an Appointment with a Public Funding Source Official

The objective of seeking an appointment is to get an interview with an administrator of the program. Start by sending or e-mailing a letter requesting an appointment. Exhibit 11.4 provides a sample e-mail you may use. You may not get a response to this e-mail/letter. Its intent is to show that you mean business. Then follow the next few steps.

1. Call and ask for the program officer or information contact.
2. Record the name of whomever you speak to and ask if they are the correct person to speak to. If they aren't, ask who is, and how and when that person can be reached.
3. Call back. Ask whether anyone else can answer technical questions about the program. You may get an appointment with an individual whose job is to screen you, but this is still better than talking to yourself. As an alternative, try to get an advocate to help you set up an appointment, or try going in cold early in the week to set an appointment for later in the week. Do not be surprised if this results in an immediate appointment. Staff members may decide they would prefer to deal with you on the spot rather than later. Be careful using elected officials to make appointments for you or to accompany you on an appointment. Bureaucrats and politicians often do not get along well.
4. When you get the program person on the phone, introduce yourself and give a brief (10-word) description of your project. Explain that

    - the need to deal with the specific problem your project addresses is extreme
    - your organization is uniquely suited to deal with this problem
    - you understand that the grantor's program deals with this need
    - you would like to make an appointment to talk about program priorities and your approach

When you get an appointment, stop and hang up. If an appointment is not possible, tell the program representative that you have some questions and ask about the possibility of arranging a 10-minute phone call for the future. If a callback is not possible, ask whether he or she could take the time to answer your questions now. Fill in any information you get (names, phone numbers, and so on) on the federal grants research form (see exhibit 10.1).

From: \<grantseeker@proactive.edu\>
To: \<contactperson@feds.gov\>
Cc:
Sent: date, time
Subject: RE: Request for an Appointment

Dear [Contact Person]:

My research on your funding program indicates that a project we have developed would be appropriate for consideration by your agency for funding under _____.

I would appreciate 5 to 10 minutes of your time to discuss my project. Your insights, knowledge, and information on any grants that have been funded using a similar approach would be invaluable.

My travel plans call for me to be in your area on _____. I will phone to confirm the possibility of a brief meeting during that time to discuss this important proposal.

Name
Title
Organization/Institution
Address
Telephone Number
Fax Number

SAMPLE E-MAIL TO A FEDERAL AGENCY REQUESTING AN APPOINTMENT

EXHIBIT 11.4

VISITING PUBLIC FUNDING SOURCES

The initial meeting is vital to getting the input you need to prepare a proposal that is tailored to the funding source. A visit also will provide you with the opportunity to update any information you have gathered on the funding source through your research.

The objective of this preproposal visit is to find out as much as possible about the funding source and how it perceives its role in the awarding of grants. Then you can use the newly acquired information to produce a proposal that reflects a sensitivity to the funding source's needs and perception of its mission. According to the theory of cognitive dissonance, the more the funding source perceives a grantseeker as different from what the funding source expects, the greater the problems with communication, agreement, and acceptance. We want the funder to love us, so we need to produce as little dissonance as possible by looking and talking as the funder thinks we should. Just remember, Washington, DC, is one of the most conservative areas in the country for dress. By dressing accordingly, you can avoid not getting heard because your attire creates dissonance.

Plan for Your Visit

When planning for a personal visit, remember that it is better to send two people than one, and that an advocate, advisory committee member, or graduate of your program has more credibility than a paid staff member. In deciding whom to send, try to match the age, interests, and other characteristics of your people with any information you have on the funding official. Before the visit, role-play your presentation with your team members and decide who will take responsibility for various parts of the presentation and what questions each will ask.

What to Take

It may be helpful to bring the following items with you on the visit:

1. Materials that help demonstrate the need for your project.
2. Your proposal development workbook (Swiss cheese book).
3. A brief video, shown on your laptop, complete with sound, that documents the problem and the unique attributes that make you a logical choice as a grantee. The video could also summarize your approach to solving the problem, but the entire presentation should be short (no longer than three minutes) and simple. You do not need a projection system and a PowerPoint presentation unless you will be meeting with five or more grantor staff members.
4. Information on your organization that you can leave with the funding official (but never leave a proposal).

Questions to Ask a Program Officer

Review the following list of possible questions to ask a program officer:

- I have located the program application on your Web site and found references to (*rules, announcements, etc.*). Are there any other sources of information I should review?
- The (*CFDA or agency publication*) lists the program funding level at ($$$$$$). How many awards will be made out of this amount and what will the overall, average grant size be?
- Your average award in this area last year to an organization like ours was ($$$$$). Do you expect that to change?
- How will successful grantees from last year affect the chances for new or first applicants? Will last year's grantees compete with new grantees, or have their funds been set aside? If their funds have been set aside, how much is left for new awards?
- Are there any unannounced program or unsolicited proposal funds in your agency to support an important project like ours?

Before each visit to a funding source, review this sheet to be sure you are taking the correct materials, advocates, and staff.

Agency Director: _____   E-mail _____

Program Director: _____   E-mail _____
Contact Person: _____   E-mail _____

Profile: Birth date: _____   Birthplace: _____

Education: College: _____

                Postgraduate: _____

Work Experience: _____
Military Service: _____
Service Clubs: _____
Interests/Hobbies: _____

Publications: _____

Comments: _____
             _____
             _____
             _____

Note: Do not ask the staff person direct questions related to these areas. Instead, record
        information that has been volunteered or gathered from comments or observations made
        in the office.

FUNDING SOURCE STAFF PROFILE

EXHIBIT 11.5

- The required matching portion is X percent. Would it improve our chances for funding if we provided a greater portion than this?

- The program announcement states that matching funds are suggested but not mandatory. I need to give my institution/organization an idea of how much match is needed to meet the "suggested" amount. Could you provide me with figure, or select three past grantees at random, and tell how much match they (the grantees) provided?

- If no match is required, would it help our proposal if we volunteered to cost share?

- What is the most common mistake or flaw in the proposals you receive?

- Are there any areas you would like to see addressed in a proposal that may have been overlooked by other grantees or applicants?

- We have developed several approaches to this needs area. From your vantage point, you may know whether one of our approaches has been fund-

Project Title: _____

Add to this sheet each time you contact a public funding source.

Agency Name: _____

Program Officer: _____

Contacted On (Date) _____

By Whom: _____

Contacted By: Letter _____ Phone _____ Fax _____ E-mail _____

               Personal Visit _____

Staff or Advocate Present: _____

Discussed: _____

_____

_____

Results: _____

_____

_____

_____

_____

_____

PUBLIC FUNDING SOURCE CONTACT SUMMARY SHEET

EXHIBIT 11.6

ed but not yet published. Could you review our concept paper and give us any guidance?

- Would you review or critique our proposal if we got it to you early?
- Would you recommend a previously funded proposal for us to read for format and style? (Remember, you are entitled to see funded proposals, but be cool.)
- What changes do you expect in type or number of awards this year (for example, fewer new awards versus continuing awards)?
- Is there a relationship between the type of project or proposal and the amount awarded? Is there a sequence or progression in the type of grant awarded? For example, do you suggest getting a consultant grant before we apply for a demonstration grant or an evaluation grant?
- We will conduct a quality circle (mock review) to improve our proposal before we submit it. Could we get more information on the review process your office will conduct? Can we get a reviewers' package including instructions, scoring information, weighting of criteria, and so on? What is the background of the reviewers? How are the reviewers selected? Could one of our team members be a reviewer? How many proposals do reviewers read? How much time do they take to read and score each proposal?

CFDA # _____   Prospect Rating   A. Excellent
Program Title _____   B. Good
Amount Requested: _____   C. Fair
Percent Match/In-kind _____

                                          Estimated Success   A. 75% +
                                                               B. 50%
                                                               C. 25%

1.   How does your grant request match with the average award size to your
      •   type of organization? _____
      •   size of organization? _____
      •   location of organization? _____
      •   proposal focus? _____

2.   What was the number of applications received versus the number of grants awarded in
      your area of interest?
      •   applications received _____
      •   grants awarded   _____

3.   How would you rate the funding staff's interest in your concept?
      •   very interested   ___
      •   interested   ___
      •   not interested   ___
      •   unknown   ___

4.   From the information you obtained on the reviewers and the review process, what should
      your writing strategy include?

5.   Based on the information you obtained on the review process, how will points be
      distributed in the funding source's evaluation process?

                  Area   *Point Value*
            _____   _____
            _____   _____
            _____   _____

TAILORING WORKSHEET

EXHIBIT 11.7

Immediately after your visit, record any information you have gathered about
the funder on the funding source staff profile (exhibit 11.5). Record the results of
your visit on the public funding source contact summary sheet (exhibit 11.6).

MAKING YOUR DECISION TO DEVELOP A PROPOSAL

So far you have not invested a tremendous amount of time in writing your proposal. You have taken time to gather data and contact potential grantors. Now
you must decide which federal grant program you will apply to.

Your best prospect is the grant program that provides the closest match between the project you want to implement and the profile you have developed of the grantor. Seldom is there a perfect fit between your project and the grantor's program, and some tailoring and changes in your program will likely add to your chances of success. Use the tailoring worksheet (exhibit 11.7) to analyze each grant or program you are interested in and to select the closest match. After reviewing your answers on the tailoring worksheet, rate your prospect. Remember that the competition (alluded to in question 1) and the award rejection ratio (alluded to in question 2) are critical to calculating your chances of success. After careful analysis, what chance do you think you have of attracting a grant from this prospect? A 25-percent chance? A 50-percent chance? A 75-percent chance?

CHAPTER 12

Planning the Successful Federal Proposal

Each federal agency has its own proposal format to which applicants must adhere. If you have been successful in obtaining a copy of a previously funded proposal, you have a quality example of what the funding source expects. After reading exemplary proposals for 30 years, I have learned that really excellent proposals do stand out. One does not have to be an expert in a proposal's particular area of interest to determine whether the proposal is good. The required components or sections of each type of proposal—a research proposal or a good proposal for a demonstration or model project—are remarkably similar. In general, federal applications include sections on

- search of relevant literature/documentation of need: to demonstrate that you have a command of the relevant studies and knowledge in the field
- what you propose to study, change, or test (for a research project, the hypothesis and specific aims; for a model project, the measurable objectives)
- proposed intervention: what you will do and why you have selected these methods or activities
- budget: the cost of the project broken down by category of expenditure
- evaluation: how you will establish the levels of change that constitute success and demonstrate that your intervention worked
- grantee credibility: unique qualities and capabilities that you possess and believe are relevant to support and complete the project

Most federal grantors will also require a summary or abstract, a title, an agreement to comply with federal assurances, and attachment of pertinent materials that the reviewer may want to refer to while evaluating the proposal. Sections on future funding and dissemination of the research findings or model also may be included.

While the inclusion of these general components seems logical, the differences in terminology, space restrictions, and order or sequence from one federal application to another can be very perplexing. The novice grantseeker frequently asks why there is not a standard federal grant application form for all programs. It seems that this would make sense but, because of the variety of federal programs and the deep-seated conviction that each area of interest is distinct, this type of standardization will probably never happen. The point is that you must follow each agency's format exactly, make no changes and no omissions, and give each agency what it calls for, not just what you want to give.

Each federal agency has its own preferences concerning the components and the order. What is similar from agency to agency is that, in one way or another, the grantseeker's proposal must establish that he/she has a project that needs to be carried out in order to advance the field of research, knowledge, or service. Chapter 13, on conducting a quality circle or proposal improvement exercise, will deal in more detail with the federal agencies' systems for evaluating and scoring proposals, including how the different sections of the proposal compare in terms of importance in the final decision. When applying to a specific agency, it is expected that you will procure a copy of the desired proposal format and develop specific insights into the agency's scoring system and an idea of what an outstanding proposal looks like by obtaining a copy of a funded proposal.

Work through this chapter and collect the materials suggested. Then develop or rearrange your proposal in the format and order required by the grantor.

DOCUMENTATION OF NEED

Most grantseekers begin their proposal with *what* they propose or want to do. Government grantors want to know *why* there is a need to do anything at all. To gain the reviewer's respect, you must show that you are knowledgeable about the need in a particular area. Your goal in this section of the proposal is to use articles, studies, and statistics to demonstrate a compelling reason or motivation to deal with the problem now.

The grantor invariably must choose which proposals to fund this year and which to reject or put on hold; therefore, you must demonstrate the urgency to close the gap between what exists now and what ought to be in your special field (see figure 12.1). Your proposed project will seek to close or reduce this gap.

In a research proposal, needs documentation involves a search of relevant literature in the field. The point of the literature search is to document that there is a gap in knowledge in a particular area. Currently in the scientific community it is necessary to enhance the motivation of the reviewer to fund your research proj-

THE GAP
What exists now. What is real. What the present situation is. _____	What could be. The goal. The desired state of affairs, level of achievement.

THE GAP DIAGRAM

FIGURE 12.1

ect by suggesting the value of closing the gap, in monetary terms or in terms of increased knowledge, and by proposing what this new knowledge can lead to.

In proposals for model projects and demonstration grants, this section is referred to as the needs statement or need documentation. To be successful in grantseeking, you must produce a clear, compelling picture of the current situation and the desired state. Grantors are buying a changed or better state of affairs.

Creating a sense of urgency depends on how well you document the need. Since not all proposals can be funded, you must make the funding source believe that movement toward the desired state cannot wait any longer. Those proposals that do not get funded did not do as good a job of

- documenting a real need (perceived as important)
- demonstrating what ought to be (for clients) or the field of interest
- creating the urgent need to close the gap by demonstrating that each day the need is not addressed the problem grows worse or that there is unnecessary suffering, confusion, and/or wasted efforts

Documenting What Is

Use the following steps to document a need in a model or demonstration grant:

1. Review the section on performing a needs survey (chapter 2) to assess whether any of the methods described could help document the need.
2. Use statistics from articles and research (e.g., "Approximately ___ women in the United States were murdered by their husbands or boyfriends last year.")
3. Use quotes from leaders or experts in the field (e.g., "Dr. Flockmeister said children who are raised in a family with spouse abuse have a ___ percent chance of being abused or of abusing their partners.")
4. Use case statements (e.g., "John Quek, a typical client of the Family Outreach Center, was abused as a child and witnessed his mother and aunt being abused.").

5. Describe a national need and reduce it to a local number that is more understandable (e.g., "It is estimated that ___ percent of teenagers are abused by their boyfriend or girlfriend by the time they reach age 17; this means that at the West Side High School ___ seniors in the graduating class may have already experienced abuse.").
6. State the need in terms of one person (e.g., "The abused spouse generally has...").
7. Use statements from community people such as police, politicians, and clergy.

When documenting what exists in a research grant, include:

1. The latest studies, research articles and presentations to demonstrate your currency in the field.
2. Studies that demonstrate the scope and sequence of work in the field and its current state, and the necessity to answer your proposed research question before the field can move ahead.
3. A thorough literature search that does not focus only on a few researchers or data that reinforces your research position. Show how the diversity or conflict in the field reinforces the need to search an answer to your question.
4. A logical flow of reference to the literature. The flow may consist of a chronological and conceptual documentation that builds to the decision to fund your work. Remember, the literature search should not be a comprehensive treatise in the field that includes references to every contributor but, rather, a convincing documentation of significant works.

Demonstrating What Ought to Be

To establish what ought to be, proven statistics may be difficult or impossible to find. Using experts' statements and quotes to document what ought to be is much more credible than using your opinion. Do not put your opinion in the needs statement. In this section you are demonstrating your knowledge of the field and showing that you have surveyed the literature.

Stay away from terms that point to a poorly documented needs statement. They include the words *many* and *most* and expressions like a *great number* and *everyone knows the need for*. Make sure your needs statement does not include any of these types of words or expressions.

It is relatively easy to say what ought to be in areas such as family violence or drug abuse but more difficult when dealing with bench or pure research. However, it is still important to demonstrate the possible uses your research could be related to even if you are working in the hard sciences. Documenting the other side of the gap is a necessity if you want to close the gap of ignorance in your field.

Creating a Sense of Urgency

The needs section should motivate the prospective funding source. One way to do this is to use the funding source's own studies, surveys, or statistics. The same basic proposal can be tailored to two different funding sources by quoting different studies that appeal to each source's own view of the need. By appealing to the views of individual sources, you will appear to be the logical choice to close the gap and move toward reducing the problem.

If the proposal format required by the funding source does not have a section that deals with your capabilities, the end of the needs statement is the best place to put your credentials. To make a smooth transition from the need to your capabilities:

- State that it is the mission of your organization to deal with this problem.

- Summarize the unique qualities of your organization that make it best suited for the job. For example, your organization has the staff or facilities to make the project work.

- Capitalize on the similarities you share with other organizations. For instance, "Our project will serve as a model to the other agencies that face this dilemma each day." Such statements will help the prospective grantor realize that the results of your project could affect many.

- Emphasize that the needs are urgent and that each day they go unmet the problem grows. For example, "Each year that teacher education colleges do an inadequate job of integrating comprehensive computer education into their curriculum, a new group of teachers with limited computer skills enter our schools unable to utilize the Internet, and the problem grows."

WHAT YOU PROPOSE TO STUDY OR CHANGE

Objectives outline the steps you propose to take to narrow or close the gap created in the needs statement. Objectives follow the needs statement because they cannot be written until the need has been documented.

Since the accomplishment or attainment of each objective will help to close the gap, you must write objectives that are measurable and can be evaluated. It is critical to be able to determine the degree to which the objectives have been attained and, thus, demonstrate the amount of the gap that has been closed. Grantseekers preparing research proposals should note that the objective of a research proposal is to close the gap of ignorance.

Government grantors have been putting increasing pressure on researchers to explain how their research can be used on a very practical level. Philosophical (and the author's) arguments aside, there are conservative elements that want a component of even basic research grants to deal with such issues as dissemination of results and how findings can be applied to benefit the general public.

Objectives versus Methods

Objectives tell the grantseeker and the funding source what will be accomplished by this expenditure of funds and how the change will be measured. *Methods* state the means to the end or change. They tell how you will accomplish the desired change. Naturally, the ability to accomplish an objective depends on the methods or activities chosen.

When in doubt as to whether you have written an objective or a method, ask yourself whether there is only one way to accomplish what you have written. If your answer is yes, you have probably written a method. For example, once a participant at one of my seminars told me that his objective was to build a visitor's center for his organization's museum. When asked why he wanted to build a visitor's center, he responded, "To help visitors understand the relationship between the museum buildings so that they can more effectively use the museum." Once he stated this out loud, he realized that his objective was really the effective utilization of the museums and that building a visitors' center was just one method for accomplishing this objective. In other words, building the visitors' center was a means to an end, just one way that my seminar participant could attempt to accomplish his objective. In fact, the reason a funding source might give money to support his project would be to help people use and appreciate the museum, not to build the visitors' center. The bricks and mortar that make up the visitors' center simply do not lend themselves to the kind of measurement that the issue of effective utilization does.

The following is a technique for writing objectives:

1. Determine result areas. Result areas are the key places you will look for improvement or change in the client population. Examples include the health of people over 65 years of age in St. Louis, better-educated minority students, and more efficient use of a museum.
2. Determine measurement indicators. Measurement indicators are the quantifiable parts of your result areas. By measuring your performance with these indicators, you will be able to determine how well you are doing. Examples include the number of hospital readmissions of people over 65 years old, scores on standardized tests, and the number of people who understand the relationship between museum buildings. Brainstorm a number of measurement indicators for each of your result areas, and then select the ones that reflect your intent and are the least difficult to use.
3. Determine performance standards. Performance standards answer the question "how much (or how little) of a change do we need to consider ourselves successful?" Using our above example, we might determine the following performance standards: a 10-percent drop in hospital readmissions, scores rising from the 80th to the 90th percentile for freshmen on the Flockman reading scale, or a 50-percent reduction in direction giving by museum staff.

4. Determine the time frame. The time frame is the amount of time in which you want to reach your performance standards. It is *your* deadline. You might decide you want to see a 10-percent drop in hospital readmissions within 6 or 18 months. Usually, this time frame is determined for you by the funding source. Most grants are for 12 months. In setting your deadlines, use months 1 through 12 instead of January, February, and so on because you seldom will start the grant when you expect to.

5. Determine cost frame. This is the cost of the methods or activities you have selected to meet your objectives. (This cost estimate can be obtained retrospectively from the project planner, the document you will fill out next.)

6. Write the objective. This step combines the data you have generated in the previous five steps. The standard format for an objective is: "To [action verb and statement reflecting your measurement indicator] by [performance standard] by [deadline] at a cost of no more than [cost frame]." For example, "To increase the reading scores of freshmen from the 80th to the 90th percentile on Flockman's reading scale in 12 months at a cost of $50,000."

7. Evaluate the objective. Review your objective and answer the question "Does this objective reflect the amount of change we want in the result area?" If your answer is yes, you probably have a workable objective. If your answer is no, chances are that your measurement indicator is wrong or your performance standards are too low. Go back to steps 2 and 3 and repeat the process.

When writing program objectives, you should follow the same seven steps.

Again, remember to emphasize end results, not tasks or methods. Do not describe how you are going to do something; instead, emphasize what you will accomplish and the ultimate benefit of your program's work.

In a research proposal, the section on what the researcher proposes to study or change is referred to as the research question and hypothesis to be tested. The development of research proposals follows an analogous route to model and demonstration grants. There must be a clearly defined problem, question, or gap to be addressed.

Researchers are inoculated with the same virus that all grantseekers share—the why virus. (Why does this happen? What can we do to change it?) The researcher asks a question and then must search the literature in the field to determine what is already known and who would care if the question was answered. (What is the value or benefit? Who would value the closing of the gap?) For example, the question of whether treatment X or Y influences the healing time of a pressure sore (bedsore) is subject to a search of the literature to see what work has already been done in this area and to determine the importance of the question. (What exists now? What is the incidence or extent of the problem, and the future impact of not addressing the question?) If there is no compelling or motivating reason to use grant moneys to answer the question, the researcher is not likely to be successful.

The research question must be specific and focused. Many researchers are overly optimistic and select too broad a question or too many questions to investigate. This sets them up for failure because they cannot control the situation. In other words, they have too many forces or variables to deal with that can influence the outcome.

Researchers must develop their questions into either a null hypothesis or an alternative hypothesis. The null hypothesis predicts that there is no basic difference between the two selected areas. For example, "There is no difference between pressure sores treated with X or Y." The researcher sets up the study to measure the outcome, or the *dependent* variable (increased healing of pressure sores). The researcher manipulates or changes the intervention, or the *independent* variable (use of treatment X or Y), to observe the effect of the two treatments on the depending variable. Just as behavioral objectives contain a measurement indicator for success (increasing reading scores from the 80th to the 90th percentile as measured by the Flockman reading scale), the researcher must select a statistical evaluation mode, before data are collected, which will be used to evaluate the differences in the intervention. When there are significant differences between two treatments, the null hypothesis is disproved and the results are based on differences in treatment rather than on chance.

The alternative hypothesis predicts that there is indeed a difference between the two treatments and suggests the direction of that difference. For example, "Treatment X will result in a healing rate that is 50 percent faster than treatment Y."

PROPOSED INTERVENTION

The methods, activities, or protocol section is the detailed description of the steps you will take to meet the objectives. Methods identify:

- what will be done
- who will do it
- how long it will take
- the materials and equipment needed

The protocol of a research proposal details how each experiment or trial will be carried out.

The methods or protocols are all a function of what you set out to accomplish. The best order to follow is to write your objectives first and then develop your methods to meet them. In making up a realistic estimate of your project costs, avoid inflating your budget. Instead, consider adding several more methods to this section than absolutely necessary to ensure that your objectives are met. When you negotiate the final award, you will gain much more credibility with the funding source by eliminating methods instead of lowering the price for the same amount of work.

Historically, final awards for research proposals were arrived at in a manner much different from that for model project proposals. Notification of a research award was frequently followed by a letter that included a dollar amount significantly less than what was applied for, and there was little or no opportunity for negotiation. Criticism of this practice led many major grantors to announce that the methods for both types of proposals should be cost analyzed and negotiated. Now both demonstration and research proposals must include an estimate of the cost of each method or activity and must show each activity's effect on the outcome.

Your methods section should:

- describe your program activities in detail and demonstrate how they will fulfill your objectives or research study
- describe the sequence, flow, and interrelationship of the activities
- describe the planned staffing for your program and designate who is responsible for which activities
- describe your client population and method for determining client selection
- state a specific time frame
- present a reasonable scope of activities that can be accomplished within the stated time frame with your organization's resources
- refer to the cost-benefit ratio of your project
- include a discussion of risk (why success is probable)
- describe the uniqueness of your methods and overall project design

The project planner (see exhibit 12.1) provides you with a format to ensure that your methods section reflects a well-conceived and well-designed plan for the accomplishment of your objectives. (The CD-ROM that accompanies this book also includes an interactive project planner that is programmed to work with Microsoft Excel.)

The Project Planner

An outcome of my 35 years of work in grant and contract preparation, the project planner is a spreadsheet-based planning tool designed to assist you in several important ways. It will help you:

- develop your budget by having you clearly define which project personnel will perform each activity for a given time frame, with the corresponding consultant services, supplies, materials, and equipment
- defend your budget on an activity-by-activity basis so that you can successfully negotiate your final award
- project a monthly and quarterly cash forecast for year 1, year 2, and year 3 of your proposed project
- identify matching or in-kind contributions

The project planner will also help you develop job descriptions for each individual involved in the project and a budget narrative or written explanation documenting your planned expenses. Several federal granting agencies have been criticized for not negotiating final awards with grantees. Their practice has been to provide grantees with a statement of the final award with no reference or discussion of how the award differs from the amount budgeted in the application or how the reduction will affect the methods and outcome. As more importance is placed on budget negotiation and the planning of project years, the more valuable the project planner will become.

You will find the following explanations of each project planner column helpful as you review the blank project planner in exhibit 12.1 and the sample project planner in exhibit 12.2.

1. Project objectives or outcomes (column A/B): List your objectives or outcomes as A, B, C, and so on. Use the terms the prospective grantor wants. For example, grantors may refer to the objectives as major tasks, enabling objectives, or specific aims.

2. Methods (column A/B): Also in the first column, list the methods or protocol necessary to meet the objectives or outcomes as A-1, A-2, B-1, B-2, C-1, C-2, and so on. These are the tasks you have decided on as your approach to meeting the need.

3. Month (column C/D): Record the dates you will begin and end each activity in this column.

4. Time (column E): Designate the number of person-weeks (you can use hours or months) needed to accomplish each task.

5. Project personnel (column F): List the key personnel who will spend measurable or significant amounts of time on this activity and the accomplishments of this objective or specific aim. The designation of key personnel is critical for developing a job description for each individual. If you list the activities for which the key personnel are responsible, and the minimum qualifications or background required, you will have a rough job description. Call a placement agency to get an estimate of the salary needed to fill the position. The number of weeks or months will determine full- or part-time classification.

   This column gives you the opportunity to look at how many hours of work you are providing in a given time span. If you have your key personnel working more than 160 hours per month, it may be necessary to adjust the number of weeks in Column E to fit a more reasonable time frame. For example, you may have to reschedule activities or shift responsibility to another staff member.

6. Personnel costs (columns G, H, I): List the salaries, wages, and fringe benefits for all personnel. Special care should be taken in analyzing staff donated from your organization. The donation of personnel may be a requirement for your grant or a gesture you make to show your good faith and appear as a better investment to the funding source. If you do make

PROJECT PLANNER™

PROJECT TITLE: _____

A. List Project objectives or outcomes A. B.	MONTH		TIME	PROJECT PERSONNEL	PERSONNEL COSTS		
B. List Methods to accomplish each objective as A-1, A-2, A-3 ... B-1, B-2 ...	BEGIN	END			SALARIES & WAGES	FRINGE BENEFITS	TOTAL
	C / D		E	F	G	H	I

© David G. Bauer Associates, Inc.
(800) 836-0732

TOTAL DIRECT COSTS OR COSTS REQUESTED FROM FUNDER ▶
MATCHING FUNDS, IN-KIND CONTRIBUTIONS, OR DONATED COSTS ▶
TOTAL COSTS ▶

THE PROJECT PLANNER

EXHIBIT 12.1

Sheet _____ of _____

Proposal Developed for _____

PROJECT DIRECTOR: _____ Proposed starting date _____ Proposal Year _____

CONSULTANTS • CONTRACT SERVICES			NON-PERSONNEL RESOURCES NEEDED SUPPLIES • EQUIPMENT • MATERIALS				SUB-TOTAL COST FOR ACTIVITY	MILESTONES PROGRESS INDICATORS	
TIME	COST/WEEK	TOTAL	ITEM	COST/ITEM	QUANTITY	TOT. COST	TOTAL I. L. P	ITEM	DATE
J	K	L	M	N	O	P	Q	R	S
						T		◄ % OF TOTAL	
								◄	
							100%	◄	

THE PROJECT PLANNER *(continued)*

EXHIBIT 12.1

PROJECT PLANNER™

A Contract for Educational Cooperation - Parents
PROJECT TITLE: Teachers & Students Charting A Course for Involvement

A. List Project objectives or outcomes A. B. B. List Methods to accomplish each objective as A-1, A-2, A-3 … B-1, B-2 …	MONTH		TIME	PROJECT PERSONNEL	PERSONNEL COSTS		
	BEGIN	END			SALARIES & WAGES	FRINGE BENEFITS	TOTAL
	C / D		E	F	G	H	I
Objective A: Increase Educational Cooperation of Teachers, Parents & Students 25% as Measured on the Educational Practices Survey in 12 Months at a Cost of $88,705							
A-1 Develop the Responsible Educational Practices Survey with the Advisory Committee	1/2		4	Proj. Dir PD Smith	West State U. PD		
a. Write questions and develop a scale of responsibility for parents, teachers and students				2 Grad students (GS)			
A-2 Administer the Survey to the Target Population	2/3		4	2 GS	' '	' '	' '
a. Develop procedure			4	PD	' '	' '	' '
b. Get human subjects approval thru West State University							
c. Graduate students to administer survey			4	2 GS	' '	' '	' '
d. Input survey data			*4	Sec'y	800	160	*960
e. Develop results			1	PD	West State U.		
A-3 Develop Curriculm	3/6						
a. Review results of pre-test given to parents, students and teachers			1	PD	' '	' '	' '
b. Develop a curriculum on responsibility concepts in education for each group (includes workbook and video on each area of curriculum)			5	PD	' '	' '	' '
			*8	Sec'y	1600	320	*1920
			8	Senior High Club - Corp.	Video Using Jones Facility		
- responsible use of time							
- homework responsibility							
- communication skills							
- developing contract for change							
A-4 Promote & Carry Out Program	6/12		24	PD	West State U.		
a. Use advisory group to announce program			24	Sec'y	4800	960	*5760
b. Public service spots on radio & television							
c. Develop and send home a program							
d. Schedule meetings with parents							
e. Develop a student video							

© David G. Bauer Associates, Inc.
(800) 836-0732

TOTAL DIRECT COSTS OR COSTS REQUESTED FROM FUNDER ▶	0
MATCHING FUNDS, IN-KIND CONTRIBUTIONS, OR DONATED COSTS ▶	8640
TOTAL COSTS ▶	8640

SAMPLE PROJECT PLANNER

EXHIBIT 12.2

Sheet __1__ of __1__

Proposal Developed for __D. Smith__

PROJECT DIRECTOR: _____ Proposed starting date _____ Proposal Year _____

CONSULTANTS • CONTRACT SERVICES			NON-PERSONNEL RESOURCES NEEDED SUPPLIES • EQUIPMENT • MATERIALS				SUB-TOTAL COST FOR ACTIVITY	MILESTONES PROGRESS INDICATORS	
TIME	COST/WEEK	TOTAL	ITEM	COST/ITEM	QUANTITY	TOT. COST	TOTAL I. L. P	ITEM	DATE
J	K	L	M	N	O	P	Q	R	S
2	1000	2000	micro/word perfect			2500			
2	500	1000	printer/modem			175			
			phone expense			150			
4	500	2000							
4	1000	4000							
4	500	2000	travel allowance			800			
			modem/phone expense			150			
1	1000	1000	micro processor			---			
1	1000	1000							
5	1000	5000	layout & print			1250			
			workbooks	10	200	2000*			
			blank tapes	2	20	40			
			video studio	5000	5hrs	25000*			
			camera edit						
			character generation						
			video camera	1000	6	6000*			
	42000					5065	47065	53%	◄ % OF TOTAL
	0					33000	41640	47%	◄
	42000					38065	88705	100%	◄

SAMPLE PROJECT PLANNER (continued)

EXHIBIT 12.2

matching or in-kind contributions, place an asterisk by the name of each person you donate to the project. Be sure to include your donation of fringes as well as wages. As you complete the remaining columns, put an asterisk by anything else that will be donated to the project.

7. Consultants and contract services (columns J, K, L): These three columns are for the services that are most cost-efficiently supplied by individuals who are not in your normal employ. They may be experts at a skill you need that does not warrant your training a staff member or hiring an additional staff person (evaluation, computers, commercial art, etc.). There are no fringe benefits paid to consultants or contract service providers.

8. Nonpersonnel resources needed (columns M, N, O, P): List the components that are necessary to complete each activity and achieve your objective, including supplies, equipment, and materials. Many a grantseeker has gone wrong by underestimating the nonpersonnel resources needed to successfully complete a project. Most grantseekers lose out on many donated or matching items because they do not ask themselves what they really need to complete each activity. Travel, supplies, and telephone communications are some of the more commonly donated items.

   Equipment requests can be handled in many ways. One approach is to place total equipment items as they are called for in your plan under Column M (item) and to complete the corresponding columns appropriately—cost per item (column N), quantity (column O), and total cost (column P). However, this approach may cause problems in the negotiation of your final award. The grantor may suggest lowering the grant amount by the elimination of an equipment item that appears as though it is related to the accomplishment of only one activity, when in actuality you plan to utilize it in several subsequent activities.

   Therefore, I suggest that if you plan to list the total cost of equipment needed in your work plan next to one particular activity, designate a percentage of usage to that activity and reference the other activities that will require the equipment. This way you will show 100-percent usage and be able to defend the inclusion of the equipment in your budget request.

   In some cases, you may choose to allocate the percentage of the cost of the equipment with the percentage of use for each activity. If you allocate cost of equipment to each activity, remember that if you drop an activity in negotiation you may not have all the funds you need to purchase the equipment.

9. Subtotal cost for activity (column Q): This column can be completed in two ways. Each activity can be subtotaled, or you can subtotal several activities under each objective or specific aim.

10. Milestones, progress indicators (columns R, S): Column R should be used to record what the funding source will receive as indicators that you are working toward the accomplishment of your objectives. Use column S to list the date on which the funding source will receive the milestone or progress indicator.

Please note that you might want to develop a computer-generated spreadsheet version of the project planner so that your objectives or other information could be easily added, deleted, or changed. This would be especially useful when the grant amount awarded is less than the amount requested, because you could experiment with possible changes without too much trouble.

Indirect Costs

An aspect of federal grants that is critically important yet poorly understood by many grantseekers and other individuals connected with grants is the concept of indirect costs. Indirect costs involve repaying the recipient of a federal grant for costs that are difficult to break down individually but are indirectly attributable to performing the federal grant. These costs include such things as

- heats and lights
- building maintenance
- payroll personnel
- purchasing

Indirect costs are calculated by using a formula that is provided by the Federal Regional Controller's Office and are expressed as a percentage of the total amount requested from the funding source (total from column Q of your project planner), or as a percentage of the personnel costs (total from column I of your project planner).

Recent developments in the area of indirect costs have led the federal government to strictly enforce of the definition of costs eligible for reimbursement under a grants direct expenditures versus those eligible under its indirect expenditures. Under the Office of Management and Budget's new guidelines, costs related to the handling of increased payroll or purchase orders are already covered under indirect costs. Therefore, any added personnel that fall under the category of secretarial support are not eligible to be added to your grant. All personnel in your grant should have a special designation, showing that their duties are not secretarial but rather extraordinary and thus eligible to be funded under the grant.

Budget

While preparing the budget may be traumatic for unorganized grantseekers, you can see that the project planner contains all the information you need to forecast your financial needs accurately. No matter what budget format you use, the information you need to construct your budget lies in your project planner. The project planner, however, is not the budget; it is the analysis of what will have to be done and the estimated costs and time frame for each activity.

PROJECT NAME: Nutrition Education for Disadvantaged Mothers through Teleconferencing	Expenditure Total	Donated/ In-Kind	Requested from This Source
	$148,551	$85,122	$63,429
1. PERSONNEL			
A. Salaries, Wages			
Project Director @ $2,200/mo.	13,200	13,200	
x 12 mos. x 50% time			
Administrative Assistant @	19,200		19,200
$1,600/mo. x 12 mos. x 100 % time			
Data Input Specialist @1,300/mo	15,600		15,600
X 12 mos. x 100% time			
Volunteer Time @ 9.00 x	36,000	36,000	
10 mos. x 400 hours			
B. Fringe Benefits			
Unemployment Insurance	1,440	450	990
(3% of first $18,600)			
FICA (6.2% of first $87,000	2,976	953	2,023
of each employee salary)			
Health Insurance ($150/mo. Per	5,400	1,800	3,600
employee x 12 mos.)			
Workmen's Compensation (1% of	480	144	336
salaries paid - $48,000)			
C. Consultants/Contracted Services			
Copy Editor ($200/day x 5)	1,000		1,000
PR Advisor ($200/day x 10)	2,000		2,000
Accounting Serv. ($250/day x 12)	3,000	3,000	
Legal Services ($500/day x 6)	3,000	3,000	
Personnel Subtotal	103,296	58,547	44,749
II. NONPERSONNEL			
A. Space Costs			
Rent ($1.50/sq. ft. x 400)	7,200	7,200	
sq. ft. X 12 mos.)			
Utilities ($75/mo. x 12 mos.)	900	900	
B. Equipment			
Desk ($275 x 1)	275		275
Computer, Printer, Copy	3,600		3,600
Machine, Rental ($300/mo x 12 mos.)			
Office Chairs ($50 x 3)	150		150
File Cabinets ($125 x 3)	375	375	

A SAMPLE PROJECT BUDGET

EXHIBIT 12.3

In most government proposal formats, the budget section is not located near the methods section. Government funders do not understand why you want to talk about your methods when you talk about money. As you know, the budget is a result of what you plan to do. If the money you request is reduced, you know you must cut your project's methods. Draw the public funding source back into your project planner so that they too can see what will be missing as a result of a budget cut. If you must cut so many methods that you can no longer be sure of accomplishing your objectives, consider refusing the funds or reducing the amount of change (reduction of the need) outlined in your objectives when negotiating

PROJECT NAME:			
Nutrition Education for Disadvantaged Mothers Through Teleconferencing	Expenditure Total	Donated/ In-Kind	Requested from This Source
	$148,551	$85,122	$63,429
Electronic Blackboard & Misc. Equip. for Teleconferencing	7,200		7,200
C. Supplies (Consumables) (3 employees x 200/yr.)	600	600	
D. Travel Local			
Project Director ($.40/mile x 500 miles/mo. x 12 mos.)	2,400		2,400
Administrative Assistant ($.40/mile x 750 miles/mo. x 12 mos.)	3,600		3,600
Out-of-Town Project Director to Nutrition Conference in St. Louis, MO			
Airfare	450		450
Per Diem ($75/day x 3)	225		225
Hotel ($100/nt. x 3)	300		300
E. Telephone			
Installation ($100/line x 3)	300	300	
Monthly Charges ($25/line x 3 lines x 12 mos.)	900	900	
Long Distance ($40/mo. x 12 mos.)	480		480
F. Other Nonpersonnel Costs			
Printing ($.30 x 25,000 brochures)	7,500	7,500	
Postage ($.34 x 25,000)	8,500	8,500	
Insurance ($25/mo. X 12 mos.)	300	300	
Nonpersonnel Subtotal	$45,255	$26,575	$18,680
Personnel Subtotal	$103,296	$58,547	$44,749
Project Total	$148,551	$85,122	$63,429
Percentage	100%	57%	43%

A Sample Project Budget *(continued)*

EXHIBIT 12.3

the amount of your award. The sample budget in exhibit 12.3 is provided for your review. In a research proposal, show how limiting your intervention or protocol will affect the reliability and validity of your research.

If you are required to provide a quarterly cash forecast, use the grants office time line in exhibit 12.4. The project activities/methods (A-1, A-2, B-1, B-2) from your project planner should be listed in the first column. The numbered columns across the top of the time line indicate the months of the duration of the project. Use a line bar to indicate when each activity/method begins and ends. Place the estimated cost per method in the far-right column. Use a triangle to indicate where milestones and progress indicators are to occur (taken from columns R and S of

Activity Number	1	2	3	4	5	6	7	8	9	10	11	12	Total Cost for Activity

	1st Quarter	2nd Quarter	3rd Quarter	4th Quarter	Total

Quarterly Forecast of Expenditures

GRANTS OFFICE TIME LINE

EXHIBIT 12.4

your project planner). By totaling costs by quarter, you can develop a quarterly forecast of expenditures. Complete a separate grants office time line and project planner for each year of a continuation grant or multi year award.

One of the more common federal budget forms for non construction projects is Standard Form (SF) 424A (see exhibit 12.5). The instructions for completing SF-424A are shown in exhibit 12.6. As with other budget forms, if you have completed a project planner, you already have all the information you need to complete SF-424A.

Many grantors also require that you submit a narrative statement of your budget, explaining the basis for your inclusion of personnel, consultants, supplies, and equipment. This is known as a budget narrative. Again, your completed project planner will help you construct the budget narrative and explain the sequence of steps. The budget narrative gives you the opportunity to present the rationale for each step, piece of equipment, and key person that your proposal calls for.

EVALUATION

Federal and state funding sources generally place a much heavier emphasis on evaluation than most private sources do. While there are many books written on evaluation, the best advice is to have an expert handle it. I suggest enlisting the services of a professional at a college or university who has experience in evaluation. Professors will generally enjoy the involvement and the extra pay and can lead you to a storehouse of inexpensive labor—undergraduate and graduate students. A graduate student in statistics can help you deal with the problem of quantifying your results inexpensively, while he or she gathers valuable insight and experience.

Irrespective of who designs your evaluation, writing your objectives properly will make the process much simpler. Most grantseekers have little problem developing objectives that deal with cognitive areas or areas that provide for results that can be easily qualified. The problems start when they move into the affective domain, because values, feelings, and appreciation can be difficult to measure. Use consultants to assist you. You will gain credibility by using an independent third party to carry out your evaluation analysis.

If you use the techniques presented in this chapter for writing objectives and ask yourself what your client population will do differently after the grant, you should be able to keep yourself on track and develop and evaluation design that will pass even the most critical federal and state standards. For example, a grant to increase appreciation for opera could be measured by seeing how many of the subjects attend an inexpensive performance after the free ones are completed.

THE SUMMARY OR ABSTRACT

The summary or abstract is written after the proposal is completed. After the title, the summary is the second most often read part of a proposal. The summary must be succinct, clear, and motivating so the reader (reviewer) does not lose interest.

In a sense, the summary or abstract has a dual purpose. Its first purpose is to provide the peer reviewer with a clear idea of what the proposed research or project entails. Its second purpose is to provide prospective grantseekers with an example of the type of research or project the federal agency funds. This second purpose occurs after the proposal is accepted, when the summary or abstract becomes public information and is placed on the funding source's Web site and in databases that are Internet accessible.

BUDGET INFORMATION

SECTION A -

Grant Program Function or Activity (a)	Catalog of Federal Domestic Assistance Number (b)	Estimated Unobligated	
		Federal (c)	No
1.		$	$
2.			
3.			
4.			
5. Totals		$ 0.00	$

SECTION B -

6. Object Class Categories	GRA	
	(1)	(2)
a. Personnel	$	$
b. Fringe Benefits		
c. Travel		
d. Equipment		
e. Supplies		
f. Contractual		
g. Construction		
h. Other		
i. Total Direct Charges (sum of 6a-6h)	0.00	
j. Indirect Charges		
k. TOTALS (sum of 6i and 6j)	$ 0.00	$
7. Program Income	$	$

Authorized for

Previous Edition Usable

STANDARD FORM (SF) 424A

EXHIBIT 12.5

- Non-Construction Programs

OMB Approval No. 0348-0044

BUDGET SUMMARY

Funds	New or Revised Budget		
n-Federal (d)	Federal (e)	Non-Federal (f)	Total (g)
	$	$	$ 0.00
			0.00
			0.00
			0.00
0.00	$ 0.00	$ 0.00	$ 0.00

BUDGET CATEGORIES

NT PROGRAM, FUNCTION OR ACTIVITY		Total	
(3)	(4)	(5)	
$	$	$ 0.00	
		0.00	
		0.00	
		0.00	
		0.00	
		0.00	
		0.00	
		0.00	
0.00	0.00	0.00	0.00
		0.00	
$ 0.00	$ 0.00	$ 0.00	$ 0.00
$	$	$ 0.00	

Local Reproduction

Standard Form 424A (Rev. 7-97)
Prescribed by OMB Circular A-102

STANDARD FORM (SF) 424A *(continued)*

EXHIBIT 12.5

SECTION C - NON-FEDERAL RESOURCES				
(a) Grant Program	(b) Applicant	(c) State	(d) Other Sources	(e) TOTALS
8.	$	$	$	$ 0.00
9.				0.00
10.				0.00
11.				0.00
12. TOTAL *(sum of lines 8-11)*	$ 0.00	$ 0.00	$ 0.00	$ 0.00

SECTION D - FORECASTED CASH NEEDS				
	Total for 1st Year	1st Quarter	2nd Quarter	3rd Quarter	4th Quarter
13. Federal	$ 0.00	$	$	$	$
14. Non-Federal	0.00				
15. TOTAL *(sum of lines 13 and 14)*	$ 0.00	$ 0.00	$ 0.00	$ 0.00	$ 0.00

SECTION E - BUDGET ESTIMATES OF FEDERAL FUNDS NEEDED FOR BALANCE OF THE PROJECT				
(a) Grant Program	FUTURE FUNDING PERIODS (Years)			
	(b) First	(c) Second	(d) Third	(e) Fourth
16.	$	$	$	$
17.				
18.				
19.				
20. TOTAL *(sum of lines 16-19)*	$ 0.00	$ 0.00	$ 0.00	$ 0.00

SECTION F - OTHER BUDGET INFORMATION	
21. Direct Charges:	22. Indirect Charges:
23. Remarks:	

Authorized for Local Reproduction

Standard Form 424A (Rev. 7-97) Page 2

STANDARD FORM (SF) 424A *(continued)*

EXHIBIT 12.5

Unfortunately, some applicants do not devote enough time to preparing their summary or abstract and the description that is made public does not do the funding agency or the project/research justice. In order to get grantseekers to pay more attention to this section of their proposals, some federal agencies have begun to score the summary or abstract in the overall proposal evaluation. Whether this area is scored or not, it plays a critical role in setting up the expectations of the reviewer before he or she gets into the body of your proposal.

In general terms, the summary is a much abbreviated version of your proposal and should contain a concise description of the need for your project, your project's goals or hypothesis, objectives or specific aims, approach or protocol, and evaluation design. Use your summary or abstract to show readers that they will find what they want in your proposal, and try to follow the same order in the summary or abstract as you do in your proposal. You can determine which of components to emphasize in your summary or abstract by reviewing the point or evaluation system the funding source will apply. Place more emphasis by devot-

---

INSTRUCTIONS FOR THE SF-424A

Public reporting burden for this collection of information is estimated to average 180 minutes per response, including time for reviewing instructions, searching existing data sources, gathering and maintaining the data needed, and completing and reviewing the collection of information. Send comments regarding the burden estimate or any other aspect of this collection of information, including suggestions for reducing this burden, to the Office of Management and Budget, Paperwork Reduction Project (0348-0044), Washington, DC 20503.

PLEASE DO NOT RETURN YOUR COMPLETED FORM TO THE OFFICE OF MANAGEMENT AND BUDGET. SEND IT TO THE ADDRESS PROVIDED BY THE SPONSORING AGENCY.

General Instructions

This form is designed so that application can be made for funds from one or more grant programs. In preparing the budget, adhere to any existing Federal grantor agency guidelines which prescribe how and whether budgeted amounts should be separately shown for different functions or activities within the program. For some programs, grantor agencies may require budgets to be separately shown by function or activity. For other programs, grantor agencies may require a breakdown by function or activity. Sections A, B, C, and D should include budget estimates for the whole project except when applying for assistance which requires Federal authorization in annual or other funding period increments. In the latter case, Sections A, B, C, and D should provide the budget for the first budget period (usually a year) and Section E should present the need for Federal assistance in the subsequent budget periods. All applications should contain a breakdown by the object class categories shown in Lines a-k of Section B.

Section A. Budget Summary Lines 1-4 Columns (a) and (b)

For applications pertaining to a *single* Federal grant program (Federal Domestic Assistance Catalog number) and *not requiring* a functional or activity breakdown, enter on Line 1 under Column (a) the Catalog program title and the Catalog number in Column (b).

For applications pertaining to a *single* program *requiring* budget amounts by multiple functions or activities, enter the name of each activity or function on each line in Column (a), and enter the Catalog number in Column (b). For applications pertaining to multiple programs where none of the programs require a breakdown by function or activity, enter the Catalog program title on each line in *Column* (a) and the respective Catalog number on each line in Column (b).

For applications pertaining to *multiple* programs where one or more programs *require* a breakdown by function or activity, prepare a separate sheet for each program requiring the breakdown. Additional sheets should be used when one form does not provide adequate space for all breakdown of data required. However, when more than one sheet is used, the first page should provide the summary totals by programs.

Lines 1-4, Columns (c) through (g)

For new applications, leave Column (c) and (d) blank. For each line entry in Columns (a) and (b), enter in Columns (e), (f), and (g) the appropriate amounts of funds needed to support the project for the first funding period (usually a year).

For continuing grant program applications, submit these forms before the end of each funding period as required by the grantor agency. Enter in Columns (c) and (d) the estimated amounts of funds which will remain unobligated at the end of the grant funding period only if the Federal grantor agency instructions provide for this. Otherwise, leave these columns blank. Enter in columns (e) and (f) the amounts of funds needed for the upcoming period. The amount(s) in Column (g) should be the sum of amounts in Columns (e) and (f).

For supplemental grants and changes to existing grants, do not use Columns (c) and (d). Enter in Column (e) the amount of the increase or decrease of Federal funds and enter in Column (f) the amount of the increase or decrease of non-Federal funds. In Column (g) enter the new total budgeted amount (Federal and non-Federal) which includes the total previous authorized budgeted amounts plus or minus, as appropriate, the amounts shown in Columns (e) and (f). The amount(s) in Column (g) should not equal the sum of amounts in Columns (e) and (f).

Line 5 - Show the totals for all columns used.

Section B Budget Categories

In the column headings (1) through (4), enter the titles of the same programs, functions, and activities shown on Lines 1-4, Column (a), Section A. When additional sheets are prepared for Section A, provide similar column headings on each sheet. For each program, function or activity, fill in the total requirements for funds (both Federal and non-Federal) by object class categories.

Line 6a-i - Show the totals of Lines 6a to 6h in each column.

Line 6j - Show the amount of indirect cost.

Line 6k - Enter the total of amounts on Lines 6i and 6j. For all applications for new grants and continuation grants the total amount in column (5), Line 6k, should be the same as the total amount shown in Section A, Column (g), Line 5. For supplemental grants and changes to grants, the total amount of the increase or decrease as shown in Columns (1)-(4), Line 6k should be the same as the sum of the amounts in Section A, Columns (e) and (f) on Line 5.

Line 7 - Enter the estimated amount of income, if any, expected to be generated from this project. Do not add or subtract this amount from the total project amount. Show under the program

SF-424A (Rev. 7-97) Page 3

INSTRUCTIONS FOR COMPLETING STANDARD FORM (SF) 424A

EXHIBIT 12.6

ing more space in the abstract or summary to the components that will be weighted more heavily in the scoring/review process. Make sure your abstract or summary is arranged so that it is easy to read. Do not crowd the contents by using every inch of space designated for this area, and highlight important parts with bullets, bold print, and so on if these visual aides are allowed.

INSTRUCTIONS FOR THE SF-424A (continued)

narrative statement the nature and source of income. The estimated amount of program income may be considered by the Federal grantor agency in determining the total amount of the grant.

Section C. Non-Federal Resources

Lines 8-11 Enter amounts of non-Federal resources that will be used on the grant. If in-kind contributions are included, provide a brief explanation on a separate sheet.

> **Column (a)** - Enter the program titles identical to Column (a), Section A. A breakdown by function or activity is not necessary.
>
> **Column (b)** - Enter the contribution to be made by the applicant.
>
> **Column (c)** - Enter the amount of the State's cash and in-kind contribution if the applicant is not a State or State agency. Applicants which are a State or State agencies should leave this column blank.
>
> **Column (d)** - Enter the amount of cash and in-kind contributions to be made from all other sources.
>
> **Column (e)** - Enter totals of Columns (b), (c), and (d).

Line 12 - Enter the total for each of Columns (b)-(e). The amount in Column (e) should be equal to the amount on Line 5, Column (f), Section A.

Section D. Forecasted Cash Needs

Line 13 - Enter the amount of cash needed by quarter from the grantor agency during the first year.

Line 14 - Enter the amount of cash from all other sources needed by quarter during the first year.

Line 15 - Enter the totals of amounts on Lines 13 and 14.

Section E. Budget Estimates of Federal Funds Needed for Balance of the Project

Lines 16-19 - Enter in Column (a) the same grant program titles shown in Column (a), Section A. A breakdown by function or activity is not necessary. For new applications and continuation grant applications, enter in the proper columns amounts of Federal funds which will be needed to complete the program or project over the succeeding funding periods (usually in years). This section need not be completed for revisions (amendments, changes, or supplements) to funds for the current year of existing grants.

If more than four lines are needed to list the program titles, submit additional schedules as necessary.

Line 20 - Enter the total for each of the Columns (b)-(e). When additional schedules are prepared for this Section, annotate accordingly and show the overall totals on this line.

Section F. Other Budget Information

Line 21 - Use this space to explain amounts for individual direct object class cost categories that may appear to be out of the ordinary or to explain the details as required by the Federal grantor agency.

Line 22 - Enter the type of indirect rate (provisional, predetermined, final or fixed) that will be in effect during the funding period, the estimated amount of the base to which the rate is applied, and the total indirect expense.

Line 23 - Provide any other explanations or comments deemed necessary.

SF-424A (Rev. 7-97) Page 4

INSTRUCTIONS FOR COMPLETING STANDARD FORM (SF) 424A *(continued)*

EXHIBIT 12.6

Many funding sources have explicit requirements concerning the summary or abstract. Some designate the space and number of words or characters that can be used, while others require potential grantees to underline a certain number of key words or phrases. Exhibit 12.7 defines what the NSF expects to be found in a project summary, and provides very specific instructions in terms of what person the summary should be written in and what it should include. NSF's guidelines even go so far as to state that the project summary should *not* be an abstract of the pro-

From the National Science Foundation Grant Proposal Guide
NSF98-2

D.   Sections of the Proposal

2.   Project Summary - Proposal Section A

The proposal must contain a summary of the proposed activity suitable for publication, not more than one page in length. It should not be an abstract of the proposal, but rather a contained description of the activity that would result if the proposal were funded. The summary should be written in the third person and include a statement of the objectives, methods to be employed and the potential impact of the project on advancing knowledge in science and mathematics education, and/or human resource development. It should be informative to other persons working in the same or related fields and, insofar as possible, understandable to a scientifically or technically literate lay reader.

(To obtain information about NSF program deadlines, to download copies of NSF publications, and/or to access abstracts of awards, visit the NSF web site at: http://www.nsf.gov)

NATIONAL SCIENCE FOUNDATION PROJECT SUMMARY

EXHIBIT 12.7

posal. Be sure to verify your funding source's rules before constructing this critical part of your proposal.

TITLE PAGE

Federal granting programs have a required face sheet or title page that must be included in your federal grant applications or proposals. The most common is Standard Form (SF) 424 (exhibit 12.8; instructions for completing the form are included in exhibit 12.9). Remember, you are dealing with a bureaucracy and, therefore, should double-check all requirements and make sure all necessary forms are completed per instructions.

The title of a proposal is very important. It is the first part of your proposal to be read by reviewers, and, if it's not good, it may be the only part read! Take the time to develop a title that ensures your proposal will get attention.

The title of your proposal should:

- describe your project
- express your project's end results, not methods
- describe your project's benefits to clients
- be short and easy to remember

APPLICATION FOR FEDERAL ASSISTANCE		2. DATE SUBMITTED January 13, 2003	Applicant Identifier		OMB Approval No. 0348-0043

APPLICATION FOR FEDERAL ASSISTANCE — OMB Approval No. 0348-0043

2. DATE SUBMITTED — January 13, 2003 — Applicant Identifier

1. TYPE OF SUBMISSION:
Application
☐ Construction
☐ Non-Construction

Preapplication
☐ Construction
☐ Non-Construction

3. DATE RECEIVED BY STATE — State Application Identifier

4. DATE RECEIVED BY FEDERAL AGENCY — Federal Identifier

5. APPLICANT INFORMATION
Legal Name:

Organizational Unit:

Address (give city, county, State, and zip code):

Name and telephone number of person to be contacted on matters involving this application (give area code)

6. EMPLOYER IDENTIFICATION NUMBER (EIN):
☐☐ – ☐☐☐☐☐☐☐

7. TYPE OF APPLICANT: (enter appropriate letter in box) ☐

A. State
B. County
C. Municipal
D. Township
E. Interstate
F. Intermunicipal
G. Special District

H. Independent School Dist.
I. State Controlled Institution of Higher Learning
J. Private University
K. Indian Tribe
L. Individual
M. Profit Organization
N. Other (Specify) _____

8. TYPE OF APPLICATION:
☐ New   ☐ Continuation   ☐ Revision

If Revision, enter appropriate letter(s) in box(es) ☐ ☐

A. Increase Award   B. Decrease Award   C. Increase Duration
D. Decrease Duration   Other(specify):

9. NAME OF FEDERAL AGENCY:

10. CATALOG OF FEDERAL DOMESTIC ASSISTANCE NUMBER:
☐☐ – ☐☐☐

TITLE:

11. DESCRIPTIVE TITLE OF APPLICANT'S PROJECT:

12. AREAS AFFECTED BY PROJECT (Cities, Counties, States, etc.):

13. PROPOSED PROJECT

Start Date	Ending Date

14. CONGRESSIONAL DISTRICTS OF:

a. Applicant   b. Project

15. ESTIMATED FUNDING:

a. Federal	$	.00
b. Applicant	$	.00
c. State	$	.00
d. Local	$	.00
e. Other	$	.00
f. Program Income	$	.00
g. TOTAL	$ 0	.00

16. IS APPLICATION SUBJECT TO REVIEW BY STATE EXECUTIVE ORDER 12372 PROCESS?

a. YES. THIS PREAPPLICATION/APPLICATION WAS MADE AVAILABLE TO THE STATE EXECUTIVE ORDER 12372 PROCESS FOR REVIEW ON:

DATE _____

b. No. ☐ PROGRAM IS NOT COVERED BY E. O. 12372
☐ OR PROGRAM HAS NOT BEEN SELECTED BY STATE FOR REVIEW

17. IS THE APPLICANT DELINQUENT ON ANY FEDERAL DEBT?
☐ Yes   If "Yes," attach an explanation.   ☐ No

18. TO THE BEST OF MY KNOWLEDGE AND BELIEF, ALL DATA IN THIS APPLICATION/PREAPPLICATION ARE TRUE AND CORRECT, THE DOCUMENT HAS BEEN DULY AUTHORIZED BY THE GOVERNING BODY OF THE APPLICANT AND THE APPLICANT WILL COMPLY WITH THE ATTACHED ASSURANCES IF THE ASSISTANCE IS AWARDED.

a. Type Name of Authorized Representative   b. Title   c. Telephone Number

d. Signature of Authorized Representative   e. Date Signed

Previous Edition Usable
Authorized for Local Reproduction

Standard Form 424 (Rev. 7-97)
Prescribed by OMB Circular A-102

STANDARD FORM (SF) 424

EXHIBIT 12.8

The best titles are like newspaper headlines, descriptive and to the point. Titles that try to entice the reader by giving only part of the story or creating a mystery seldom work.

Do not use jargon, buzzwords, biblical characters, or Greek gods in your proposal title, since you cannot be sure that the funding source will be familiar with your reference. For example, calling your solar energy project "Apollo's Flame" could work to your disadvantage if the reviewer does not know who Apollo is or fails to make the connection.

INSTRUCTIONS FOR THE SF-424

Public reporting burden for this collection of information is estimated to average 45 minutes per response, including time for reviewing instructions, searching existing data sources, gathering and maintaining the data needed, and completing and reviewing the collection of information. Send comments regarding the burden estimate or any other aspect of this collection of information, including suggestions for reducing this burden, to the Office of Management and Budget, Paperwork Reduction Project (0348-0043), Washington, DC 20503.

PLEASE DO NOT RETURN YOUR COMPLETED FORM TO THE OFFICE OF MANAGEMENT AND BUDGET. SEND IT TO THE ADDRESS PROVIDED BY THE SPONSORING AGENCY.

This is a standard form used by applicants as a required facesheet for preapplications and applications submitted for Federal assistance. It will be used by Federal agencies to obtain applicant certification that States which have established a review and comment procedure in response to Executive Order 12372 and have selected the program to be included in their process, have been given an opportunity to review the applicant's submission.

Item:	Entry:
1.	Self-explanatory.
2.	Date application submitted to Federal agency (or State if applicable) and applicant's control number (if applicable).
3.	State use only (if applicable).
4.	If this application is to continue or revise an existing award, enter present Federal identifier number. If for a new project, leave blank.
5.	Legal name of applicant, name of primary organizational unit which will undertake the assistance activity, complete address of the applicant, and name and telephone number of the person to contact on matters related to this application.
6.	Enter Employer Identification Number (EIN) as assigned by the Internal Revenue Service.
7.	Enter the appropriate letter in the space provided.
8.	Check appropriate box and enter appropriate letter(s) in the space(s) provided:
	-- "New" means a new assistance award.
	-- "Continuation" means an extension for an additional funding/budget period for a project with a projected completion date.
	-- "Revision" means any change in the Federal Government's financial obligation or contingent liability from an existing obligation.
9.	Name of Federal agency from which assistance is being requested with this application.
10.	Use the Catalog of Federal Domestic Assistance number and title of the program under which assistance is requested.
11.	Enter a brief descriptive title of the project. If more than one program is involved, you should append an explanation on a separate sheet. If appropriate (e.g., construction or real property projects), attach a map showing project location. For preapplications, use a separate sheet to provide a summary description of this project.

Item:	Entry:
12.	List only the largest political entities affected (e.g., State, counties, cities).
13.	Self-explanatory.
14.	List the applicant's Congressional District and any District(s) affected by the program or project.
15.	Amount requested or to be contributed during the first funding/budget period by each contributor. Value of in-kind contributions should be included on appropriate lines as applicable. If the action will result in a dollar change to an existing award, indicate _only_ the amount of the change. For decreases, enclose the amounts in parentheses. If both basic and supplemental amounts are included, show breakdown on an attached sheet. For multiple program funding, use totals and show breakdown using same categories as item 15.
16.	Applicants should contact the State Single Point of Contact (SPOC) for Federal Executive Order 12372 to determine whether the application is subject to the State intergovernmental review process.
17.	This question applies to the applicant organization, not the person who signs as the authorized representative. Categories of debt include delinquent audit disallowances, loans and taxes.
18.	To be signed by the authorized representative of the applicant. A copy of the governing body's authorization for you to sign this application as official representative must be on file in the applicant's office. (Certain Federal agencies may require that this authorization be submitted as part of the application.)

SF-424 (Rev. 7-97) Back

INSTRUCTIONS FOR COMPLETING STANDARD FORM (SF) 424

EXHIBIT 12.9

Acronyms should be used only if the funding source has a preference for them. Trying to develop a title that describes the benefits of your project is difficult enough without trying to use specific words that will result in a catchy acronym.

Since you have written the proposal, it is easy for you to develop tunnel vision and attribute more meaning to the words in the title than a person reading it for the first time would. To make sure this does not happen, read your title to other people who know little or nothing about your proposal, and then ask them what they think the proposal is about based on the title. You may find that you are not the best person to write the title. Have friends read the proposal and ask them for title suggestions.

Titles can vary in length and can be up to 10 to 13 words. Some federal programs have rules on the number of characters or spaces used in a title. Check the rules.

The key to writing a good title is to ask funding officials what they prefer and to examine a list of titles used by past grantees. This will give you a more accurate idea of what the funding source really likes.

FUTURE FUNDING

Most funding sources are buying a piece of the future. It is in their best interest to see any project they fund continue. This way, they are able to take credit for the project and its benefits over a greater length of time. Unfortunately, many grantseekers ignore the funding sources' need to keep their investment alive and neglect to mention a future financing plan in their proposal. If you cannot think of ways to finance your project after your federal grant funds run out, think again. Perhaps you could continue your project through

- service fees
- membership fees
- support from agencies such as the United Way
- big gift campaigns aimed at wealthy individuals
- an endowment program
- foundation and corporate grants
- a direct-mail campaign
- other fundraising mechanisms

Include the cost of one or more of these activities in your expenses, and budget them in the grant. You are not automatically considered an ingrate for doing this; rather, you may come across as a good executor of the funding source's estate. You are planning for continuation.

DISSEMINATION

In addition to the good that will come from meeting the objectives and closing the gap established in your needs statement, much good can come from letting others know what you and the funding source have accomplished. Others in your field will come to know your name and ask you to enter into consortia with them. In addition, other funding sources will solicit your application.

You can disseminate the results of your grant by

- mailing a final report, quarterly journal, or a newsletter to others in your field
- sponsoring a seminar or conference on the topic
- attending a national or international conference to deliver the results of the project (many government funding officials cannot travel to conferences, but they can fund you to go and disseminate the results)
- producing a CD or video of the project

Activities aimed at disseminating project results are viewed positively by most funding sources. In general, they want their agency and program name up in lights and are willing to pay for it. So, build the costs related to dissemination into your budget.

ATTACHMENTS (APPENDIX)

The attachments can provide the winning edge when your proposal is compared to a competitor's. Throughout the proposal development process, you should be gathering materials that could be used in the attachment section of your proposal. Your final task is to select which materials to include. Naturally, you want to choose those that will best support your proposal and build credibility. Whether the funding source skims over them or examines them in detail, attachments may include

- studies or research, tables, and graph
- vitae of key personnel
- minutes of advisory committee meetings
- list of board members
- auditor's report or statement
- letters of recommendation or endorsement
- copy of your IRS tax-exempt designation
- pictures or architect's drawings
- copies of your agency's publications
- list of other funding sources you will approach for support

Check funding source rules to determine how long your attachments section can be. Guidelines may state the maximum number of pages it can have, or that it can be up to twice as long as the proposal. Many funding sources will not want you to include the full vitae of key staff, and will specify that you attach abbreviated resumes instead.

Also check funding source rules for the appropriate appendix format. Provide a separate table of contents for your appendix, and number the pages for easy reference.

WRITING YOUR FEDERAL OR STATE PROPOSAL

Your proposal must reflect what the funding source wants and what the reviewers will be looking for. To create a winning proposal

- follow the guidelines exactly (even when they seem senseless, or when you think you are repeating yourself)
- fill in all the blanks
- double-check all computations
- include anything the funding source asks for, even if you think you already provided the information under another section of your proposal

When writing your proposal, keep in mind that it must be readable and easy to skim. Place special emphasis on vocabulary, style, and visual attractiveness and, above all, consider the intended audience (the reviewer).

Vocabulary

Your contact with a past reviewer will have given you an idea of the reviewers' level of expertise and their depth of knowledge in your subject area. Be sure your proposal uses language appropriate to the reviewers. Shorter words are generally better than long, complex words, and avoid buzzwords unless you are sure the reviewer expects them. Define all acronyms, or avoid them completely.

Writing Style

By now you should know the background of the typical reviewer selected by the grantor agency and how much time the reviewers spend reading each proposal. These peer reviewers are under pressure to use their time efficiently, so you must produce a proposal that is poignant, yet organized and easy to read.

- Use simple sentences (no more than two commas) and short paragraphs (five to seven lines).
- Begin each section with a strong motivating lead sentence.
- Make sure your writing style cannot be construed as cute or offensive to the reader. Avoid stating the obvious and talking down to the reviewer.
- Develop a user-friendly proposal. One of the peer reviewers may be chosen to defend your proposal to the rest of the review panel. In this case, you want to be certain to make the reviewer your friend by organizing

and referencing attachments in such a way that they can be used to mount a good defense and to answer the other panelists' questions.

Visual Attractiveness

Even scientific research need not look boring to the reviewer. To enhance the readability of your proposal and make your points stand out, use:

- underlining
- bullets
- different fonts
- various margins and spacing
- bold headings
- pictures and graphics
- charts and tables
- handwriting

While you must follow the grantor's rules regarding type font, number of characters per inch, line spacing, and so on, your computer and laser printer can provide you with a wealth of creative ways to make your proposal more readable.

You will understand how important readability, writing style, and visual attractiveness are after you read several samples of funded proposals followed by your own. Tired reviewers need all the help you can give them to locate and score the important sections of your proposal. Avoid creativity for its own sake, but think of the reader and your goal as you write your proposal.

Keep foremost in your mind that these federal funds are the result of taxes paid by individuals like you, as well as corporations. It is your responsibility to make the plan for how you propose to spend these moneys as precise and as clearly related to the project outcome as possible. The tendency to round numbers up and pad budgets is a threat to your credibility and could affect your ability to gain the peer reviewers' and federal staff's confidence.

Remember, do not leave anything to chance. All required forms must be completed precisely.

Online Proposal Preparation

The federal government is moving toward the congressional mandate for a paperless environment. This mandate has met with varying amounts of success within the different government departments. Through your research you will learn where and how to apply for your specific grant.

The Department of Education has a pilot program called e-application, which allows applicants to apply online for a specially selected group of grants. The *Fed-*

eral Register notice for each program will indicate whether the program is accepting e-applications as part of the department's pilot program. To determine if your program is accepting electronic applications, visit the department's link to *Federal Register* notices at <http://www.ed.gov/legislation/FedRegister/announcements/>. If the program is accepting electronic applications and you are a new user, you will need to register to use e-application at <http://e-grants.ed.gov/>. You will then be given a user name and password, and be able to access your unique application. You can complete the application and all necessary forms online. However, only authorized individuals from your organization can submit the application. Check with your certifying official or sponsored research office before submission.

Formerly known as e-GAPS, the Department of Education's pilot program is currently being expanded and soon its online grant application process will be available to many discretionary and formula grant program applicants. It's only a matter of time before many other government departments will be implementing a similar application system.

All federal agencies are moving toward meeting Congress's paperless environment mandate, and how it impacts proposal creation and submission is different in each agency. For example, the NSF is still fine-tuning its FastLane electronic submittal system. Check with your federal program's Web site and with the program officer for the latest changes in its system.

While electronic systems are seeking to make proposal creation and submittal simple and accurate, there still are some shortcomings. For example, most of the existing systems do not allow for spell- or grammar-check. In some cases, you are instructed to download to perform those functions, and then include the corrected narrative as an attachment. Obviously, there are many new and interesting challenges as we move toward the electronic grant application system and away from print copy. One really important advantage is the time and effort these systems save, not to mention a forest or two.

CHAPTER 13

Improving Your Federal
Proposal
The Grants Quality Circle

THE GRANTS QUALITY CIRCLE

Consistently funded grantees usually take advantage of a pre submission review of their proposals by a colleague or two. While this technique is positive, its value depends on how knowledgeable those reviewing your proposal are of the field and how much they know about the actual peer review system that will be used by the actual reviewers. For example, while a four-hour review of your proposal by one of your colleagues will be quite detailed, it may actually be counterproductive in its suggestions, if the real reviewer is going to spend just one hour reviewing it. The secret to improving your federal proposal is to conduct a mock review that emulates the actual review system as closely as possible. Of course, the first step is to be proactive and to make sure you have enough time to take advantage of this most valuable technique.

Proactive grantseekers initiate proposal development early in the federal grant cycle and therefore have sufficient time to have their proposals reviewed by their peers before submission. You will improve your proposal and significantly increase your chances for success by asking several colleagues or members of your grants advisory committee to voluntarily role-play the review team that will ultimately pass judgment on your proposal. This presubmission review process is really a test run or mock review, and the group conducting it is your quality circle, as described in W. Edward Deming's work in total quality management (TQM).[1] If you follow the TQM model, you will not pay your mock reviewers to take part in the activity. They should be motivated by their desire to help you improve your proposal, increase its probability of acceptance, and, thus, enhance the image of your organization. It is to everyone's advantage to position your institution in the most favorable manner. In many institutions, the grants office will assist you in setting up this improvement exercise and when necessary, may even pay the mock reviewers a small stipend.

The grant office at Eastern Michigan University (EMU) offers a quality circles training session to educate faculty members how to lead quality circles. There are incentives involved, such as course release time, for leading these mock reviews. Contact Brian Anderson at EMU for more information ([734]487-3090). Western Michigan University (WMU) uses a similar process to impact the quality and success of their proposals. For more information, contact Dr. Eileen Evans, Associate Vice President for Research, WMU ([269]387-8298).

As previously mentioned, the most significant factor in the success of this improvement exercise is how closely each aspect of the mock review resembles the actual federal or state review. The benefits you can derive from this technique are directly related to your ability to create the scenario in which the actual reviewers will find themselves.

To arrange a mock review that is similar to what the actual review will be like, procure a list of last year's reviewers, a copy of the scoring system that will be used, and a sample of an exemplary proposal. Through preproposal contact (see chapter 11), you should already have information about the setting in which your proposal will be reviewed.

To make this exercise as valuable as possible, provide your mock review group or grants quality circle with data on the following:

- the training each reviewer receives.
- the setting in which proposals are reviewed (the federal agency, the reviewer's home, both sites, and so on).
- the review process: Does one reviewer defend the proposal while others try to locate flaws or weaknesses?
- the scoring system: Are scores averaged? Are the highest and lowest scores eliminated and the remainder averaged?
- the amount of time spent reviewing each proposal

It is essential that you instruct the members of your grants quality circle to spend only the same amount of time reviewing your proposal as the actual reviewers will. Some of your mock reviewers may mistakenly think they will be helping you by taking an inordinate amount of time to read your proposal carefully. However, if actual reviewers will skim parts of the proposal, then your mock reviewers should do the same. Remind your quality circle participants that they should be trying to *mirror* the actual reviewers, not to do a better job than them! If the actual reviewers will invest over 90 minutes reviewing and scoring each proposal, consider distributing your draft proposal to the members of your grants quality circle before

Date

Name
Address

Dear _____:

I would like to take this opportunity to request your input in helping our [organization, group, team] submit the very best grant proposal possible. We are asking that you review the enclosed proposal from the point of view of the federal reviewer. The attached materials will help you role-play the actual manner in which the proposal will be evaluated.

Please read the information on the reviewers' backgrounds and the scoring system and limit the time you spend reading the proposal to the time constraints that the real reviewers will observe. A grants quality circle worksheet has been provided to assist you in recording your scores and comments.

A meeting of all mock reviewers comprising our quality circle has been scheduled for [date]. Please bring your grants quality circle worksheet with you to this meeting. The meeting will last less than one hour. Its purpose is to analyze the scores and brainstorm suggestions to improve this proposal.

Sincerely,

Name
Phone Number

SAMPLE LETTER INVITING AN INDIVIDUAL TO PARTICIPATE IN A GRANTS QUALITY CIRCLE

EXHIBIT 13.1

they come together. If a corporate or foundation official is likely to spend 10 minutes reviewing it, then disseminate the proposal at your quality circle meeting.

The sample letter inviting an individual to participate in a grants quality circle (exhibit 13.1) and the grants quality circle worksheet (exhibit 13.2) will help you carry out this valuable exercise. After the suggestions from your mock review have been incorporated into your final proposal, you are ready to move on to submission.

In some cases it is not feasible to assemble a group of volunteers for a quality circle. There may be too few colleagues in your organization to conduct a role-playing activity such as this, confidentiality may be an issue, personality problems may exist, or competition in the field could rule out the possibility of such an activity occurring. However, one option in these instances would be to ask one or two individuals that you trust from outside your organization or off campus to review your proposal. Provide them with the same data and worksheets discussed

The following information is designed to help you develop the proper focus for the review of the attached proposal.

1.   The Review Panelists

     Proposals are read by review panelists with the following degrees and backgrounds:

     Degrees: _____

     _____

     Backgrounds (Age, Viewpoints, Biases, and So On): _____

     _____

     _____

2.   The Time Element and Setting

     Number of proposals read by each reviewer: _____

     Average length of time spent reading each proposal:_____

     Proposals are read at the: _____ reviewer's home
                                     _____ reviewer's work
                                     _____ funder's location
                                     _____ other site

3.   The Scoring System

     a. The scoring system that will be employed is based on a scale of: _____

     _____

     _____

GRANTS QUALITY CIRCLE WORKSHEET

EXHIBIT 13.2

above, and, if necessary, offer them an honorarium for their efforts ($200 is common). You could request that they sign a nondisclosure agreement. Most university grant offices have these agreement forms and will be happy to share a copy with you. This way you can tailor the agreement to your project with minimal effort. Seldom are these extraordinary security measures necessary with colleagues, but this is an option you may want to consider to insure that no one steals your idea.

A look at a few selected scoring systems reveals the importance of knowing how your proposal will be reviewed and how important it is to share this information with your mock reviewers. The first example from the Office of Educational Research and Improvement is characterized by a specific point system, heavily weighed toward national significance and project design.

b. The areas to be scored are (list or include attachment):

Area	Total Possible Points	Your Score

c. According to the total points per area, how many points represent an outstanding, superior, adequate, weak, or poor score? For example, if the total points possible for one area are 25, 0-8 = poor, 9-12 = weak, 13-19 = adequate, 20-23 = superior, and 24-25 = outstanding.

d. After recording your scores, list the positive points of the proposal that may appeal to the actual reviewer. Also list those areas that seem weak and may cost valuable points. List suggestions for improvement.

GRANTS QUALITY CIRCLE WORKSHEET *(continued)*

EXHIBIT 13.2

Example 1

National significance	30 points
Quality of project design	30 points
Quality of potential contribution of personnel	15 points
Adequacy of resources	15 points
Quality of management plan	10 points
Total	100 points

In examples 2 and 3, the National Institute on Aging (example 2) and the NSF (example 3) do not use evaluation systems based on points. In situations like these, the grantseeker must ask more questions of the grantor so that he or she can ascertain what looks good under each criterion. After all, to play the game you need to know *all* the rules!

Example 2

- Scientific, technical, or medical significance
- Appropriateness and adequacy of approach
- Qualifications of principal investigator/staff

- Availability of resource
- Appropriateness of budget
- Adequacy of plans to include both genders and minorities
- Protection of human subjects

Example 3

- Criterion 1: What is the intellectual merit of the proposed activity?
- Criterion 2: What are the broader impacts of the proposed activity?

Few techniques suggested in this book will have a more dramatic effect on the quality of your proposals than the grants quality circle. Support for this activity will be rewarded through the promotion of a better image with reviewers and federal staff, as well as an increase in quality proposals from staff members participating in the activity.

NOTE

1. Gary Fellers, *The Deming Vision: SPC/TQM for Administrators* (Milwaukee: ASQC Quality Press, 1992).

CHAPTER 14

Submission
What To Do and What Not To Do

Although this chapter addresses the federal grants area, much of the information it contains also can be applied to other government funding sources such as state, county, and city. Irrespective of which type of public funding source you are submitting your proposal to, you do not want to do anything at this late stage that may have a negative impact on your submitted proposal's outcome.

WHAT TO DO

Submit your proposal a day or two before the deadline. Do not position yourself as a last-minute applicant who beats the deadline by a few minutes. After all your hard work you do not want to position yourself as a loser. Grantors have told me that they worry about funding last-minute Herculean proposal developers because they are likely to experience problems with their expenditure rates (i.e., having leftover money that ends up as a grant continuation or extension), late or missing reports and evaluations, and a host of other maladies that could make the grantor's program look bad to Congress.

Follow all instructions and every rule. Do not wait until your proposal has been written, has undergone a mock review, and is ready to be sent out before you read the submission rules. Review the submittal requirements early to make sure you have enough time to comply with them. Do not jeopardize your chances for success by failing to show funders that you have read and complied with their rules for submission.

Since each government agency and even some of the grant programs within agencies have different submittal procedures, they cannot all be listed here. Several federal programs require you to initial a special sign-on section or provide signatures next to each of the requirements that are most often overlooked. Others call for the inclusion of notarized copies of the board minutes and resolutions that authorized your organization's approval to submit the proposal (especially when matching or in-kind contributions are required). Many agencies require letters of commitment from consortia members.

Unfortunately, many grantseekers read the requirements too late and find that their board will not meet again before the grantor's deadlines. They then include a note with their proposal saying that they will forward the necessary documents at a later date. This is a red flag to grantors and alerts them that this applicant may be a problem.

Even with extensive instructions, grantseekers make mistakes in obtaining appropriate or authorized signatures, page length, number of pages, assurances, and so on. In fact, it would be too time-consuming to list all of the problems federal grantors have in gaining compliance with their rules. Review and follow the submittal procedures contained in your application package carefully.

Keep the cover clear and simple. If the grantor requires a special cover sheet, use it. If the grantor does not require a special cover sheet, make sure the cover you place on the application does not interfere with the handling of your proposal. Your cover should act as a luggage tag, allowing for the easy identification of where your proposal is going and where it came from. The cover should clearly designate the office, division, mail stop, and so on; the program title and CFDA number, the name and phone number of the program officer; your organization's name and return address; and your name. Remember, as the principal investigator or proposal developer you are not usually authorized to submit a proposal nor enter into any legal agreements. Check with your grants office early for their rules on how much time they need to review your budget. Complete all the assurances, and so on. Most larger nonprofit institutions have a sign-off process to obtain required signatures. You may be required to go around and get these signatures. So, be sure to leave enough time to do so. Remember, asking for and receiving advance approvals on your preproposal summary and approval form (chapter 4, exhibit 4.2) streamlines the sign-off process and avoid problems with matching funds, released time, space, and equipment usage.

WHAT NOT TO DO

It is recommended that you limit the use of elected representatives in the grants process, especially at submittal time. Federal bureaucrats view the use of congresspeople and their aides as potentially unethical and possibly illegal. Elected officials want to be viewed by you, the voter, as ready to help in any way, but their assistance should be limited to preproposal contact and gathering information about past grantees and reviewers when you are unable to get the information on your own.

Do not ask for extra time or a later submittal date, and do not ask to send in any parts of the proposal after the deadline. Do not contact federal bureaucrats after submission. This is viewed as an attempt to influence the grantor's review process and decision. On a rare occasion, an advancement in the field could dramatically effect a proposal you have already submitted. In this instance, you should alert the program officer of the ramifications of the advancement and how they will affect your proposal's protocol or budget. Send the program officer an e-mail explaining the situation and let him or her decide whether to send the new information to the reviewers, and so on.

OTHER SUBMISSION TECHNIQUES

Several optional techniques may be helpful.

1. You could hand-deliver your proposal (and all the copies the agency could use) to the designated grants logging center for that agency. While doing so, stop by the program office to thank staff members for their assistance.
2. Most federal agencies are required to have an electronic submittal process in place in 2003. Since you are proposing that your project approach reflects the most current views in your field, use the most modern mode of submission. It is becoming more common for federal programs to have their application forms available online and to encourage and accept proposals submitted electronically over the Internet. For example, the NSF uses an interactive, electronic submittal system known as *FastLane*. The purpose of the program is to use the World Wide Web to facilitate business transactions and the exchange of information between NSF and its client community. (To obtain instructions on how to use *FastLane*, visit <http://www.fastlane.nsf.gov/>.) Internet transmittal is becoming so common that now it is even the preferred method for peer reviewers to submit their proposal critiques.

   While the use of the Internet is growing in this field, it is still a good idea to check to see what your proposal looks like when received by electronic submission. What happens to graphics and to the layout and design? A little care may pay off dramatically.

   Double-check with our institution's grants office to see when they need the proposal by to do their job and who is the authorized agent to make the transmittal official.
3. You could send (or deliver) a copy of your proposal abstract or summary to your congressperson's office. Advise the congressperson that you do not want or expect any intervention at this point, but let him or her know the approximate or anticipated date of the notice of award (usually several months

away). Many times, federal granting officials will inform the congressperson of awards before they notify the grantee. Therefore, it is important to alert your congressperson that you have submitted a proposal and that you will contact him or her again closer to the notification date. Let your congressperson know that you would appreciate it if he or she would contact you immediately if they receive notice of your award first, so that you can prepare a joint public relationships release.

Check with your program officer or contact person to confirm the preferred method of submission.

Submission is the final step in demonstrating your ability and desire to comply with the federal granting source's rules and regulations. Hopefully your attention to detail will lead the grantor to believe that you will be equally precise in executing your funded grant. One thing is certain, however; if you fail to comply with all submission rules, you will lose your credibility and drastically diminish your chances of being funded.

CHAPTER 15

Federal Grant Requirements

Many nonprofit agencies exhibit great fear and trepidation over the rules regarding federal grant moneys. These fears are basically unwarranted and should be of concern only to nonprofit organizations that do not have adequate fiscal rules and regulations. The restrictions governing usage of federal funds are understandable and in most cases reasonable. Yes, there are instances of disallowed expenditures two or three years after a grant has been completed, but they are avoidable. Most people remember the exception rather than the rule. Over $150 billion in federal grant funds are awarded each year, and only a small fraction of grantees have their expenditures disallowed or experience a problem with an audit. Most likely, your existing personnel, accounting, and purchasing procedures will be adequate. If you must make changes in your system to ensure the adequate handling of federal funds, however, do so. Such changes will increase the credibility of your system.

The federal grants requirement worksheet (see exhibit 15.1) will help you comply with most federal grant requirements. If your institution has a grants administration office, this worksheet may not be necessary, but you, the project director, still need to know the facts so that you can help in the overall administration of your grant.

FEDERAL GRANTS REQUIREMENT WORKSHEET

The federal grants requirement worksheet will help you familiarize yourself with and keep abreast of the basic obligations your nonprofit organization agrees to fulfill by accepting federal grant funds.

Project Title: _____

Project Director: _____

Federal Account Identification Number: _____

Agency Staff: _____

Agency Phone Number: _____ Agency Fax Number: _____ Agency Email: _____

Notification of Award Received on (Date): _____

Start Date of Project: _____

End Date of Project: _____

Dates Reports are Due: _____

Final Report Due On (Date): _____

Number of Years Funding Can Be Applied For: _____

Matching or In-Kind Requirements: _____% $ _____

Where Matching or In-Kind Records Will Be Kept: _____

Who Will Be Responsible for Keeping Them: _____

Federal Rules Governing This Grant

- OMB Circulars/Guidelines Governing Grant Expenditures:

  _____

  _____

  _____

- Location of OMB Circulars/Guidelines Governing Grant Expenditures:

  _____

  _____

  _____

- Special Rules and Federal Management Circulars (List from Assurances Section of Proposal):

  _____

  _____

  _____

- Location of Special Rules and Federal Management Circulars:

  _____

  _____

  _____

FEDERAL GRANTS REQUIREMENT WORKSHEET

EXHIBIT 15.1

1. Complete the first section of the worksheet when you receive notice of funding. Include the federal account identification number and all other information you can supply. It is critical that you record the actual start date or date funded so that you do not change any part of the grant before its official award date. Review your project planner and record the dates on which you must supply progress indicators.

2. List the Office of Management and Budget (OMB) circulars that will govern your grant expenditures and where the circulars are located.

3. Record any information about the number of years of funding that can be applied for.

4. Indicate the percentage and dollar total of the cost-sharing requirements, where the records will be kept, and who will be responsible for keeping them.

5. Acceptance of federal funds require that your organization have a policy regarding drug use and counseling of employees.

6. If your grant calls for the creation of unique materials, make note of the rules regarding ownership and use. Noting these in advance reduces problems later.

7. The fair and equal employment rules are reasonable and should pose no problems for most nonprofit organizations.

8. List the office or person responsible for approval of projects that involve copyrights or patents, or the use of human and animal subjects, recombinant DNA, radioactive material. If you work for an organization that already has institutional review boards, be sure to check with those groups. If your organization does not have institutional review boards or committees, do not initiate them. Instead, involve a university-or-college related individual on your grants advisory committee, and ask him or her to use their institution's review boards.

Even though your proposal may not call for the performance of hard-core research, the federal government is very broad in its interpretation of what activities pose a potential danger to humans. In fact, federal officials even require human subjects approval for some needs assessment surveys, model projects, and demonstration grants.

RAISING AND DOCUMENTING MATCHING FUNDS

One of the more confusing areas of federal grants is the requirement of matching funds or in-kind contributions (also known as cost sharing). An organization can be asked to supply either cash, services, or facilities to match a percentage of the grant. This requirement may change over the years that federal funds support the project. For example, year 1 may require a 20-percent match, year 2 a 40-percent match, and year 3 a 50-percent match.

In some cases, the federal instructions state that a match is not required but encouraged. If you have inquired into this matter, discovered that a match will help you get funded, and have designated a specific amount in your budget for a match or in-kind contribution, be aware that this match must be documented and will be subject to an audit to verify the amount. It is always wise to document and list the efforts and costs that will be provided by your organization and partners. Review your project planner for any personnel, consultants, contract services, supplies, equipment, or materials that will be contributed to your project. Remember, not to list anything that is being supplied to this grant that was provided under any other federal program.

The worksheet on sources of matching funds (see exhibit 15.2) can help you plan a successful matching funds campaign before you approach federal agencies. The worksheet contains several standard methods for cost sharing and provides

Project Title: _____

Total Project Cost: $ _____

Match Required: _____ % $ _____

Review each of the following sources of matching funds. Check with federal officials to ensure that your match is in compliance with their rules and will be accepted. Make sure that nothing listed under your match has been provided from federal funds.

1. Personnel - List the percentage of time and effort of each individual who will be contributing to the match. Include salaries, wages, and fringe benefits.

   Options:

   • Include the time and effort of volunteers, consultants, and/or corporate sponsors if allowable by the grantor.

   • If the project calls for staff training or development, will your organization be required to increase salaries? If so, check with the grantor to see whether this can be listed as a match.

2. Equipment - List any equipment that will be purchased primarily to carry out this project. Include the cost of each piece and the total equipment cost.

3. Facilities - List the location, square footage, and cost per foot for each facility and the total facilities (space) cost.

4. Foundation/Corporate Grantors - What other grantors could you approach for a grant to match this grant?

   • Foundations:

   • Corporations:

5. Fundraising Activities - In some cases you may have to resort to fundraising activities to develop your matching portion. List the activities and the net return expected from each.

   • Special Events (Dance, Raffle, etc.):

   • Sales of Products:

   • Other:

WORKSHEET ON SOURCES OF MATCHING FUNDS

EXHIBIT 15.2

an evaluation system for each method. (This worksheet can also be useful when working with foundations and corporations that request matching support.)

FEDERAL GRANTS MANAGEMENT CIRCULARS

The highly regulated, detailed rules about grant management are probably the most imposing characteristic of federal grants. These rules may specify allowable costs, indirect cost rates, accounting requirements, and the like. Before getting involved in government grants, you and/or your accounting department should review the appropriate grants management circulars. Such a review usually diminishes fears about your organization's ability to comply with federal grant requirements. In most cases, you will find that your organization has safeguards in effect that meet the requirements.

The OMB produces circulars outlining uniform standards for financial dealings with government granting agencies. These circulars can be accessed online at <http://www.whitehouse.gov/omb/grants/>. To obtain circulars that are not available online, call the OMB's information line at (202)395-3080.

The following section is a broad description of OMB Circular A-110.

OMB Circular A-110

OMB Circular A-110 is entitled "Uniform Administrative Requirements for Grants and Agreements with Institutions of Higher Education, Hospitals and Other Nonprofit Organizations." This circular, along with its updates and attachments, budget forms, and cash request instructions, is a guide to the rules regarding federal grants. The circular is divided into four subparts:

- Subpart A—General
- Subpart B—Pre-Award Requirements
- Subpart C—Post-Award Requirements
  Financial and Program Management
  Property Standards
  Procurement Standards
  Reports and Records
  Termination and Enforcement
- Subpart D—After-the-Award Requirements

Attachments to the circular cover the following areas:

- cash depositories
- bonding and insurance
- retention and custodial requirements for records

- Cost Principles
  A-21, Educational Institutions
  A-87, State and Local Governments
  A-122, Non-Profit Organizations

- Administrative Requirements
  A-102, State and Local Governments
  A-110, Institutions of Higher Education, Hospitals, and Other Organizations

- Audit Requirements
  A-133, States, Local Governments, and Non-Profit Organizations

GRANTS MANAGEMENT OMB CIRCULARS

EXHIBIT 15.3

- program income
- cost sharing and matching
- standards for financial management systems
- financial reporting requirements
- monitoring and reporting program performance
- payment requirements
- revision of financial plans
- close-out procedures
- suspension and termination
- standards for applying
- property management standards
- procurement standards

Colleges and universities will also be interested in OMB Circular A-21, which defines cost principles for federal research and development grants to educational institutions. All nonprofit organizations should familiarize themselves with OMB Circular A-122, "Cost Principles for Non-Profit Organizations," and state and local governments must also review OMB Circular A-87, "Cost Principles for State, Local and Indian Tribal Governments," and OMB Circular A-102, "Grants and Cooperative Agreements with State and Local Governments." Please be advised that you should always refer to the most current circular for the specific rules and regulations in your area.

Exhibit 15.3 lists all of the grants management OMB circulars in numerical sequence. Fears concerning the expenditure of federal grant funds are reduced when you request the appropriate OMB circulars for your type of organization and review the rules with your fiscal staff. From purchasing to personnel, your organization will most likely already have the necessary safeguards in place. Those areas that look as if they will pose a problem can be addressed in a general manner, for all federal grants, or handled separately, case by case, to avoid any difficulties.

CHAPTER 16

Dealing with the Decision of Public Funding Sources

The federal government is attempting to streamline the grants process. This includes making award determinations that are understandable and the same across all granting programs. Instead of making determinations that left grantseekers confused (such as "supportable but not fundable"), the federal government is now using these determinations:

- accepted (as written)
- accepted with modifications (usually budget modifications, which will affect some activities)
- rejected (the proposal did not reach the level or score required for funding)

ACCEPTED

If your proposal is accepted, consider taking the following steps:

1. Thank the grantor. Whether you are notified by phone, letter, or e-mail, send the program or project officer a thank-you letter expressing your appreciation for the time and effort staff and reviewers expended on your proposal.
2. Request the reviewers' comments, and include a self-addressed label for the funding source's convenience.
3. Ask the federal official for insight into what you could have done better.
4. Invite the program or project officer for a site visit.
5. Ask the official what mistakes successful grantees often make in carrying out their funded grant so you can be sure to avoid these errors.

163

6. Review the reporting structure. What does the grantor require and when? Will your dates for milestones and progress indicators be helpful?

ACCEPTED WITH BUDGET MODIFICATIONS

Should your proposal receive this response, do the following:

1. Send the funding source a thank-you letter.
2. Call the funding source and suggest that the program officer refer to your project planner to negotiate the budget terms.
3. Discuss the option of eliminating some of the project's methods or activities.
4. If several activities must be eliminated, consider dropping the accomplishment of an objective or reducing the expected degree of change.
5. If you are forced to negotiate away the supporting structure necessary to achieve your objectives, be prepared to turn down the funds. After all, you do not want to enter into an agreement that will cause you to lose credibility later.

REJECTED

If your proposal is rejected, take the following actions aimed at developing insight into the changes you need to make in your proposal for the next submission cycle:

1. Send the funding official a thank-you letter in appreciation for his or her time and effort as well as that of the reviewers and staff. Let the funding official know that although you were aware of the risk of failure before you invested your time in applying, you would appreciate assistance in reapplying.
2. Request the reviewers' comments. Enclose a self-addressed label for their convenience.
3. Ask the funding official for his or her suggestions.
4. Find out whether your proposal could possibly be funded as a pilot project, as a needs assessment, or in some other way.
5. Ask whether there are any ways the funding source could assist you in getting ready for the next submission cycle, such as conducting a preliminary review.
6. Ask whether it would be wise for you to reapply. What are your chances and what would you have to change?
7. Ask whether you could become a reviewer to learn more about the review process.

By examining the reviewers' comments you may find that some reviewers scored a section of your proposal as outstanding, while others gave the same section a low score. This situation can create a dilemma. Changing your proposal to reflect one reviewer's comments may negate another reviewer's comments, and your changes could result in resubmission scores that are just average. Ask the grantor what you can do about this situation. Also, ask an outside expert to review your proposal; even if you must pay someone to review the proposal, you need insight into what is causing this discrepancy.

Some federal agencies inform grantseekers at the time of rejection whether they should change their proposal and reapply or avoid resubmittal and develop an entirely new approach. In fact, new agency reviewing procedures call for a process that eliminates proposals with a low likelihood of funding from a thorough review. Some grantors even require that 25 percent of the applications they receive are given this brief and expedited review, and then returned to the applicants without detailed reviewer comments. Many of the rejected applications that are not read thoroughly or evaluated and scored are cited for errors in the application itself or for nonallowable costs and/or inappropriate ideas.

No matter what the determination (accepted, accepted with modifications, or rejected), or the degree to which your proposal was reviewed, your response to your grant application's outcome must be positive. Whether you are jubilant or depressed, thank the grantor and seek to learn as much as possible from the experience. Demonstrate your willingness to learn from the funding source's feedback. You will find reinforcement for your positive behavior and become aware of how to avoid making the same mistakes.

CHAPTER 17

Follow-Up with Government Funding Sources

The object of follow-up is to position yourself as an asset to funding sources and not as a pest. You want to develop professional relationships and maintain contact with funding sources throughout the grants process, not just at submittal and award time. In addition to advising funders of your willingness to serve as a reviewer, consider:

- forwarding notes on special articles or books in your area to them
- inviting them to visit your organization
- asking whether they would like to speak at your professional group or association's conference, or at a special grants conference
- asking them what meetings or conferences they will be attending so that you can look them up
- requesting information about what you can do to have an impact on legislation affecting their funding levels or allocations

By remaining on grantors' mailing lists and reviewing their agency publications (i.e., NSF Guide, NIH Bulletin) and/or the *Federal Register*, you will gain advance knowledge of the next funding opportunity. Do not wait until next year's deadline to begin thinking about your ensuing application. Start to plan for next year right after funding decisions are made for the current year.

The best way to learn what is going on is to visit the funding source personally. Keep in touch. Watch for meeting announcements in the *Federal Register*. Testify at committee hearings that will affect the agency and its funding level. Send the agency blind copies of your efforts to have an impact on legislation for them (and yourself). Use your association memberships and legislative committees to push for changes that benefit the particular agency, and write to Senate and House appropriations committees to increase funding. Attend professional meetings and sessions that program officers are speaking at, and ask questions.

DEVELOPING CONTINUED GRANT SUPPORT

The key to continued success is to repeat the steps that have brought you to this point. If you have used the concepts presented in this manual to develop a proactive grants process, you have a system that alerts you to changes in program rules, deadlines, and the like through the *Federal Register,* mailing lists, personal contacts, and established links.

Although federal officials may change jobs and positions, their names seem to reappear again and again. A systematic approach to recording research on funding sources and officials will prove useful as you come across old friends and make new ones. By maintaining your relationship, whether you have received funding or not, you demonstrate to funding sources that you plan to be around for awhile and that you will not forget them as soon as you receive their check. Unfortunately, changes in staffing at government agencies make maintaining contacts more difficult. Just when things are going great, the program officers you have been working with will move on. But take heart; they may appear again somewhere down the grants road, so keep on their good side!

PART THREE

....

Private/Foundation Funding Opportunities

CHAPTER 18

Understanding the Private Foundation Marketplace

This dynamic and fascinating source of grant funds can be a virtual gold mine for the astute grantseeker. This area is often misunderstand and, subsequently, approached for funding for inappropriate projects and exorbitantly large grant amounts. If you have not already taken the marketplace quiz in chapter 8, do so now and then return to this chapter.

After taking the quiz and reviewing the correct answers you were probably surprised at how far off your guesses were. If so, you are not alone. Ninety percent of my seminar participants believe that foundation grants are a major portion of the $241 billion philanthropic marketplace. The real numbers often scare grantseekers away, when, in reality, they should deepen their resolve to do a little more research to take advantage of these funds.

Private foundations have experienced the same financial challenges that taxpaying individuals have faced in recent years. While required to grant 5 percent of the market value of their assets, private foundations have historically granted much more than that. But times are changing. Foundation giving increased by 20.4 percent between 1998 and 1999, by 19.6 percent between 1999 and 2000, but by only 5.4 percent between 2000 and 2001. The 2001 and 2002 drops in the stock market and the onset of a recession have had a dramatic effect on this marketplace. Some foundations had large holdings in areas of the private sector that experienced 40 to 50 percent decreases in value. Needless to say, this affected their asset bases substantially. Because of this, your research on the foundations that share an interest in your area of concern will have to include an assessment of the forecasted changes in their asset bases and how these changes will affect their future granting programs. Once you locate a prospective foundation funding source, you will need to examine a copy of its IRS tax return to determine what stocks and other assets it holds (more on this in chapter 19). From this you will be able to estimate the minimal amount the foundation will need to award in grants to comply with the 5-percent IRS regulation.

On the bright side, not all foundations experienced a decrease in their asset bases in the last few years. Despite challenges to Microsoft and a decline in its stock value, the Bill and Melinda Gates Foundation's $20 billion asset base actually grew slightly. The Gates Foundation had its assets in bonds and certificates of deposit and, therefore, its base did not decrease like those of the foundations that were heavily invested in stocks. However, Surdna Foundation executive director Edward Sklott stated that most foundations experienced a 10- to 30-percent decline in their asset bases over the last two years.[1] It remains to be seen if any of them will dig into their asset bases to maintain or even surpass their past levels of giving at this very critical time.

To fully understand private foundations, you need to think like the wealthy individuals who create them. Let's assume you have created a foundation to move vast sums of your wealth into a tax-deductible entity that will allow you, your family, and your friends to fund projects and organizations that further your values, beliefs, and life's work. According to IRS rules, you must give away at least 5 percent of the market value of your foundation's assets each year to the groups your by-laws designate as recipients or pay a tax. However, the costs related to the administration of your foundation (i.e., staffing, office space, equipment, travel, board salaries, etc.) are included in this 5 percent. For instance, if the market value of your foundation's assets is $10 million, and you decide to disburse the minimum required amount of 5 percent or $500,000, you must subtract from this the cost of your director, support staff, office, and overhead, which could easily reach $250,000, leaving you only $250,000 to give away in the form of grants. So what can you do to reduce your administrative costs and increase the portion of the 5 percent you distribute through the grants process? You can decide not to hire a director or create an office, or have a staff. After all, you don't need a staff or reviewers. You know what you want to fund, and you want to make as much money as possible available for grants. Now that you are thinking like the creator of a foundation, here are the facts.

- There are approximately 60,000 private foundations.
- Of the 60,000 foundations, it is estimated that 2,000 or less have a dedicated office, and that the total number of foundation employees is less than 2,000.
- Less than 2,000 foundations have Web sites and, of these, only a few accept online transmittal of proposals.
- Foundations granted $26.9 billion in 2002.

- The largest 1,000 foundations made $12 billion in grants—almost one-half of the $26 billion.
- Of the $26 billion in foundation grants, there were approximately 125,000 grant awards for over $10,000. Grants of less than $10,000 were too numerous to count, and very likely to be in the hundreds of thousands.

Now the good news. Most foundations use a letter proposal or short concept paper (two to three pages in length) as the primary component of their application process. Unfortunately, the brevity of the process can encourage grantseekers to simply locate the name and address of 20 or 30 foundations and send the same letter proposal to each of them. This "dear occupant, please send foundation grant" approach is a fatal mistake, usually resulting in rejection and negative positioning.

To be a successful foundation grantseeker, you must discover what your prospective foundation funding source values, seek to understand how they look at the world, and present your project in such a way that to reject it would conflict with the foundation's values, stated beliefs, and past giving pattern. To assist you in this research process, read the following brief descriptions of the basic types of foundations and then review the Grantseeker's Private Foundation Decision Matrix (table 18.1) to help you select which of the four basic types of private foundations is right for your project—national general purpose, special purpose, community, or family.

NATIONAL GENERAL PURPOSE FOUNDATIONS

To be designated as a national general purpose foundation, a foundation does not need to fit a hard-and-fast definition. *National general purpose* refers to the foundation's scope and type of granting pattern. Foundations in this group have a philanthropic interest in several subject areas and make grants for proposals that will have a broad-scale impact across the United States and the world. They prefer model, creative, innovative projects that other groups can replicate to solve similar problems. Since national general purpose foundations like to promote change, they do not usually fund deficits, operating income, or the many necessary but not highly visible or creative functions of organizations.

National general purpose foundations have staff and in some instances use professional consultants as reviewers. Their applications are usually longer than those of the other types of foundations and they often have more rules and regulations. They expect those they fund to have major players on staff and in consortia, but their grant size is larger than those of the other foundations.

Of the 60,000-plus foundations, there are probably less than 200 national general purpose foundations. Even though there are so few, most people have no trou-

TABLE 18.1

GRANTSEEKERS' PRIVATE FOUNDATION DECISION MATRIX

TYPE OF FOUNDATION	GEOGRAPHIC NEED	TYPE OF PROJECT	GRANT AWARD FOR SIZE FOR FIELD OF INTEREST	IMAGE	CREDENTIALS OF P.I./P.D.	PRE-PROPOSAL CONTACT	APPLICATION	REVIEW SYSTEM	GRANTS ADMIN. (RULES)
NATIONAL GENERAL PURPOSE	National need-local regional population	Model Innovative	Large Medium	National image +	National +	Write, phone	Short concept paper - longer form if interested	Staff and some peer review	Few audits and rules
SPECIAL PURPOSE	Need in area of interest	Model Innovative Research	Large to Small	Image not as critical as solution	Image in field of interest +	Write, phone	Short concept paper-longer form if interested	Board review (some staff)	Few audits and rules
COMMUNITY	Local need	Operation Replication Building/ Equipment	Small	Local Image +	Respected locally	Write, phone, go see	Short letter proposal	Board review	Few audits and rules
FAMILY	Varies - but geographic concern for need	Innovative Replication Building/ Equipment Some Research	Medium Small	Regional image +	Local / Regional	Write, phone	Short letter proposal	Board review	Very few audits and rules
NONPROFITS, SERVICE CLUBS, ETC.	Local	Replication Building/ Equipment Scholarship	Small	Local image and member involvement	Local	Write, phone, present to committee or members	Short letter proposal	Committee review and/or member vote	Few audits and rules

ble naming one, such as the Rockefeller Foundation or the Ford Foundation. This is because they get a lot of attention for the size of the awards they make and the initiatives they launch. Unfortunately, the public image of these well-known foundations is what leads many grantseekers into thinking that the foundation marketplace in general makes more and bigger grants than it actually does.

SPECIAL PURPOSE FOUNDATIONS

Often confused with national general purpose foundations because some are very large and financed by unusually large asset bases, special purpose foundations are different in that they define their area of concern quite specifically. For example, the Robert Wood Johnson Foundation is a special purpose foundation synonymous with the health field, and the Exxon Education Trust and Carnegie are special purpose foundations focusing on education. While grant sizes can be considerable, special purpose foundations put the applicant's likelihood of making a contribution or a breakthrough in their area of concern foremost, and *may* put less importance on staff prestige, publishing, and so on.

There are probably only a few hundred of these dedicated special purpose foundations, and the key to success in this marketplace is to match your project with the foundation's specific area of interest and to demonstrate how your project will impact it.

COMMUNITY FOUNDATIONS

According to a study by the Columbus Foundation, there were 582 community foundations in the United States in 1999. Although they use a variety of geographic parameters to define *community*, community foundations are easy to identify because their name denotes the area they serve (e.g., San Diego Foundation, Cleveland Foundation, North Dakota Foundation, Oregon Foundation).

Some think that community foundations are family foundations that restrict their granting to a particular state, city or Zip code. This is not the case. Community foundations fund projects and programs that no other type of foundation would consider supporting. From program deficits, to operating funds, to seed money for a needs assessment that might lead to a larger state or federal grant, community foundations exist to deal with local needs. They do not care if prospective grantees have national stature in their field. They just want to make sure that the funds they grant will be used to make a difference in the communities they serve. In general, community foundations are concerned with what works and are more interested in supporting the replication of successful projects than in taking chances with experimental approaches or research.

FAMILY FOUNDATIONS

Family foundations account for approximately one-half of the 60,000 foundations. Because their granting patterns represent the values of the family members whose interests have been memorialized by the creation of the foundations, granting patterns of family foundations vary widely from foundation to foundation and change frequently. Therefore, you must research them thoroughly to keep abreast of changes in interests and commitment.

Three-fifths of all family foundations have assets of $1 million or less and most fund locally and in small amounts. However, if they value what you propose, and you are in the right locale, you should consider them when developing your grants plan.

NONPROFIT ORGANIZATIONS, MEMBERSHIP GROUPS, PROFESSIONAL SOCIETIES, AND SERVICE CLUBS

In addition to the four basic types of private foundations, many nonprofit organizations, membership groups, professional societies, and service clubs award grants, and some even have foundations attached to them. The awards made through these groups are usually small and limited to a special field of interest. For example, a Kiwanis group may choose to provide support only for the purpose of improving business education in local schools.

The application forms used by these groups are typically short and easy to complete, and they will often provide funding for things that the four basic types of foundation would not consider supporting. While they have been know to provide matching funds for government grants, support for travel to conferences and meetings and honorariums for experts and guest lecturers, they are particularly interested in funding things that will improve their image and the image of their members in their community.

TYPES OF INVESTMENTS MADE BY PRIVATE FOUNDATIONS

The major vehicle of support by private foundations is a cash grant or award. The majority of foundations do not make grants to individuals except in the form of scholarships, and even those may be made through institutions. Most private foundations prefer that the third-party 501(c)3 tax-exempt organization affiliated with the grantee handle and disburse the award.

Program Related Investments (PRIs) are a new and growing alternative to cash grants and awards, and foundations that make them, make them as a supplement to their existing grant programs. In the PRI vehicle, your organization applies to a foundation for a loan, venture capital, or an investment in a charitable-use property. In 1999, 200 foundations used PRIs for a total of $266.6 million. While this is only a small percentage of the $25.9 billion in total foundation giving, it is a growing interest and should be considered as a potential component of your grants plan.

PRIs are often made to organizations with an established relationship with the grant maker. A large portion of PRI dollars support affordable housing and community development. However, PRI support also has been provided for a variety of capital projects such as preserving historical buildings, repairing churches, emergency loans to social service agencies, and protecting and preserving open space and wildlife habitats.

Another type of foundation that is becoming a financial force in more and more local communities is the health conversion foundation. Federal law requires that proceeds from the sale of assets of tax-exempt entities go to charity. One way this requirement can be met is to establish a foundation to benefit the community previously served by the nonprofit; and approximately 160 foundations have been created as a result of nonprofit hospitals and Health Maintenance Organizations (HMOs) converting to for-profit status. Most of these foundations are dedicated to funding health-related projects, although some define health broadly and do provide funding for a variety of community purposes.

GRANTSEEKERS' PRIVATE FOUNDATION DECISION MATRIX

The Grantseekers' Private Foundation Decision Matrix (see table 18.1) summarizes the principal types of private foundation funding sources, their major funding characteristics and preferences, and their similarities and differences. Familiarizing yourself with this information will help you to create a prioritized list of the best foundations to approach and to determine the appropriate amount of funding to request from each.

Keep in mind that the majority of foundation grant award sizes are smaller than grantseekers think. Instead of making the mistake of asking for an inappropriate amount of funding from one foundation, consider breaking your proposal into fundable parts with each part appealing to the values of a different type of foundation funder.

Column 1 of the matrix lists the major foundation funding source types. Columns 2 through 10 provide information on variables such as geographic area/need, type of project, and award size. Please note that the matrix is meant to point you in the right direction only. Follow-up research will allow the proactive grantseeker to further estimate the funder's interest, the appropriateness of the project, and the proper grant size to request before proposal preparation and submission.

To achieve grants success, you must be vigilant in attempting to consider all aspects of your proposal from the grantor's point of view. It should be increasingly

TABLE 18.2

FOUNDATION GRANTS BY RECIPIENT CATEGORY

RECIPIENT CATEGORY	PERCENT OF FOUNDATION GRANTS
Education	25.3%
Human Services	17.2%
Health	16.2%
Arts / Culture	12.1%
Public / Society Benefit	12.1%
Environment / Animals	6.1%
Science / Technology	3.0%
International	3.0%
Religion	3.0%
Social Science	2.0%

TABLE 18.3

PERCENT OF FOUNDATION GRANTS BY EDUCATION SUBCATEGORY

EDUCATION SUBCATEGORIES	PERCENT OF EDUCATION GRANTS BY SUBCATEGORY
Policy Management	0.02%
Elementary / Secondary	6.40%
Vocational / Technical	0.02%
Higher Education	11.00%
Graduate / Professional	3.90%
Adult / Continuing	0.20%
Library Science / Libraries	1.50%
Student Services	0.10%
Education Services	0.90%
Miscellaneous	1.26%
Total % of Foundation Grants to Education	**25.30%**

evident that the "one proposal fits all" method of grantseeking will not meet with a positive response from such a diverse group of private grantors.

WHO AND WHAT PRIVATE FOUNDATIONS FUND

Combined, the 60,000 foundations granted $26 billion to many of the 900,000 eligible 501(c) nonprofit organizations, including 3,500 colleges and universities. As you can see from table 18.2, education is the largest recipient of foundation funds. Table 18.3 further breaks down education funding into subcategories.

In the example, it is clear that higher education receives almost twice the support that its nearest competition, elementary and secondary education, receives. Information such as this could be used in many ways. For instance, it could be used to help you select the lead organization in a consortia project based on grantor preference. If you are interested in pursuing foundation funding for a subject area other than education, you should research subcategory-giving patterns within that specific area. Chapter 19 will instruct you how to gather this information.

Most foundations award the majority of their funding in the states where they are located and, unfortunately, there is great disparity in the number of foundations from state to state. In fact, 621 of 1,009 largest foundations in the United States are located in just 9 of the 50 states (California, Florida, Georgia, Illinois, Massachusetts, New York, Ohio, Pennsylvania, and Texas), as well as the District of Columbia, and of the 125,000 grants of $10,000 or more, these 621 foundations made 62 percent of them.

If you are located in one of the other 41 states, remember that even nonprofit organizations in states with none of 1,009 largest foundations still attract *some* grants from foundations located in other states. For example, Montana, a state with none of the largest foundations, was still able to draw 289 grants totaling $19,364,000 in 2000 from foundations in other states. In addition, you may be able to select a consortia partner located in a state with more foundations, and win a foundation grant that you could share through a subcontract agreement.

Not only is the private foundation grants marketplace misunderstood by individual grantseekers but also entire institutions have added to the confusion by arbitrarily deciding that government grant applications and contracts should go through a university grants office, and that foundation grant proposals should be handled by an institution's development office. One reason in support of this decision is that the development office in most universities is tied to a university foundation—the 501(c)3 entity required to submit proposals. However, the problem lies in the fact that many development offices limit the access that faculty have to private foundations so that they (the development office) can use the foundation marketplace to attempt to fund administrative priorities, such as capital campaigns and endowments. This problem is compounded by the fact that only a small percentage of foundations dollars are actually awarded to fund these types of capital support projects. For example, a quick review of table 18.4 (types of support) demonstrates clearly that foundations *prefer* to fund the types of project that emanate from faculty such as program and research grants.

While some universities have dealt with this issue by developing two separate 501(c) tax-exempt entities, one for the university's overall grants effort and another for its development effort, one thing is critical for the grantseeker to understand. The quest for a private foundation grant needs to be coordinated within your institution or organization so that you can make sure you do not approach a

TABLE 18.4

TYPES OF SUPPORT AWARDED BY DOLLAR VALUE OF GRANTS

TYPE OF SUPPORT	DOLLAR VALUE OF GRANTS
General Support	**13.7%**
Capital Support	**24.2 %**
Capital Campaigns	3.2%
Building/Renovation	11.8%
Computer Systems/Technology	1.1%
Equipment	1.4%
Land Acquisition	0.6%
Endowments	5.1%
All Other	1.0%
Program Support	**43.9%**
Program Development	33.3%
Conferences/Seminar	1.2%
Faculty/Staff Development	1.0%
Curriculum Development	3.3%
All Other	6.1%
Research	**11.2%**
Student Aid Funds	**5.4%**
Other	**1.6%**

foundation that is already being approached by several of your colleagues. Not only is this embarrassing but also it presents the prospective grantor with a negative image of you and your institution.

Many foundations only allow one proposal from one institution at one time, and will immediately disallow all of the proposals submitted by the institution if they receive multiple applications. To avoid this type of problem, use one or more of the research tools presented in chapter 19 to locate the foundation most suited to fund your project, and then develop a profile of what it funds. Take this profile to your grants office (or any other pertinent office) to gain approval to make pre proposal contact. This will provide your institution with the heads-up it needs to insure its integrity with prospective funding sources, and move you one step closer to grants success.

NOTE

1. Michael Anft and Ian Wilhelm, "Off the Charts: As the Stock Market Gyrates, Charities Face Tough Times," *The Chronicle of Philanthropy* (August 8, 2002):25.

CHAPTER 19

Researching Potential Private Foundation Grantors
How to Find the Foundation That Is Best Suited to Fund Your Project

A key to successful grantseeking with foundations is to gather the most complete and accurate information possible on funding sources before you approach them. The foundation research form (see exhibit 19.1) will help you do this. Complete one worksheet for each foundation you research. Try to provide as much information on the form as possible, but remember that even a partially completed worksheet will help you make a more intelligent decision on whether you should solicit grant support from a particular funding source. Enlist volunteers to ferret out the information you need. Let your research guide your solicitation strategy and proposal development process. Talk to your college or university librarian after you read this chapter to see what additional resources and techniques he or she suggests.

Bauer Associates' Winning Links software program has been designed to assist you in recording and accessing data in an efficient manner. (For ordering information, see the list of resources available from Bauer Associates at the end of the book.)

In addition to the research you conduct on grant making foundations, you should also uncover and record as much information as possible on the decision makers in those foundations. The funding executive research worksheet (see exhibit 19.2) is designed to help you do this.

Naturally, you do not have to have information on a foundation's executives (i.e., directors, trustees, board members, contributions officers, etc.) in order to consider submitting a proposal, but it will increase your chances of success. The information you collect and record on your funding executive research worksheet will help you in two major ways.

The following form outlines the data you need to collect in order to make a decision to seek funding from this grant source. Your attempts to collect as much of this information as possible will prove rewarding. (When feasible, record the source of the information and the date it was recorded.)

1. Name of Foundation: _____
   Address: _____
   Phone: _____ Fax: _____ E-mail: _____
   Web site: _____

2. Contact Person: _____
   Title: _____
   Any Links from Our Organization to Contact Person: _____
   _____
   _____

3. Foundation's Areas of Interests: _____
   _____
   _____

4. Eligibility Requirements/Restrictions:
   a. Activities Funded/Restricted: _____
   _____

   b. Organizations Funded/Restricted: _____
   _____

   c. Geographic Funding Preferences/Restrictions: _____
   _____

   d. Other Requirements/Restrictions: _____
   _____
   _____
   _____
   _____

FOUNDATION RESEARCH FORM

EXHIBIT 19.1

1. It will allow you to determine, in advance, likely preferences and biases you will encounter if you are lucky enough to arrange an in-person meeting.
2. It will make it easier to locate links between your organization and a funding source.

Recording accurate research on foundation decision makers will raise your chances of success. In addition, your ability to attract future funding will increase as you develop a history and file on each of the grantors you are interested in.

FOUNDATION FUNDING SOURCE RESEARCH TOOLS

Basic research tools for developing your list of potential foundation grantors can be accessed at little or no charge and usually within a short distance from your

5.   Information Available

<u>In Possession Of</u>

IRS 990-PF Tax Return (Year)   _____
Guidelines   _____
Newsletters   _____
Annual Report   _____

_____   _____
_____   _____

6.   a. Board Members:

_____
_____
_____

     b. Staff   Full Time   Part Time

_____   _____   _____
_____   _____   _____
_____   _____   _____

7.   Deadline: _____

     Application Process/Requirements:

_____
_____
_____

8.   Financial Information

Asset Base: $_____
Are there current gifts to build the asset base?   Yes _____   No_____
If yes, how much? $_____
Total number of grants awarded in 200_: _____
Total amount of grants awarded in 200_: $_____
High Grant: $_____
Low Grant: $_____
Average Grant: $_____
In our interest area there were _____ grants, totaling $_____
High grant in our interest area: $_____

FOUNDATION RESEARCH FORM *(continued)*

EXHIBIT 19.1

workplace. Before you begin searching for your best possible grantor, review the following resources. Although you may purchase resources or access them through electronic transmission, first explore the hard copy version to determine your level of usage and the cost-effectiveness of purchasing versus traveling to a cooperating collection housed at your public college, or university library.

The whole point of your research effort is to focus on the sources most likely to fund your proposal. Even if you are a novice grantseeker, do not be tempted to send letter proposals to any and all foundations that are even remotely related to

Low grant in our interest area: $_____
Average grant in our interest area: $_____

9.   Grants Received Versus Grants Funded
      Number of proposals received in 200_: _____
      Number of proposals funded in 200_: _____

10.   Sample Grants in Our Area of Interest:

              Recipient Organization   Amount
      _____   _____
      _____   _____
      _____   _____
      _____   _____

FOUNDATION RESEARCH FORM *(continued)*

EXHIBIT 19.1

your project area. If preproposal contact is allowed or a proposal format is provided or suggested, take every opportunity to develop an individualized, tailored proposal for each of your best prospects.

THE FOUNDATION DIRECTORY

The Foundation Directory is the major source of information on larger foundations. Available in hard copy, CD-ROM, and through an online subscription plan, the 2003 edition provides information on approximately 10,000 of the 60,000-plus foundations. These 10,000 foundations hold assets in excess of $434 billion. The foundations described in *The Foundation Directory* make grants totaling over $24 billion each year, or approximately 92 percent of all foundation funding. To be included in *The Foundation Directory* a foundation must:

- hold assets of at least $2 million, or
- distribute $200,000 or more in grants each year.

The directory contains information on independent, community, and company-sponsored foundations. (Company-sponsored foundations are foundations that corporations have initiated as part of their philanthropy program. Only those company-sponsored foundations that meet the criteria outlined above appear in the directory.) Foundations included in the directory appear in numerical order, and each has its own entry number.

The directory contains seven indexes to assist you in your search for appropriate funding sources:

1. Index to donors, officers, and trustees
2. Geographic index

1. Funding Source Name: _____
2. Name of Contact Person/Director/Contributions Officer: _____
3. Title: _____ Birth Date: _____
4. Business Address: _____
    _____
5. Home Address: _____
    _____
6. Education:
    Secondary: _____
    College: _____
    Post Graduate: _____
    Military Service: _____
7. Clubs/Affiliations: _____
    _____
8. Corporate Board Memberships: _____
    _____
9. Business History (Promotions, Other Firms, etc.): _____
    _____
    _____
10. Other Philanthropic Activities: _____
    _____
    _____
11. Newspaper/Magazine Clipping(s) Attached: _____ yes _____ no
12. Contacts in Our Organization: _____
    _____
    _____
13. Recent Articles/Publications: _____
    _____
14. Awards/Honors: _____
    _____
    _____

FUNDING EXECUTIVE RESEARCH WORKSHEET

EXHIBIT 19.2

One technique that will add a whole new dimension to your foundation grants effort is to become adept at using the index to donors, officers, and trustees. When your organization's friends provide you with their links, pay special attention to those people who list board memberships or friends on foundation boards. In most cases, your friend will be willing to discuss your project with fellow board members or with friends who serve on other boards.

The Foundation Directory Part 2 is also available for your use. The 2003 edition of this directory includes the next 10,000 largest foundations by total giving, and features 1,500 foundations that are covered for the first time and over 36,000 grant descriptions.

In addition to these two directories, you may also access *The Foundation Directory Supplement*, which provides revised entries for hundreds of foundations in *The Foundation Directory* and *The Foundation Directory Part 2*. Changes in giving interests, and updates on staff, financial data, and contact information are provided in the *Supplement*.

The two directories and the supplement are published by the Foundation Center, 79 Fifth Avenue, New York, NY 10003. For more information and/or to order one of these products, call the foundation's customer service line at (800) 424-9836 or visit the foundation's Center's Web site at <http://fdncenter.org/marketplace>.

Using *The Foundation Directory*

The most productive approach to using the directory is to first review chapter 5 on redefining your project idea. After identifying key words and fields of interest (e.g., environment, health education curriculum development, folk arts for children), you can use the directory's subject index to determine which foundations have an active interest in the area for which you are seeking grant support. Another approach is to use the types of support index to identify foundations interested in your type of project (e.g., conferences/seminars, building/renovation, equipment, program development, matching or challenge grants).

Before you rush into reviewing the actual foundation entries, remember that a significant portion of foundations possess a geographic homing device. In other words, they give only where they live. The directory's geographic index will point you in the direction of those foundations that may be interested in your project because of its location.

The best match will be a foundation that funds your subject area, type of project, and geographic area. Do not despair if the use of the geographic index produces limited prospects. Many foundations have a national and even international interest in certain areas. While these foundations may not have granted funds in your state or community before, they may do so if approached properly.

As you do your research, be sure to record the name of the foundation, the state, and the directory entry number for each foundation you are interested in. Recording this information will help you refer to the foundation quickly.

The contents of the entries in *The Foundation Directory* vary but in general, the entries consist of

- entry number
- name, address, telephone, and fax number of foundation
- contact person
- donors

- foundation type
- financial data—including year-end date of foundation's accounting period, assets at market value (M) or ledger value (L), total expenditures, amount and number of grant paid, high and low grants, and separate information on amount and number of employee matching gifts, grants to individuals, or loans. (One important variable that is not covered in this section is which areas of interest received the high and low grants. You will need to do more in-depth research to uncover this information.)
- purpose and activities—what areas the foundation prefers to support. (This information does not include how much of the foundation's grant money is attributed to each area.)
- fields of interest—the stated interests of the funding source. (Use this information to narrow down your funding source choices by comparing your proposal to the foundation's stated interests.)
- types of support—the funding mechanisms used by the grantor to support its stated fields of interest. (Use this information to match your proposal with the type of grant the foundation supports. For example, if the foundation prefers research over model or demonstration grants, you could consider adding a research component to your proposal.)
- limitations—including geographic preferences, restrictions by bases on subject area, or types of support
- publications or other printed materials distributed by the foundation
- application information—including the preferred form of application, the number of proposal copies requested, application deadlines, frequency and dates of board meetings, and the general amount of time the foundation takes to notify applicants of the board's decision. Some foundations will indicate that they contribute to preselected organizations only, that applications are not being accepted, or that their funds are currently committed to ongoing projects. When this occurs, your only chance for a grant is to review the list of officers and trustees with your grants advisory group to see whether you have a link to the foundation. In other instances, foundations will state that they do not allow preproposal contact and that the desired contact is by letter only. The letter they are referring to and its development are the focus of chapter 22.
- officers, principal administrators, trustees, directors, or distribution committee members—names and titles of members of the foundation's governing body
- number of staff—number of professional and support staff employed by the foundation and the part-time or full-time status of these employees
- EIN—Employer Identification Number assigned by the Internal Revenue Service
- list of selected grants

A fictitious *Foundation Directory* entry is provided in exhibit 19.3. For the purpose of explanation, assume that the grantseeker is interested in securing grants for projects related to substance abuse services. Entry number 5218, the Jon Foundation, is a good choice for the prospective grantee to examine further because the grantseeker's project falls within the foundation's stated fields of interest and will take place in the foundation's preferred geographic funding area—New York State. The prospective grantee will have to conduct more in-depth research to discover how much money the Jon Foundation has actually awarded to projects related to substance abuse services and the high and low grants in that particular area.

THE FOUNDATION GRANTS INDEX

The Foundation Grants Index on CD-ROM contains over 125,000 descriptions of grants of $10,000 or more, awarded by over 1,000 of the largest, independent, corporate, and community foundations in the United States. You can use this reference to search for grantors that have funded nonprofit organizations similar to yours, uncover foundations that favor your geographic area, and identify grantors with funding patterns that demonstrate a strong commitment to your area of interest. The *Index* contains 12 search fields to choose from, including: recipient name, recipient state, recipient city, recipient type, grant maker name, grant maker state, geographic focus, subject, types of support, grant amount, year authorized, and text search.

In our example, we can use a variety of key terms to uncover foundations that have funded substance abuse projects in the past or have given to a related field. For instance, we could search in the subjects index, under *substance abuse services, drug/alcohol abusers, alcoholism*, or *abuse prevention*. Let's assume we look under *substance abuse services*. The grant search results would alphabetically list all the foundations in the *Index* who have awarded a grant in this area. The list would include the grant maker's name and state, the recipient's name and state, the year the grant was awarded, and the amount of the award.

In general, the foundation information provided in the *Foundation Grants Index* is not as detailed as the information in *The Foundation Directory*. Therefore, you will have to go to the *Directory* to gather more information on the potential grantor you uncover through the use of the *Index*.

If you locate a prospective funding source in *The Foundation Directory* first, then you can use *The Foundation Grants Index on CD-ROM* to find out how many of the foundation's grants in excess of $10,000 went to each of their interest areas. For example, using the grant maker name index in *The Foundation Grants Index on CD-ROM* you could look up all the grants for over $10,000 that were awarded by the fictitious Jon Foundation.

Exhibit 19.4 illustrates the search window elements of the *Foundation Grants Index on CD-ROM*. In this sample, the grantseeker is looking for grants awarded

---

5218
The Jon Foundation
108 9ᵗʰ Ave., 18ᵗʰ Fl.
New York, NY 10019 (212)849-8777
Contact: Larry T. Jon, Pres.
FAX: (212)849-6246

Trust Established in 1990 in NY.
Donor(s): Larry T. Jon, Sally M. Lyon.
Foundation type: Independent
Financial data (yr. Ended 12/31/00): Assets, $25,240, 036 (M); expenditures $1,253,373; qualifying distributions, $856,460; giving activities include $846,320 for 75 grants (high: $240,000; low: 700; average: $25,000-$30,000).
Purpose and activities: Giving primarily for human services, social services, arts, and for special needs populations such as children, youth, disadvantaged families, and substance abusers.
Fields of interest: Human services; children & youth, substance abuse services, arts/cultural programs, women, economically disadvantaged.
Types of support: General/operating support; capital campaigns; building/renovation; program development, continuing support, equipment, emergency funds.
Limitations: Giving primarily in the city of New York and the northeastern U.S. No grants to individuals.
Publications: Annual report (including application guidelines), application guidelines.
Application information: Application form required.
  Initial approach: Letter requesting application form
  Copies of proposal: 1
  Deadline(s): None
  Board meeting date(s): Quarterly
Officers and Trustees: *Larry T. Jon, Pres.; *Sally M. Lyon, Exec. Dir.; Stephen Mardner, Marsha Raydeck, John Sloan.
Number of staff: 1 full-time professional; 1 part-time support.
EIN: 258000113
Selected grants: The following grants were reported in 1999.
$240,000 to Blake Hall for Women, NYC, NY. For renovation of substance abuse recovery center.
$100,000 to New York City Children's Collaborative, NYC, NY. For continued support
$50,000 to the Northeast June Arts Festival, Boston, MA. For general support.
$35,000 to the Family Preservation Center, NYC, NY. For program development.
$20,000 to the Kowl Children and Youth Learning Assessment Center, Hartford, CT. For equipment.
$25,000 to the Addiction Prevention Program, NYC, NY. For expansion of services.
$10,000 to the Harlem Churches, NYC, NY. To start-up neighborhood credit.

FOUNDATION DIRECTORY ENTRY (FICTITIOUS DATA)

EXHIBIT 19.3

---

in the area of folk arts. The grants search results are listed on the search screen. The index window tells the grantseeker the number of grants listed in the *Index* that are related to his/her subject area.

INTERNAL REVENUE SERVICE TAX RETURNS

Form 990-PF is the annual tax return that U.S. private foundations must file with the IRS. Federal law requires that all foundations provide their tax returns for pub-

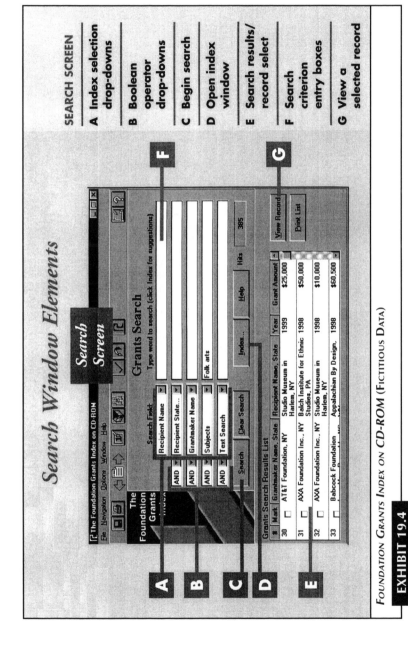

Search Window Elements

SEARCH SCREEN

A Index selection drop-downs

B Boolean operator drop-downs

C Begin search

D Open index window

E Search results/ record select

F Search criterion entry boxes

G View a selected record

FOUNDATION GRANTS INDEX ON CD-ROM (FICTITIOUS DATA)

EXHIBIT 19.4

190

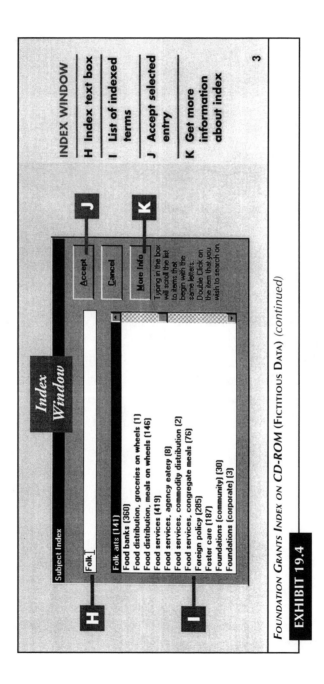

FOUNDATION GRANTS INDEX ON CD-ROM (FICTITIOUS DATA) (continued)

EXHIBIT 19.4

lic information purposes. A foundation's 990-PF return gives fiscal details on receipts and expenditures, compensation of officers, capital gains or losses, and other financial matters, and provides the foundation's application guidelines, the names of its board members/officers/trustees, and a complete list of the grants it has paid.

While *The Foundation Directory* and *Foundation Grants Index on CD-ROM* are useful reference tools, they are basically compilations of information from many sources, and there is no guarantee as to the accuracy of the information provided. In fact, *The Foundation Grants Index* is based on only 60 percent of the actual total foundation grants.

The IRS, however, deals in specifics. By reviewing the returns of the private foundations you believe to be your best funding prospects, you can find valuable information such as the actual amount of assets, new gifts received, total grants paid out, and so on. Most important, you can view a list of all the grants they have paid, including grants for less than $10,000.

Larger foundations often issue annual reports and/or have Web sites that contain a listing of their grants. But the IRS form 990-PF may be the only source in which you can find a complete grants list for smaller and mid-sized foundations.

Exhibit 19.5 is a sample of the first page of form 990-PF. Finding the information you need on a 990-PF is relatively easy.

- page 1, top section and line 25 provides date, name, address, assets, and grants paid
- page 6, part VIII, line 1 provides the list of board members/officers/trustees
- page 9, part XV, line 2, a, b, c, d, provides application information
- page 10, part XV, line 3 provides grants paid

For more detail, visit <http://fdncenter.org/learn/demystify/index.html> to find a tutorial on how to read a 990-PF.

Copies of tax returns for the past three years for all 60,000 foundations can be viewed free at the Foundation Center's reference collections in New York City and Washington, DC. The Atlanta, Cleveland, and San Francisco offices of the Foundation Center contain IRS Form 990-PF returns for the Southeastern, Midwestern, and Western states, respectively.

You can also access foundation tax returns on the Web in PDF format at the following sites:

- Foundation Finder or 990 PF Search, at <http://Inp.fdncenter.org/finder.html>
- Guidestar, at <http://www.guidestar.org/>
- Grantsmart, at <http://www.grantsmart.org/search/search.html>

Please note that the tax returns you will be able to access will typically be one to two years behind. In addition, if you cannot find a particular organization's 990-

Form **990-PF**	**Return of Private Foundation** or Section 4947(a)(1) Nonexempt Charitable Trust Treated as a Private Foundation	OMB No. 1545-0052
Department of the Treasury Internal Revenue Service	**Note:** *The organization may be able to use a copy of this return to satisfy state reporting requirements.*	**2001**

For calendar year 2001, or tax year beginning _____ **, 2001, and ending** _____ **, 20** ___

G Check all that apply: ☐ Initial return ☐ Final return ☐ Amended return ☐ Address change ☐ Name change

Use the IRS label. Otherwise, print or type. See Specific Instructions.	Name of organization	**A** Employer identification number
	Number and street (or P.O. box number if mail is not delivered to street address)	Room/suite	**B** Telephone number (see page 10 of the instructions) ( )
	City or town, state, and ZIP code	**C** If exemption application is pending, check here ▶ ☐

H Check type of organization: ☐ Section 501(c)(3) exempt private foundation
☐ Section 4947(a)(1) nonexempt charitable trust ☐ Other taxable private foundation

D 1. Foreign organizations, check here . . ▶ ☐
2. Foreign organizations meeting the 85% test, check here and attach computation . . ▶ ☐

I Fair market value of all assets at end of year *(from Part II, col. (c), line 16)* ▶ **$** _____

J Accounting method: ☐ Cash ☐ Accrual
☐ Other (specify) ....
(Part I, column (d) must be on cash basis.)

E If private foundation status was terminated under section 507(b)(1)(A), check here . . ▶ ☐
F If the foundation is in a 60-month termination under section 507(b)(1)(B), check here . . ▶ ☐

Part I **Analysis of Revenue and Expenses** *(The total of amounts in columns (b), (c), and (d) may not necessarily equal the amounts in column (a) (see page 10 of the instructions).)*

		(a) Revenue and expenses per books	(b) Net investment income	(c) Adjusted net income	(d) Disbursements for charitable purposes (cash basis only)
Revenue	**1** Contributions, gifts, grants, etc., received (attach schedule)				
	Check ▶ ☐ if the foundation is **not** required to attach Sch. B				
	2 Distributions from split-interest trusts				
	3 Interest on savings and temporary cash investments				
	4 Dividends and interest from securities				
	5a Gross rents				
	b (Net rental income or (loss) _____)				
	6a Net gain or (loss) from sale of assets not on line 10				
	b Gross sales price for all assets on line 6a _____				
	7 Capital gain net income (from Part IV, line 2). .				
	8 Net short-term capital gain				
	9 Income modifications				
	10a Gross sales less returns and allowances _____				
	b Less: Cost of goods sold . .				
	c Gross profit or (loss) (attach schedule). . . .				
	11 Other income (attach schedule)				
	12 **Total.** Add lines 1 through 11				
Operating and Administrative Expenses	**13** Compensation of officers, directors, trustees, etc.				
	14 Other employee salaries and wages				
	15 Pension plans, employee benefits				
	16a Legal fees (attach schedule)				
	b Accounting fees (attach schedule)				
	c Other professional fees (attach schedule). . .				
	17 Interest				
	18 Taxes (attach schedule) (see page 14 of the instructions)				
	19 Depreciation (attach schedule) and depletion . .				
	20 Occupancy				
	21 Travel, conferences, and meetings				
	22 Printing and publications				
	23 Other expenses (attach schedule)				
	24 **Total operating and administrative expenses.** Add lines 13 through 23				
	25 Contributions, gifts, grants paid				
	26 **Total expenses and disbursements.** Add lines 24 and 25				
	27 Subtract line 26 from line 12:				
	a Excess of revenue over expenses and disbursements				
	b Net investment income (if negative, enter -0-) .				
	c Adjusted net income (if negative, enter -0-). .				

For Paperwork Reduction Act Notice, see the instructions. Cat. No. 11289X Form **990-PF** (2001)

IRS FOUNDATION ANNUAL RETURN (FIRST PAGE)

EXHIBIT 19.5

PF, it may be because the organization you are looking for files a 990 instead. In general, churches, hospitals, schools, and publicly supported organizations file 990s.

THE FOUNDATION CENTER

Incorporated as a nonprofit organization in 1953, the Foundation Center was formed by foundations as an independent national service center. Part of the Foundation Center's mission is to provide accurate information on philanthropy with special emphasis on foundation grant making. The center covers its operating expenses through grants from foundations and corporations, the sale of publications, and fee-based subscriber services. The center operates five reference collections, one in New York City, one in Washington, DC, one in Cleveland, one in San Francisco, and one in Atlanta. Each of these is staffed by Foundation Center employees.

There are also over 200 Foundation Center Cooperating Collections operated by libraries, community foundations, and other nonprofit agencies throughout the United States.

Locate the Collection nearest you by visiting <http://fdncenter.org/collections/>. In addition to having a core collection of the Foundation Center's publications, many Cooperating Collections have IRS tax returns for their state and/or neighboring states. The Collections will also have several other valuable grants resource materials including:

- computer-generated printouts or guides that list grants by subject area
- state foundation directories
- other publications from the Foundation Center (see the list of resources for more detail).
- searchable foundation grant related databases

ELECTRONIC RETRIEVAL AND DATABASE SEARCHES

Many public libraries, university libraries, and higher education grants offices are able to perform electronic searches of *The Foundation Directory* and other resources containing foundation grants information. Explore the possibility of computer search and retrieval by contacting an established grants office near you.

The Foundation Center offers *FC Search: The Foundation Center's Database on CD-ROM*. It includes over 70,000 grant makers (foundations, corporate givers, and grant making public charities), describes over 339,000 grants, and lists approximately 300,000 trustees, officers, and donors. It also provides links to approximately 2,400 grant maker Web sites and over 1,500 corporate Web sites, and in-depth program descriptions for 1,000 top funders and enhanced application guidelines for 6,700 funders. In addition, the Foundation Center offers free ses-

Grant
Guidelines

Application
Procedure

Grants List

Trustees and
Staff

THE
FOUNDATION
CENTER

THE
JEAN & LOUIS DREYFUS
———— FOUNDATION, INC.

Suite 626
420 Lexington Avenue
New York, NY 10170
Tel: 212-599-1931
Fax: 212-599-2956
E-mail: jldreyfusfdtn@hotmail.com

SAMPLE FOUNDATION WEB SITE

EXHIBIT 19.6

HOME

Grant
Guidelines

Application
Procedure

Grants List

Trustees
and Staff

GRANT
GUIDELINES

THE
JEAN & LOUIS DREYFUS
———— FOUNDATION, INC.

The Jean and Louis Dreyfus Foundation, Inc. was established in 1979 from the estate of Louis Dreyfus, a music publisher, and that of his wife, Jean. The mission of the Foundation is to enhance the quality of life of New Yorkers, particularly the aging and disadvantaged. Grants are disbursed mainly within the five boroughs of New York City, and primarily in fields supportive of aging, arts-in-education, education and literacy, and social services.

The Foundation is committed to funding direct service organizations and those projects which will produce systemic change. To this end the Foundation supports pilot programs which can eventually be replicated or which will be funded by independent or government sources in the future. Occasionally organizations will be awarded grants to strengthen their infrastructure or for general operating support. The Foundation encourages matching funds from other charitable organizations, public financial drives, individuals, and government bodies.

Grants are made only to organizations whose tax exempt status has been recognized by the IRS. Grants are never made to individuals.

SAMPLE FOUNDATION WEB SITE *(continued)*

EXHIBIT 19.6

	APPLICATION	THE ———————
HOME	PROCEDURE	JEAN & LOUIS DREYFUS
		———— FOUNDATION, INC.

Grant
Guidelines

Application
Procedure

Grants List

Trustees
and Staff

Initial inquiries should consist of a one to two page letter describing the grantee organization and outlining the project in question. Letters should be sent by mail to:

> Ms. Edmée de M. Firth
> Executive Director
> Jean and Louis Dreyfus Foundation, Inc.
> Suite 626
> 420 Lexington Avenue
> New York, NY 10170
> Tel: 212-599-1931 • Fax: 212-599-2956
> E-mail: jldreyfusfdtn@hotmail.com

All such inquiries will be acknowledged indicating whether or not a general application is justified (the Foundation uses its own application form). Letters of inquiry are due no later than February 1st and August 1st for the Spring and Fall board meetings respectively. Letters received later than these deadlines will be held over until the next review cycle. Any discussion or indications of interest concerning a grant application should not be construed as a commitment by the Foundation. All requests will be approved or rejected in writing.

Any questions about the Foundation and its application procedure should be directed to Jessica Keuskamp, Program Assistant (please see contact information above).

SAMPLE FOUNDATION WEB SITE *(continued)*

EXHIBIT 19.6

---

sions on the effective utilization of *FC Search* in all five Center libraries and some Cooperating Collections.

There are several other electronic funding databases and CD-ROMs available are accessible by subscription only, which offer current and in-depth information and vary in price.

- The Dialog Corporation offers over 600 databases, some of which are aimed at doing funding searches (<http://www.dialog.com/info/products>)

- Orxy Press produces *GrantSelect*, which indexes thousand of grants including some offered by private foundations (<http://www.grantselect.com>)

- *The Chronicle Guide to Grants* presents all corporate and foundation grants listed in *The Chronicle of Philanthropy* since 1995 (<http://www.philanthropy.com/grants>)

| HOME | GRANTS LIST | THE JEAN & LOUIS DREYFUS FOUNDATION, INC. |

<table>
<tr><td>

HOME

Grant Guidelines

Application Procedure

Grants List

Trustees and Staff

</td><td colspan="2">

On December 31, 2001, the unaudited market value of the Foundation was approximately $22,000,000. Grants paid during 2001 totaled $1,352,500 and were awarded to 81 organizations for 85 projects.

Grants for:
9/11 Relief | Aging | Arts
Education | Social Service

</td></tr>
</table>

GRANTS FOR 9/11 RELIEF	
Alliance for the Arts The Arts Rebuild New York.	$15,000
The Bridge Fund of New York Project Recovery.	$15,000
Holy Apostles Soup Kitchen Emergency grant for September 11th relief.	$30,000
New York Foundation for the Arts New York City Arts Recovery Fund.	$15,000
Total Grants for 9/11 relief	**$75,000**

GRANTS FOR AGING	
Alzheimer's Association Safe Return Program.	$10,000
Brookdale Center on Aging at Hunter College Money Management Clinic Program.	$10,000
Burden Center for the Aging Endowment Campaign.	$25,000
Casita Maria Homebound Senior Visitor's Program.	$15,000
Cobble Hill Health Center Health Education and Wellness Center.	$15,000
Columbia University, Health Sciences Division Social Worker for Taub Institute for Research on Alzheimer's Disease and the Aging Brain.	$30,000
Council of Senior Centers and Services of	$20,000

SAMPLE FOUNDATION WEB SITE *(continued)*

EXHIBIT 19.6

- *Taft's Prospector's Choice* provides profiles of nearly 10,000 foundations and corporate giving programs including up to 50 grants per profile, total giving figures, contact person information, and application guidelines (<http://www.taftgroup.com>)

Foundation Web Sites and the Internet

The use of the Internet to research private grantors is limited. Only 1 to 2 percent of all private grant makers currently have Web sites. There are a variety of reasons for this, including lack of staff and geographic giving interests. Many foundations only give locally and do not want the unsolicited "worldwide" proposals that having a Web site may bring. Some private grantors, particularly those that are technology-based, do allow Internet submittal of proposals, but the number that do is also surprisingly small.

Through portals such as the Foundation Center's Grantmaker Search (<http://www.fdncenter.org/funders/grantmaker/index.html>), grantseekers can find links to the Web sites of more than 2,000 foundations, corporate grant makers, grant making public charities, and community foundations. In addition, the Council on Foundations (<http://www.cof.org/links/memberindex.htm>) offers links to over 1,800 of its members' Web sites, and Philanthropy News Network Online (<http://www.pnnonline.org>) provides links to many private foundations, corporations, and community foundations.

Exhibit 19.6 is a sample of a foundation's Web site, and the type of information you can sometimes gather online. In this example, you can obtain the Jean and Louis Dreyfus Foundation's guidelines, application procedure, grants list, and roster of trustees and staff from its Web site. However, for the majority of grant makers, you will still need to use alternative research methods for obtaining this information.

Several nonprofit organizations have developed Web sites with grantor information. There are also bulletin boards and chat rooms that focus on foundation and corporate grantors. Check with your membership groups and your peers to see what is available, or perform your own Internet search.

Research to locate your most likely foundation grantor need not be labor intensive or costly. Using electronic databases and Web sites in your search will save you time, but the actual information you will find is identical to that in the print form. The key is to locate the data that will enable you to estimate your chances for success before you invest any more time in seeking a foundation grant.

CHAPTER 20

Contacting a Private Foundation Before Submission

Contacting the private foundation before you write your proposal will help you validate your research and gather additional information about the grantor's priorities and interests. More importantly, preproposal contact will allow you to tailor your proposal according to the particular approach or method that each private foundation will find interesting, and provide you with the information needed to determine the appropriate amount to request. You also can use this contact to explore the grantor's feelings about funding only a portion of the total amount your project requires, and the other funders you will be approaching. The purpose of this contact is not to convince the grantor to fund your proposal but to ensure that your approach will meet the grantor's needs. By contacting the foundation funding source you increase your chances of success over five times. Do not miss out on this tremendous opportunity.

HOW TO CONTACT PRIVATE FOUNDATION GRANTORS

Now that you realize how important preproposal contact is, here's the bad news. Most private foundations are understaffed and many have no staff. Therefore, making contact with them is very difficult. Many private foundation application instructions state "no contact except by letter," and your research will show that many addresses for private funding sources are actually addresses for trust departments of banks or accountants' offices.

Naturally, you do not want to talk to a trust officer at a bank, but speaking with a foundation board member would be a big help. With less than 2,000 foundations occupying their own offices, the chances of talking to a foundation's director or staff are limited to the largest foundations. What is significant, however, is that each foundation usually has 8 to 10 board members. This means that there are approximately 500,000 board members serving the 60,000 foundations, and you may be surprised at how many your advocates know! These board members are the actual decision makers, and they can be contacted effectively through your webbing system.

One foundation director underscored the importance of using links to board members when she told me:

- one-third of her foundation's grants will be awarded to her board members' favorite nonprofit organizations
- one-third will go to her board members' friends' favorite nonprofits
- one-third will be up-for-grabs to those who write creative, persuasive proposals that match the interests and values of her foundation

At this point your research should already include the names of your best prospects' decision makers and board members. Ask the leaders of your organization whether they know any of these people and, if so, whether they would help you by using this informal means of contact. Perhaps, your link can set up lunch or a conference call. (See chapter 7 for more information on how to use webbing and linkage information.) If you do not uncover a link, your plan should be to follow the grantor's guidelines as outlined in the various resource publications.

If there is an office and contact is not ruled out or discouraged, you should:

- write an inquiry letter
- telephone to set up a visit or phone interview
- make a personal visit to the grantor

Contact by Letter

Be very selective when sending a letter requesting an appointment and information on a grantor's program. Since very few private foundations have the staff resources necessary to respond to written requests, do not be surprised if you receive a rejection notice even though you only asked for application guidelines.

Exhibit 20.1 provides a sample inquiry letter. (This letter could be sent as an e-mail, but only a few foundations provide e-mail addresses for correspondence purposes.) Please note that this is not a letter proposal or a letter of intent. The letter proposal will be described in chapter 21.

Contact by Telephone

Telephone contact with a private foundation may take the place of face-to-face contact or may be used to set up a visit. When you are successful at telephoning

Date

Name
Title
Address

Dear _____:

I am developing a project which deals with _____ and provides benefits to [or in]
_____. My research indicates that this area is an important concern of the
[name of foundation].

Please use the enclosed label to send me your current priority statement and information on your
desired format for proposals or other guidelines. I would also appreciate it if you could add us to
your mailing list so that we could receive your annual reports, newsletters, and any other
materials you think might be useful to us as we work on this and related projects.

Thank you for your cooperation.

Sincerely,

Name/Title
Organization
Address

SAMPLE INQUIRY LETTER TO A PRIVATE FOUNDATION

EXHIBIT 20.1

a private foundation, you can be sure you have contacted one that falls within two percent that have an office and a paid staff. Even if you are telephoning the grantor in hopes of setting up a visit, be ready to discuss your project. Many grantors use the telephone very effectively for assessing projects and their interest in them before agreeing to discuss the project face to face, or inviting you to make a written application. After all, it is much easier to tell a grantseeker that they are not really interested in a project over the telephone than it is in person, or to have to read about an idea that is not going to make it.

If the grantor wants to discuss your project before giving you an appointment, ask whether you could fax, e-mail, or mail a one- or two-page concept paper and call back when he or she has your outline in hand.

If they agree to a visit, set the date. Do not offer any more information at this time, but do ask them what they recommend that you bring. Also ask about

- the use of audiovisual equipment in your presentation (restrictions, availability of electrical outlets, etc.)

- the number of staff to be present so that you can bring the appropriate number of copies of information about your organization
- the possibility of their making a visit to your location
- their travel plans, whether they will be near your, or whether they will be attending any conferences or meetings you will be attending or where you will be presenting

If a personal visit is not possible, you will be forced to discuss your project over the telephone. The questions you ask over the phone will actually be the same as those you would ask if you were to make a personal visit. Therefore, review the following section on the visit and questions to ask a funding source.

The Visit

Visiting in person is the best way to get to know the foundation, but visits can be difficult to arrange since foundations are not heavily staffed. If you are fortunate enough to get a visit, use your time wisely.

Who Should Go? Your credibility will be higher if you take a nonstaff representative with you. An articulate, impressive volunteer, advocate, or advisory committee member is an excellent choice. Two people is the maximum. You do not want to overpower the grantor by sending three or more people. Use the information you collected from your webbing and linkages to choose a close match to the funding source. Use age, education, club affiliation, and other personal characteristics as the basis for your choice. Dress according to the information you have about the funding source. Dress in the foundation world is generally conservative, and usually it is better to be overdressed than underdressed. Dress codes differ in the East, West, South, and Midwest, so be aware of geographic influences. The best person to ask about the appropriate dress for a particular funding source is a link who knows the grantor or a past grantee.

Materials to Bring. The materials you will need to bring are those you have already gathered and organized in your proposal development workbook (Swiss cheese book). You may also want to bring simple audiovisual aids that document the need in a more interesting or vivid manner and help show the funding source how important it is to meet the need *now*. If you do use audiovisual aids, make sure they are in balance with your request. A three- to five-minute video would be appropriate if you are making a large request ($250,000) but inappropriate for a smaller ($5,000) request. At this point it is still proper to have several possible approaches to meeting the need. Therefore, you should have the cost and benefits and pros and cons of each approach outlined and ready for presentation. You want to learn which approach the prospective funding source likes best; you are not trying to convince the grantor that you have the one and only way to solve the problem. Your cost-benefit analysis worksheet from chapter 4 will usually elicit more than enough response to begin a conversation.

Be ready to use the various parts of your Swiss cheese book for answers to questions such as "Why should we give the money to you instead of some other organization?" Refer to your section on the uniquenesses of your organization (personnel, mission, and so on).

Questions to Ask a Foundation Funding Source. Review these questions to determine which would be the most appropriate to ask based on your current knowledge of the funding source. You may want to assign specific questions to each of the two individuals going to the meeting and prepare for the visit by role-playing various answers.

1. We have developed several feasible approaches. Would you please look at them and comment on which one looks the most interesting to you (or would look the most interesting to the board)?
2. Last year, your foundation awarded $___ to our kind of project and the average size was $___. Will this remain consistent?
3. Our research indicates that your deadlines last year were ___ and ___. Will they be the same this year?
4. Does it help you if proposals are submitted early? Do proposals that are submitted early receive more favorable treatment?
5. How are proposals reviewed by your foundation? Who performs the review? Outside experts? Board members? Staff? Is there a scoring system or checklist they use that you could share with us?
6. Are there more current granting priorities? (Give them a copy of your research sheet to determine whether your research accurately reflects their priorities.)
7. What do you think of submitting more than one proposal in a funding cycle?
8. Is the amount we are requesting realistic in light of your current goals?
9. Have you ever provided grant support jointly with another funding source and, if so, is that approach appropriate here?

The following two questions should be asked only when the grantor seems very encouraging.

10. Would you look over our proposal before our formal submission if we finished it early?
11. May I see a proposal you have funded that you think is well written? This would provide us with a model for style and format.

Ask question 12 only if the grantor is not very encouraging.

12. Can you suggest any other funders who may be appropriate for this project?

Complete one of these forms after each contact with a private foundation.

Funding Source: _____

Funding Source Address: _____

_____

Funding Source Contact Person: _____

Telephone Number: _____   Fax:_____   E-mail: _____

Contacted On (Date): _____

Contacted By (Name): _____

Type of Contact: Phone _____   Visit _____   Other (Explain) _____

Objective of Contact: _____

_____

_____

_____

Results of Contact: _____

_____

_____

_____

Follow-up: _____

_____

_____

_____

PRIVATE FOUNDATION REPORT FORM

EXHIBIT 20.2

Private Foundation Report Form

Each time a member of your staff contacts a funder in person, over the phone, or through e-mail, he or she should complete and file a private foundation report form (see exhibit 20.2). This simple procedure has a number of important benefits. It will keep you from damaging your credibility by repeating the same questions or having the funder say, "I gave that information to ___ from your organization. Don't you people ever talk to each other?" Also, it will allow another person from your organization to pick up where you leave off.

Successful grantees will recognize the importance of contacting the funding source before writing the proposal. The purpose of the contact is not to make small talk but to validate research and gather data needed to address the grantor's hidden agenda. Using the techniques in this chapter to contact and record contact with private grantors will be an essential part of your grantseeking strategy.

CHAPTER 21

Applying for Private Foundation Funds
Creating a Winning Letter Proposal

Historically, private foundations have used the letter proposal format as the primary component of their application process. Now federal and state granting programs are showing a shift in this direction, and many have instituted a preapplication process that is similar to creating a letter proposal or concept paper. Public funding sources may call the letter proposal a white paper or preproposal concept paper or a letter of intent. In some cases they will not send a prospective grantee an application package unless they like the approach outlined in this paper or letter. Although this preproposal screening may sound negative at first, it really is not such a bad idea, because it prevents grantseekers from completing a more lengthy application for a project that the prospective grantor has little interest in funding or reviewing.

Foundations use the letter proposal format simply because they do not have the time or staff to read long, tedious proposals. They *want* short, concise letters and grant billions of dollars each year based on two to three pages of content.

Letter proposals are often read by board members during relatively brief meetings. A survey of foundations revealed that most foundations meet one to three times a year for an average of one to three hours each time. Within this short time frame, they must read an overwhelming number of letter proposals; therefore, it is imperative that your proposal attract and retain their interest.

If your research provides you with an application format to follow, use it exactly as outlined. However, review the components presented here to be sure that the suggested areas are included in your prospective funding source's required format. Some of the foundations that have a Web site provide an application form that can be printed offline, but the majority still request a letter proposal.

CONSTRUCTING A LETTER PROPOSAL

The main components of a letter proposal are:

- an introductory paragraph stating the reason for writing
- a paragraph explaining why this grantor was selected
- a needs paragraph
- a solution paragraph
- a uniqueness paragraph
- a request for funds paragraph
- a closing paragraph
- signatures
- attachments, if allowed

Introductory Paragraph

Begin by stating your reason for writing to the funding source, and mention your link to the grantor when possible. In some cases, your link may prefer to remain anonymous and endorse your proposal at a board meeting. In other instances, your link may actually instruct you to refer to him or her in your proposal. If so, you could say something such as:

> Kate Macrae [your link, a past board member, trustee, or staff member of the foundation] and I have discussed the mutual concerns of the Kleineste Foundation [funding source] and my organization in meeting the nutritional needs of the elderly [subject area or problem].

If you cannot mention a link, begin your letter proposal with the next most important factor—why the grantor was selected for solicitation or how you knew it would be interested in your proposal.

Why the Grantor Was Selected

Foremost in the reader's mind is why he or she should be reading your proposal. This is your opportunity to position yourself and your organization as winners that do their homework. You want the prospective funding source to know you are not blanketing the foundation world with a "one proposal fits all" approach. What you need to make clear in this paragraph is that, based on what you have discovered through your research, you believe the funding source is likely to find your proposal interesting. This means saying something such as: "Our research indicates that your foundation is committed to the support of health care for the indigent. In the last three years you have dedicated over $400,000 to this important area." In this example, you could also refer to the percentage of the funding source's total grant dollars that went to supporting health care for the indigent or mention a major or significant accomplishment made in this area through a previously awarded grant.

This paragraph need not be long. You want to demonstrate that you have taken the time to research the funding source's interests and that your proposal will address an issue that has been a concern of the grantor's. By doing so, your proposal will command the respect of the reader and warrant the investment of time he or she will make to review it At this point, it is obvious that this proposal is tailored to this foundation.

Again, you are following Festinger's theory of cognitive dissonance. To keep the reader interested in your proposal, you are going to have to present a proposal that reinforces his or her values and feelings of worth and importance. Seek to align your organization with the values of the grantor by adding something such as, "It is with our mutual concern for (or commitment to) the welfare of the indigent that we come to you with this proposal."

Needs Paragraph

If you have constructed a proposal development workbook as suggested in chapter 3, you already have gathered statistics, case studies, quotes, and articles to document a compelling statement of need for action. The main difference between stating the need in a letter proposal to a foundation and stating it in a federal grant application is that you have the opportunity to incorporate the human element in your appeal to the private grantor. While your letter proposal must be based on fact, you can motivate the foundation funding source with the more human side of the problem. The challenge is to portray a compelling need without overusing either the facts (by quoting too many research articles) or the human-interest aspects of the problem.

Select the components of the need that will most likely convince the grantor that the gap between what is and what ought to be must be closed *immediately*. To accomplish this you must have done research on the values and perspective of the grantor. Use what you have learned to describe the gap in a manner that is tailored to each particular funding source. With today's technology you could even scan a picture into your needs paragraph that may be worth a thousand words.

In a few paragraphs, your letter proposal must:

- include a few well-chosen statistics
- exhibit sensitivity to the geographic perspective of the grantor
- portray the human side of the problem

Whether your proposal is for a model project, research, or a service model, your statement of need must be more compelling than your competitor's to keep the reader interested. Readers must want to read the rest of your proposal to discover

what you are going to do about closing the gap you have so eloquently and suc-
cinctly documented. Many novice grantseekers overlook or underestimate the importance of the needs section of their letter proposal; they assume readers must
already know about the need since they have granted funds to this area in the past.
This assumption is a mistake. Grantors do know about the need, but they expect
you to command their respect by proving *your* expertise in the field as in the following example:

> The need for cancer prevention and treatment in the United States continues to
> grow—but not equally for all races. If you were diagnosed with cancer in 1950, you
> would have a slightly higher survival rate if you were black. Today, however, the sta-
> tistics are dramatically reversed. In a study by Stotts, Glynn, and Baquet, African
> Americans were ranked first among U.S. ethnic groups with the lowest cancer survival
> rate and first with the highest age-adjusted rates of cancer incidence and mortality.

Solution Paragraph

What will you do to close the gap you have just documented? The solution section of your proposal calls for a brief description of the approach you propose to
use to solve the problem. In most cases your approach will not totally eliminate
the problem, but you must describe how much of the gap you will close (your objective). While describing how you will close the gap, include the measurement
indicator you will use to evaluate the success of your approach. Review the section in chapter 12 on writing objectives.

Depending on the number of pages allowed, you may have to limit this section
to one or two paragraphs of five to seven lines. While you need to have a legitimate plan, you must guard against making the methodology too elaborate. Since
you are the content expert, you may have difficulty viewing your proposal from
the reader's point of view. Ask yourself the following questions:

- How much does the reader really need to know?
- Will the reader understand my plan?
- Will the words used in the description of my solution be familiar to the
  reader?
- Is all the information included critical to convincing the funder that I have
  a sound, worthwhile plan, or am I including some of it just for myself?

Remember, while you are concerned with how you will solve the problem,
grantors are concerned with what will be different after their money is spent. If
possible, use this section to summarize your approach and objectives and refer the
funder to your project planner for more information as in the following example:

> What can we do in Smithville to promote the sharing of responsibility for education
> among schools, parents, and children? At Smithville Elementary School we have
> developed a program aimed at increasing responsible behavior and encouraging

parental involvement in the classroom and at home. Teachers will actually work with parents and students to develop tailored, individual contracts to produce increases in all levels of education and the quality of course work. The attached project planner outlines each objective and the activities that will foster the changes we desire. Through the education and involvement of parents in their children's responsible use of out-of-school time, our program will provide the catalyst for decreasing television viewing of students, increasing the completion of homework assignments, and improving test scores.

Uniqueness Paragraph

In the uniqueness paragraph, you want to assure the grantor that your organization is the best choice for implementing the solution. Assuming you have held the reader's interest up to this point, he or she knows:

- why you have selected the funding source
- that there is a compelling need
- that you have a plan to address this need

The key question in the grantor's mind at this critical moment is whether your organization is the right one to address the problem.

If you have completed the uniqueness exercise in chapter 6, you already have a list of your organization's uniquenesses and, if appropriate, the unique advantages of your consortia members. Select items from the list to include in this section of your letter proposal. Choose credibility builders that will convince the grantor that you have the commitment, staff, skill, buildings, and equipment to do the job. For example, you could say something like:

Serving the elderly has been the sole mission of Rock of Ages Home for over 50 years. Since our inception we have continually received superior ratings from the state board. Our staff members represent over 300 years of experience, and their commitment to doing more than their call of duty is exhibited by their willingness to *volunteer* time to develop this model approach for serving Alzheimer patients.

Request for Funds Paragraph

You must make a precise request for money. If you want to demonstrate that you have done your homework, refer to the fact that your request is (or is close to) the grantor's average size award for your area of interest.

If your request from this grantor does not cover the entire cost of the project, mention those other sources that have already given support, list the others you will be approaching, or mention that such a list is available on request.

You can summarize the budget categories that make up your total request, or you can provide prospective grantors with the portion of the budget that you would like them to fund. Since you are working under a severe space limitation, your

May 5, 2003

Abraham Donaldson, Executive Director
Foundation for the Terminally Ill
One East Third Avenue
Washington, DC 22222

Dear Mr. Donaldson:

       While working with your colleague David Ketchum, I learned of your foundation's
efforts to support the hospice movement. Your underwriting of a book on AIDS and your
concern for serving AIDS patients have prompted us to write this letter and request your
foundation's support of the Central Aids Hospice Project. This is a unique project that will serve
over 1,000 AIDS patients in Georgia over the next five years.
       The Central Hospital is located in Smithville and adjoins Central Medical College. A
leader in caring for medically under served minorities, Central has been in the forefront of health
promotion since 1904.
       The current AIDS epidemic has hit our minority population hard. The enclosed chart
illustrates the cumulative number of AIDS patients diagnosed in Georgia and those who were in
the active stage as of January 1, 2003. Central Hospital lies in Region I - Middle Georgia. In
addition to serving the 987 known cumulative cases and the 842 active cases in our region, we
also serve AIDS patients in the west and south districts, which pushes our totals to 1,129 known
cumulative and 906 active cases. Naturally, these figures represent a conservative estimate of the
true number of cases.
       Some of our AIDS patients have family members and friends to take care of them at
home at the onset of their disease. Others are alone and destitute. Because our catchment
population consists primarily of the medically under served, we know many do not enter our
treatment system until the later stages of their disease. No matter what the individual situation
may be, it is at this final stage of life that our AIDS patients so desperately need an in-patient
hospice facility to care for them.
       Central Hospital has agreed to provide 20 patient rooms for an AIDS hospice unit. We
have the space, we have the patients, and we have the commitment and support of the hospital
and the medical college. What we don't have are the funds for furniture (estimated at $16,000),
renovations (estimated at $18,000), or special staff training (estimated at $5,000).
       Our plan of action is outlined on the project planner found on page two. (A complete and
itemized budget is available upon request.) We will start with a 6-bed unit, then increase it to 8,
then to 10, and so on. We forecast that the unit will be self-sufficient through third party
payments by the sixth month of operation.

SAMPLE LETTER PROPOSAL TO A PRIVATE FOUNDATION

EXHIBIT 21.1

budget summary should be arranged in paragraph form or in several short columns.
If you submit your project planner with your proposal, you can refer to the column subtotals in your planner. For example: "The salary and wages, including
fringe benefits, total $24,000. The work of the project director and other employees
called for in this proposal is documented on page 3 in columns G, H, and I of the
project planner."

   To keep the focus on the value of the project and the results that you are seeking, you may want to divide the cost of the project by the number of people who
will benefit from it. Consider the effect your project may have over several years,
and calculate a cost per person served or affected by the project. For example: "In
the next five years the equipment that you provide under this grant will touch the

We feel confident that this project is a meaningful contribution to the Smithville community and Georgia for many years to come. First, look at our mission. Central Hospital and Central Medical College are unique in their extraordinary and admirable mission to provide medical training *and* patient care to minorities. Second, consider our graduates. Over 75 percent of Central's graduates go on to choose medically under served urban and rural settings in which to practice medicine. And finally, look at our staff. The hospital staff members responsible for developing this project and for operating it, Dolores Levell and Mel Campo, have over 61 years of cumulative experience in nursing and long-term patient care!

It will take $39,000 to make our AIDS in-patient hospice facility a reality. However, a $15,000 grant from the Foundation for the Terminally Ill would give us the boost we need to solicit the rest of the funds locally. Your foundation's investment in our project will provide us with the motivation, positive image, and credibility we need to raise the remainder.

In recognition of your generous and truly caring gift, we would like to dedicate the entire 20-room facility to the Foundation for the Terminally Ill and have you and your board members attend our ribbon-cutting ceremony here in Smithville. You will also be proud to know that your foundation's name will be placed on 10 of the rooms and that you and your donors, through a grant of $15,000, made a needed, meaningful contribution to the disadvantaged minority population of Georgia.

Please call Dolores Levell at _____ to discuss this further and to arrange a visit to Central Hospital and Central Medical College.

Sincerely,

Thomas Watkins, Ph.D.
Chief Executive Officer
Central Hospital

Adele Trent, M.D.
President
Central Medical College

Sample Letter Proposal to a Private Foundation *(continued)*

EXHIBIT 21.1

lives of approximately 5,000 students by helping them to read on grade level for the first time, and at a cost of only $5.63 per person served."

Closing Paragraph

Many grantseekers close their letter proposal with a statement reflecting their willingness to meet with the prospective grantor to discuss their proposal. Unless the prospective grantor is a large foundation with a staff, any reference to such a meeting is usually futile. Instead, use the closing of your proposal to underscore your willingness to provide any further documentation or information the funding source may desire.

This brings up the question of who from your organization will be the best person to communicate with the prospective grantor. While you may have written the proposal, you probably will not be the individual to sign it. Therefore, in your closing paragraph, request that the prospective grantor contact you (or the individual responsible for the project) for more information or to answer any questions. For example, "I encourage you to telephone me at my office or to call Ms. Connors directly at ___ to respond to technical questions or for additional information." Be sure to include a telephone number and extension, and test the line that will be used for this purpose to be certain that it is answered by a courteous and knowledgeable representative of your organization.

The closing paragraph is also the appropriate place to include your organization's designation as a 501(c)3 organization.

Signatures

Since this is a grant application and constitutes an agreement between your organization and the grantor if it is accepted, the administrator or officer who holds rank and responsibility should sign it. If the link to the grantor is not your chief operating officer or chief executive officer, there is no reason why two individuals cannot sign the proposal—the link and the administrator.

Because the board is legally responsible for the consequences of your organization's actions, including a board member's signature along with the chief executive officer's may impress the grantor. Just remember that the purpose of the signature is to provide the proposal with legal commitment and credibility.

Attachments, if Allowed

Most foundations do not encourage prospective grantees to submit any additional materials with their proposal. This includes attachments as well as videotapes, audiotapes, compact discs, and so on.

Consider including your project planner as a page in your proposal rather than as an attachment, and be sure to always refer to it by page number. In general, your proposal should give the impression that you have more information you are willing to give the prospective grantor if desired. Including too much with the proposal, however, may reduce the likelihood that it will be read.

In general, use more white space, bullets, and short inviting paragraphs. Never use small font. Use 12 to 13 characters per inch. Some grantors may require double spacing. Read and heed all application guidelines.

The letter proposal follows an orderly progression that focuses on the needs and interests of the funding source. As you gain insight into your prospective grantor, you will develop the ability to write grant-winning foundation proposals.

A sample letter proposal to a foundation (see exhibit 21.1)

CHAPTER 22

Proposal Submission, the Decision, and Follow-Up
Private Foundation Funding Sources

The deadlines set by private foundation funding sources must be taken just as seriously as those of the government. If you cannot meet a deadline, you will appear to be a poor steward of funds, so try to be prompt, or, better yet, early. Private foundations, unlike the government, have been known to give a few extra days' grace period when the prospective grantee has a good explanation for the delay and the benefit of personal contact. However, it still does not look good when you need extra time, especially when the deadline has been published for a year or more.

When you are submitting your request to a large foundation, you can deliver it in person or have an advocate or board member deliver it for you. Although there is not as much advantage to hand delivery in the private sector as in the public sector, hand delivery makes an impression and helps avoid problems with delivery service. In other words, you can be sure the proposal is there! If you decide to mail your proposal, send it by certified mail with a return receipt requested. You can also obtain a signed receipt when using United Parcel Service (UPS), Federal Express, or the United States Postal Service's priority and next day services. This way, you will have proof that your proposal arrived on time.

A few of the private foundations that have Web sites offer online proposal submittal. While very few offer this option, if your prospective funding source has a Web site be sure to check if this alternative method of submittal is available to you. Even if you submit your proposal electronically, print it off and send a hard copy also so that you can make sure that electronic submittal did not somehow affect its visual attractiveness. Note on each copy that a duplicate has been provided, and be sure to get both copies (the electronic and the print version) in before the deadline.

Make note of the following:

- Send the contacts or people you discovered through the webbing and linkage process a copy of your letter proposal.
- Ask these friends to push for your proposal at the board meeting or to contact their friends or other board members to encourage a favorable decision.
- Minimize personal contact once you have submitted your proposal to avoid appearing pushy.

THE DECISION AND FOLLOW-UP

Private foundation grantors are generally more prompt than government funders at letting you know their decision about your proposal. They will give you a simple yes shortly after the board's scheduled meeting. If the answer is yes, you should immediately:

- Send a thank-you letter to the funding source. One foundation trustee told me that one of the only records they keep on grantees is whether or not they thank the foundation. She said, "If an organization that receives a grant doesn't thank us, they do not receive another grant from us."
- Find out the payment procedures. Usually the acceptance letter comes with a check. If a check is not enclosed, the letter will at least inform you of when you will receive payment. Because of staff shortages, small foundations will usually grant the entire amount requested in one lump sum. Large foundations with staff may make partial or quarterly payments based on your cash forecast.
- Check on any reporting procedures that the funding source may have.
- Ask the funding source when you might visit to report on the grant, and invite funders to visit you when traveling in your area.
- Ask, or have your link ask, the funding source what was best about your proposal and what could have been better. Although most grantors will not comment on your proposal, it cannot hurt to ask.

Most funding sources feel neglected once they have given away their money. You can get on their list of good grantees by following up. Your follow-up checklist should include

- putting funding sources on your public relations mailing list so that they will receive news or press releases
- keeping your funding source files updated and having a volunteer maintain current lists of grants funded by each of your grantors

- writing to funding sources two years after they have funded you to let them know how successful you are and to thank them again for their far-sightedness in dealing with the problem

If the answer is no, make the most of it by learning as much as you can from the experience.

- Send a thank-you letter to the funding source. Express your appreciation for the time and effort spent on reviewing your proposal.
- Remind the funder of what an important source of funds it is.
- Ask for helpful comments on your proposal and whether the funding source would look favorably on resubmission with certain changes.
- Ask whether the funder could suggest any other funding sources that may be interested in your project.

If the foundation has no staff and you have no links, you may not find answers to your questions. Try again. Successful grantseekers are persistent! However, you should also be aware of the fact that you may not hear *anything* from the funding source. Some private foundations send out acceptance notices only. After six months have passed, you can probably assume that your proposal was rejected.

The steps suggested in this final follow the unifying principle of this book; that is, look at everything you do from the perspective of the grantor. From preproposal contact, to writing your thank-you letter, to follow-up, consider how you would want to be appreciated and recognized for your contribution now and in the future.

PART FOUR

....

Private/Corporate Funding Opportunities

CHAPTER 23

Understanding the Corporate Marketplace

To understand the present corporate marketplace and to predict its future, one must look at corporate grants and corporate philanthropy from a historical perspective.

The concept of self-interest as the guiding principle of corporate philanthropy actually has it basis in law. The Internal Revenue Act of 1935 made it legal for corporations to deduct up to 5 percent of their pretax revenues for charitable donations. The general consensus was that these gifts (which many still view as the purview of the stockholders and not the corporation) were to be used for purposes that directly benefited the corporation's business or interests.

However, in 1953 in *A. P. Smith Manufacturing Co. v. Barlow, et al.*, the New Jersey Supreme Court ruled that corporate contributions for purposes other than a direct benefit to the business are legal. The case involved a contested gift of $1,500 made by the A. P. Smith Manufacturing Company's board of directors to Princeton University for general maintenance. Until that time, the company's corporate practice had been only to sponsor educational research projects that related to the company's business. The stockholders charged that the gift was a misappropriation of corporate funds, but the Supreme Court ruled otherwise. This ruling has been referred to as the "magna carta" of corporate philanthropy, and ultimately changed the ground rules for corporate contributions forever.

Even though 2003 will mark the 50th anniversary since it became legal for a corporation to award gifts and grants that do not directly benefit its business, corporate giving is still motivated by corporate self-interest. Corporate giving is usually a "this-for-that" exchange. Corporations do not usually *give away* money; they invest it. As a corporate grantseeker, you must view their proposed investment in your organization (your grant) through their values glasses.

Toward that end, the fields of education and health and human services are the two biggest recipients of corporate contributions.

Historically, education has received the largest portion of the corporate philanthropic dollar. As you ponder your ability to attract corporate support for your college, university, school, or educationally related nonprofit group, you need to consider the following. Traditionally, higher education has been industry's subcategory of choice. Corporations figured out long ago that, without the raw ingredient of a trained workforce, they could not produce salable products or services. Today, they realize that they need higher education graduates to maintain a competitive place in an increasingly global marketplace. However, higher education cannot assume that it will always receive the largest share of the corporate education dollar. Recently, a considerable challenge has been successfully mounted by secondary education, elementary education, and even preschool education.

For example, while working at an institution of higher education in Alabama, I noticed that many grants were going directly to local elementary and secondary schools from automobile and technology dependent companies new to the area such as Mercedes Benz. When I inquired why our institution's higher education proposals were not being funded, the corporations' hidden agenda became obvious. In order to recruit the highly technical personnel they needed, they had to insure their prospective employees that the K–12 education their children would receive on relocation would be of the highest quality. Of course, another reason to support the schools was to provide a future workforce.

The bottom line is that as you develop your corporate grants strategy, you must review your institution's or organization's ability to provide corporations with what they value.

While education has historically attracted the greatest cash share of corporate philanthropy, health and human services is now receiving a greater percent of total corporate contributions when you consider all forms of support (cash and noncash). One reason for this shift may be the escalating costs of health care and the fact that health and human services programs, projects, and research may provide direct benefits to employees, which decreases the need for services and, hence, lowers the corporation's employee health costs.

While one could argue that support for education and health and human services makes a company look good and enhances the general community, how would you explain a corporation's interest in culture and arts or civic and community affairs? As a past board member and grantseeker for a museum, I once asked a corporate contributions' committee member how I could make my museum proposal more attractive to the committee. I was told I should document certain overriding factors, such as

- the use of the museum by current corporate employees, their families, and their friends
- the number of corporate employees and/or their family members who volunteer at the museum
- how the museum interfaces with the local Chamber of Commerce and how its presence promotes tourism and visitors to the area
- the existence of programs designed to provide family tours and so on to those who the corporation is seeking to recruit

Whether a corporation supports education, health and human services, culture and the arts, or civic and community affairs, you can be sure that its expenditures, be they philanthropic dollars or noncash gifts, are related to its enlightened corporate self-interests.

Before you begin to refine your approach, consider the varied mechanisms that companies employ to make their corporate investments.

CORPORATE INVESTMENT MECHANISMS

Corporations use four basic mechanisms for investing in and making grants to nonprofit organizations.

1. Corporate Contributions Program

Corporate contributions programs are the mechanism of choice in corporate philanthropy. Usually, high-ranking corporate officials decide what portion of their corporation's net earnings before taxes (the bottom line of profits after manufacturing, sales, and marketing costs have been deducted) will be made available as gifts and grants. This money is then deducted from the corporate taxes due to the government, and directed to a corporate contributions committee to disperse to nonprofit organizations that the corporation values. Interests vary from company to company but generally fall within the categories listed above (education, health and human services, culture and arts, and civic and community affairs). Committee members may be corporate executives and/or representatives of employee groups or unions. Since many of the existing five million corporations are relatively small, with only a few employees, it can be surmised that the larger the company, the more likely it is to have a corporate contributions program and to engage in this mechanism of corporate philanthropy.

The latest IRS rule allows corporations to donate up to 10 percent of their pretax income (bottom line) in gifts and grants to nonprofit organizations as a tax deduction. However, the practice of donating a *set* percentage annually is not widespread. In fact, estimates are that of the five million corporations in the United States, only 35 percent dedicate *any* funds to nonprofit organizations.

At the beginning of the twenty-first century, the Bush administration backed a change in legislation to increase the corporate profits write-off from 10 percent to 20 percent. Even if passed, the current upper limit of 10 percent of deductions has never been approached. For example, when the limit was 5 percent, the average pretax profits donated was just over 2 percent. When the limit was raised to 10 percent, the average declined to around 1 percent, and remained there. Efforts to allow 20 percent will likely have little if any impact on increasing this average. In fact, if history is any indicator, charitable corporate write-offs could even decrease.

It is interesting to note that corporate philanthropic contributions are not required to be reported to stockholders in an itemized format. Stockholders are not *entitled* to a list of recipient organizations and the associated amounts of grant support. Only the IRS receives such a list with the corporate tax return, and it is not at liberty to share it with anyone.

Since the current stock market declines and decreases in profits, some stockholders have become very critical of the legitimate corporate write-offs made by corporate contributions committees because they are not involved in the selection process, or even privy to the name and amounts granted to each nonprofit organization. Because of the paranoia surrounding corporate contributions programs, it is no wonder that some corporations are deciding to opt out of the process altogether, pay more taxes, and let their individual stockholders deal with their own personal tax burdens.

2. Corporate Foundations

In this investment mechanism, companies designate a portion of their entitled write-off of pretax profits to be transferred to a foundation (usually named after the corporation) from which grants are paid. The main reason for initiating a corporate foundation is to stabilize a corporation's philanthropy program. Corporate foundations lead to a more uniform and stable approach to corporate social philanthropy than giving programs that rely solely on a percentage of company profits. Programs tied to company profits are subject to the so-called seesaw effect, because profits can vary widely from year to year.

Many corporations maintain a corporate contributions program *and* a corporate foundation. This allows the company some flexibility in making grants. For example, if profits are down one year, the corporate contributions program can be supported by expending some of the assets that have built up in the foundation. The corporation can level out the highs and lows of its corporate contributions over periods of high, low, and no profits, and still attain some level of support for its favorite nonprofit organizations. While all foundations are required to pay out

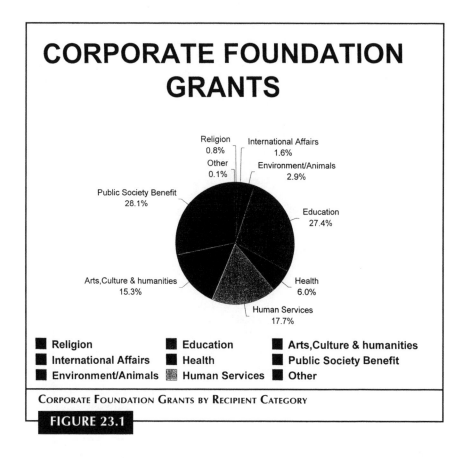

CORPORATE FOUNDATION GRANTS

Religion 0.8%

International Affairs 1.6%

Other 0.1%

Environment/Animals 2.9%

Public Society Benefit 28.1%

Education 27.4%

Arts,Culture & humanities 15.3%

Health 6.0%

Human Services 17.7%

- Religion
- International Affairs
- Environment/Animals
- Education
- Health
- Human Services
- Arts,Culture & humanities
- Public Society Benefit
- Other

CORPORATE FOUNDATION GRANTS BY RECIPIENT CATEGORY

FIGURE 23.1

a minimum of 5 percent of its assets, corporate foundations have historically paid out a much higher percentage, especially in the years marked by recession or low corporate profits.

Like the other types of foundations discussed in chapter 18, corporate foundations must list the benefactors of their grants and make their tax returns available for public viewing. This requirement can become a problem for corporations when their stockholders object to the types of organizations or specific projects that the corporate foundation supports. In addition, the public scrutiny to which the corporate foundation is subject allows for social activists and leaders of particular causes to research the foundation's giving pattern and arrange for demonstrations, which could result in a negative public relations. To avoid such problems, many corporations only make noncontroversial grants through their foundation; they make all other grants through their corporate contributions program, which does not require public disclosure.

Since corporate foundations are an extension of a profit-making company, they tend to view the world and your proposal as any corporation would. They must

Analyze how your project fulfills various corporate self interests, and then compare these interests to the funding criteria of the four basic corporate grant making mechanisms to determine which vehicle best fits your project.

Corporate Self Interest	Corporate Contributions Program	Corporate Foundation	Marketing	Research Program
Ability to Attract High Quality Personnel				
Benefits Workers and/or their Families				
Benefits Overall Community Where Parent Corporation has Factory or Special Interests				
Positions Product in such a Way that it Results in Future Sales				
Product Development - Tests, Improves, or Creates a New Product				
Research - Furthers Knowledge in Corporation's Field of Interest				
Other:				

CORPORATE GRANTS SUPPORT WORKSHEET

EXHIBIT 23.1

see a benefit in all of the projects they fund. Many of these foundations fund grants only in communities where their parent corporations have factories or a special interest. Figure 23.1 shows that the largest recipient of corporate foundation grants is different than either of the two largest recipients of total corporate support (education and health and human services). Proposals related to public society benefit are the top recipients of corporate foundation grants. For the most part, every grant made by a corporate foundation must benefit either the corporation or its workers or enhance the corporation's ability to attract high-quality personnel to the community.

3. Marketing

While it is estimated that 25 percent of corporate support to nonprofits comes in the form of donated products, this figure is probably deceptively low. Corporate support in the form of products is likely to be far greater than the reported levels, but data on the marketing mechanism is difficult to collect and analyze.

Many corporate contributions of products may not be recorded as gifts per se because they are being used in a product positioning effort that the company believes will result in future sales. In essence, these product gifts could be questioned by the IRS because they do not qualify as true gifts, some *quid pro quo* (or this-for-that) is involved in these transactions, and the company writes off the associated costs before net earnings are ever calculated.

4. Research Program

Corporations have traditionally supported colleges, universities, and nonprofit organizations' attempts to apply science to further the development of new technologies, patents, and breakthroughs in their fields of interest. Some corporations also contribute to nonprofit organizations based on the nonprofit's ability to contribute to the testing, improvement, or creation of a new product. The litmus test as to whether the support provided is really a grant is whether the nonprofit that is involved in the receipt of corporate support is acting as a free agent, or is a captive contractor for the corporate sponsor of the proposed work.

To be considered a true corporate grant, the results of the research must be published and shared for the "greater good" of the field. If the work is to be prescribed by the corporation, and/or the freedom to publish the resulting data is restricted, and any patents derived are the sole ownership of the corporation, the corporation's support will not be viewed by the IRS as a grant but, rather, as a fee for services rendered or a corporate contract. If the support is viewed as a corporate contract, it is not allowed to be written off as a charitable contribution. However, it could be considered as a research or marketing cost and as such could be deducted before the company arrives at its net earnings before taxes.

While you do not need to be concerned with how the company deducts these costs from its balance sheet, it is crucial to both you and your institution/organization to clarify the intellectual property rights (copyrights, patents, etc.) before entering into any research-related agreement.

Review your proposed project and consider how it provides your prospective corporate grantor with what it values. Then, based on these variables, determine which corporate grant making mechanism best fits your project (see exhibit 23.1).

CHAPTER 24

Researching Potential Corporate Grantors
How to Find the Corporate Funding Source That Is Best Suited to Fund Your Project

To be a successful corporate grantseeker, you will need to gather accurate information on your prospective corporate grantors before you approach them. The corporate research form (exhibit 24.1) outlines what information you will need to collect.

How you research the corporate marketplace depends on many factors, including the type of corporate grants mechanism you are pursuing. You must ask why a corporation would be interested in your proposal. If your project is related to products, product positioning, product development, or research, you can cast a wide corporate net. In fact, you can move beyond local boundaries and look all across the country for the corporations best suited to fund your project.

To do so, you must first determine which major corporations could possibly be affected by your project. Develop a list of the products and services (the keywords) that could be related to your project, and then access the *NAICS (North American Industry Classification System) Manual* at your university or public library. This publication references companies by the types of good they produce. By searching the *NAICS Manual* using your keywords, you can discover the names of the corporations that might be interested in your project. For example, if your project uses innovative ways to educate people with visual impairments, you might use the *NAICS Manual* to locate companies that manufacture state-of-the-art telecommunications equipment that could be used in your solution.

Please note that while the *North American Industry Classification System* (*NAICS*) has replaced the U.S. Standard Industrial Classification (SIC) for statistical purposes, you will still find references to SIC codes in many publications. Like the NAICS, the SIC is a system for classifying establishments by type of eco-

The following form outlines the data you need to collect in order to make a decision to seek funding from this grant source. Your attempts to collect as much of this information as possible will prove rewarding, (When feasible, record the source of the information and the date it was recorded.)

1. Name of Corporation: _____
   Name of Corporate Foundation: _____
   Name of Corporate Contributions Program: _____
   Address: _____
   Phone: _____ Fax: _____ E-mail: _____
   Web site: _____

2. Contact Person: _____
   Title: _____
   Any Links from Our Organization to Contact Person: _____
   _____
   _____

3. Corporation's Areas of Interests: _____
   _____
   _____

4. Eligibility Requirements/Restrictions:
   a. Activities Funded/Restricted: _____
   _____

   b. Organizations Funded/Restricted: _____
   _____

   c. Geographic Funding Preferences/Restrictions: _____
   _____

   d. Other Requirements/Restrictions: _____
   _____
   _____
   _____
   _____

CORPORATE RESEARCH FORM

EXHIBIT 24.1

nomic activity. Although the principles of the systems are the same, NAICS codes are longer (6 digits) and may vary considerably from the SIC codes.

You will also want to find out if there are any major industry specific associations or membership groups that fund research or projects in your field. For instance, the Society of Manufacturing Engineers funds beneficial research in their field, and there are many more like them.

While you should look outside of your local area for corporate grantors when your project is related to research and product development, remember that most corporations give where they live. Therefore, you may find yourself targeting cor-

5.   Information Available

                            In Possession Of

        IRS 990-PF Tax Return (Year)   _____ (Corp. Foundation Only)
        Guidelines   _____
        Newsletters   _____
        Annual Report   _____

        _____   _____
        _____   _____

6.   a. Contributions Committee Members/Board of Directors/ Foundation Officers:

        _____
        _____
        _____
        _____
        _____

7.   Deadline: _____

        Application Process/Requirements:

        _____
        _____
        _____

8.   Financial Information

        Fiscal Year: _____
        Corporate Sales: $_____
        Parent Company: _____
        Corporate Sites: _____
        # of Employees: _____
        Credit Rating: _____ Source: _____
        Private or Publicly Held: _____
        If Publicly Held: Stock Price $_____
                                 Dividend: $_____
        Products Produced/Distributed: _____

        _____
        _____

CORPORATE RESEARCH FORM *(continued)*

EXHIBIT 24.1

porations that are hundreds or thousands of miles away, as well as some that are nearby.

Checking with your grant office and development office is always recommended when dealing with out-of-the-area corporations, and absolutely essential when contacting companies close to home. Corporate people assume that anyone who submits a proposal or contacts them has the approval of the institution or organization they represent, and you risk negative positioning if the right hand does not know what the left is doing. This does not mean that you should not consid-

For Corporate Foundations:

Asset Base: $_____

Are there current gifts to build the asset base?   Yes _____   No_____

If yes, how much? $_____

Total number of grants awarded in 200_: _____

Total amount of grants awarded in 200_: $_____

High Grant: $_____

Low Grant: $_____

Average Grant: $_____

In our interest area there were _____ grants, totaling $_____

High grant in our interest area: $_____

Low grant in our interest area: $_____

Average grant in our interest area: $_____

Grants Received Versus Grants Funded

Number of proposals received in 200_: _____

Number of proposals funded in 200_: _____

9.   Sample Grants in Our Area of Interest:

Recipient Organization	Amount
_____	_____
_____	_____
_____	_____
_____	_____

CORPORATE RESEARCH FORM *(continued)*

EXHIBIT 24.1

er local corporations, but do your research and make a case to your organization as to why you and your project should be allowed to proceed to submittal with each target corporation.

There are several great sources of information on corporate support. The Foundation Center, in particular, is a good resource for information on corporate foundation grants. One of its publications, the *National Directory of Corporate Giving*, provides information on 2,100 corporate foundations and 1,300 direct giving programs, and descriptions for over 6,500 recently awarded grants are included among the corporate entries. *Corporate Foundation Profiles*, also published by the Foundation Center, contains grants information on 187 of the largest corporate foundations in the United States—grant makers that each give at least $1.2 million annually. The *Corporate Giving Directory*, published by Taft Group, is another good source. It provides profiles on 1,000 of the largest corporate foundations and corporate direct giving programs. (See List of Resources for ordering information.) In addition, the annual 990-PF tax returns for corporate foundations can be ac-

	Birmingham Metropolitan Statistical Area Largest Employers	
1.	University of Alabama at Birmingham	15,505
2.	U.S. Government*	9,000
3.	BellSouth	8,250
4.	State of Alabama	6,150
5.	Baptist Health System	5,800
6.	Bruno's Inc.	5,700
7.	Jefferson County Board of Education	5,301
8.	City of Birmingham	4,500
9.	Birmingham Public Schools	4,200
10.	Jefferson County Government	4,077
11.	Wal-Mart	4,000
12.	SouthTrust Bank	3,400
13.	USX	3,000
14.	AmSouth Bank	3,000
15.	American Cast Iron Pipe	2,800
16.	Alabama Power Company	2,713
17.	Parisian, Inc.	2,700
18.	Brookwood Medical Center	2,600
19.	Drummond Company	2,560
20.	Carraway Methodist Medical Center	2,002
21.	Children's Hospital	2,000
22.	Shelby County Board of Education	1,986
23.	Compass Bank	1,886
24.	EBSCO	1,700

* Includes 3,820 U.S. Post Office employees, 1,900 Social Security Adminstration Employees, and 1,000 VA Medical Center employees

Note: Employment figures reflect both full-time and part-time employees

CHAMBER OF COMMERCE LIST

EXHIBIT 24.2

cessed through the Foundation Center's regional and cooperating collections and on the Web (see chapter 19).

While it still makes sense to check out the corporate grant resource books available in your local public library and at the Foundation Center's regional collections, a more important source for data is your local Chamber of Commerce, which can provide you with a list of local corporations and information on number of employees, total value of payroll, and products and services provided. You can obtain this list by visiting or phoning your chamber, and, in some instances, from its Web site.

This list is most valuable as you begin to target your local grantors and develop your strategy on why they should be interested in your proposal. For example, when I was an associate professor at the University of Alabama, Birmingham, I asked for and received a list of the areas largest employer from the local chamber of commerce (see exhibit 24.2). By reviewing the information on the list, I discovered the following facts:

- The university I was employed by was the area's largest employer.
- Of the top 10 largest employers, only three were profit-making corporate prospects.
- Fifty percent of the 10 largest employers were nonprofit organizations and in competition with me for corporate support.

In addition to having to deal with the harsh reality of these facts, I also had to come to terms with the fact that the rest of my university had designs on the same local corporations that I did, and that I would have to plead my case for approval to submit a proposal to a development team comprised of representatives from colleges and departments other than mine.

If your institution or organization is not in a large metropolitan area, and there is no Chamber of Commerce, contact your nearest economic development agency, industrial park headquarters, or business incubator. One of these groups should have the data you need to uncover the corporations in your geographic area.

Once you identified your distant and nearby potential corporate funding sources, your public library of local college library will have several resources to help you gather more information to determine your best prospects for funding. Any one of the Dun & Bradstreet research tools or Standard & Poor's publications will provide the basic information you will need.

Dun & Bradstreet's Million Dollar Directory is a set of five volumes that is published annually. The set consists of an alphabetic listing in three volumes and geographic and industry cross-reference volumes. Each volume includes both a numerical and an alphabetic index of SIC codes. The print version of the directory should be available in your public library or local college library. Also available online, on a subscription basis, as part of the *Million Dollar Directory Suite*, *Dun & Bradstreet's North American Million Dollar Database* provides information on approximately 1,600,000 U.S. and Canadian leading public and private businesses. (See List of Resources for ordering information.)

Exhibit 24.3 is an example of what an entry in *Dun & Bradstreet's Million Dollar Directory* looks like. As you can see, entries in the directory include the following information on corporations:

- D-U-N-S number
- company name, address, and phone number
- state of incorporation
- primary and secondary SIC codes
- sales volume
- number of employees
- parent company and location
- year started/ownership date
- key executives' names and titles

D-U-N-S 00-656-4690
HENTLEY & CO (DE)
10 SE Main St, Washville, IL/++/

Zip 81829   *Tel* (309)545-2000
Sales 11100MM   *Emp* 49900

Tkr sym BTL   *Exch* BSE CIN MSE NYS PBS
                                                     PCS
SIC 7361 7363 Employment agencies; temporary help service
BK Congressional Bk NA, Chicago, IL
Accts Proven Way
*Mark V Franz   Ch Bd CEO
*James C. Luch   Pr
 Ken A Ruchan   Sec
 Thomas Glianno   Ex VP, Finance
 Stefan Ziegler   Sr VP
 Karl Boggle   VP, Sales

ENTRY FROM *DUN & BRADSTREET'S MILLION DOLLAR DIRECTORY* (FICTITIOUS DATA)

EXHIBIT 24.3

- primary bank and accounting firm
- import/export designation
- stock exchange symbol and indicator for publicly owned companies
- line of business description
- trade name
- directors other than officers

The *Standard & Poor's Register of Corporations, Directors, and Executives* provides information on over 100,000 public and private corporations. The user can access key corporate facts including address/phone, officers/directors, sales volume, number of employees, SIC codes, and business descriptions. The *Register* consists of three volumes: volume 1 provides information on both public and private corporations, volume 2 contains biographical information on corporate executives and directors, and volume 3 contains indices.

Volume 1 of *Standard & Poor's Register of Corporations, Directors, and Executives* provides similar information as *Dun & Bradstreet's Million Dollar Directory* (see exhibit 24.4).

Because a corporation's executives often make up its contributions committee, I have chosen to show a sample entry from volume 1 of *Standard & Poor's Register of Corporations, Directors and Executives* in exhibit 24.4.

In both *Dun & Bradstreet's Million Dollar Directory* and volume 1 of *Standard & Poor's Register of Corporations, Directors and Executives*, the names designated with an asterisk appear in each publication's companion book (or volume) on directors and executives. For example, after searching in volume 1 of *Standard & Poor's Reg-*

AMERICAN COMMUNICATIONS CO.
99 Brady Ave., New York, NY 10007
Tel. 212-897-8888

*   Chrm & Chief Exec Officer - Charles L. Brown
*   Pres & Chief Oper Officer - William M. Ellinghouse
*   Vice-Chrm & Chief Fin Officer - William S. Chasel, Jr.
     Exec V-P (Business) - Thomas E. Bolger
     Exec V-P (Network) - Richard R. Hough
     Exec V-P - Charles E. Hugel
     Exec V-P - Morris Tanebaum
     Exec V-P (Residence) - Kenneth J. Whaling
     Exec V-P - S.R. Wilcox
     V-P & Asst to Chrm - Alvin von Auw
     V-P (Bus Services) - Robert E. Allen
     V-P (Network Plan & Design) - Jack A. Baird
     V-P (Fed Reg Matters) - James R. Billings
     V-P (Pub Rel & Empl Inf) - Edward M. Block
     V-P (Residence Mktg Sales & Serv) - John L. Clendenin
     V-P & Treas - Virginia A. Dwyer
     V-P (Pub Affairs) - John G. Fox
     V-P (Pres - Long Lines Dept) - Robert W. Kleinert
     V-P (Tariffs & Costs) - Walter B. Kelly
     V-P (Bus Mktg) - Archie J. McGill
     V-P (State Reg Matters) - Alfred G. Hartoll
     V-P (Labor Rel Cor Per & Policy Seminar) - Rex V. Reed
     V-P (Fin Mgt) - John L. Segally
     V-P (Plan & Admin D) - William G. Sharell
     Secy - Frank A. Hutson, Jr.
     Accts - Coopers & Lybrand
     Revenue: $45.41 Bil Employees 984,000
     Stock Exchange(s): NYS, BST, PAC, MID, CIN, PSE
*   ALSO DIRECTORS - Other Directors Are:
     Edward W. Carter   Catherine M. Bleary
     Archie W. Davis   John D. de Butts
     BUSINESS: Communications
     S.I.C. 4844; 4833

ENTRY FROM VOLUME 1 OF *STANDARD & POOR'S REGISTER OF CORPORATIONS, DIRECTORS, AND EXECUTIVES* (FICTITIOUS DATA)

EXHIBIT 24.4

ister of Corporations, Directors, and Executives, you may decide you want to locate more information on William S. Chasel Jr., vice chairman and chief financial officer of American Communications Company. There is an asterisk next to his name in volume 1 of the *Register*, so you can look for further information in volume 2. Exhibit 24.5 is a sample of what you might find.

As you can see, the information provided in volume 2 of *Standard & Poor's Register of Corporations, Directors, and Executives* includes the age, educational background, and residence of the corporate executive, as well as his or her other corporate

CHASEL, WILLIAM S., JR. (b. 1944 Brooklyn - Dartmouth Coll. (Amos Tuck Sch. of Bus. Admin., 1966) - Vice-Chrm, Chief Fin Officer & Dir., American Communications Co., 99 Brady Ave., New York, NY 10007
        Campbell Soup Co., Dir
        Southside Telephone Company, Dir
        Manufacturers Hanner Corp. & Trust Co., Dir
        Philadelphia Fund Savings Group, Trustee

CHASHELL, GEORGE R. (b. 1939 Mansfield, OH - BPOE) - Secy, Bopping Paines, Inc., 664 S. West St., Mannington, OH 44902 - Res: 355 Oak St., Mannington 44904
        Bopping Paines Inc. (California), Secy
        Bopping Paines Inc. (Delaware), Secy
        Bopping Disc Inc., Asst Secy
        Smith Water System Co., Secy
        National Construction Sacky Credit Group, Mem

CHASIN, EDWARD A. (b. 1941 Duluth, MN - Univ of Chicago, 1961) - Exec. V-P & Dir (Mktg Sales), Complete Controls Inc., 6777 Washington St., Minneapolis 56654 - Res: 555 Shoreside Ave., Wayzata, MN 55392
        Fireside Country Club, 1st V-P & Dir

CHASMAN, EDMUND JOSEPH (b. 1942 Rockville Square, NY - St. Patrick's Coll, 1964) - Exec V-P & Dir Hoggens Mason Wood Walker, Inc., 6 Maple Ave., Baltimore, MD 32241 - Res: 7878 A Frame Rd., Huxton, MD 32256
        Peacon Picture Services, Inc., Dir
        RFS Financial Services (subs Hoggens Mason), Dir
        Garden Capital (subs Hoggens Mason), Dir

CHASMANN, GEORGE D. (b. 1939 NYC) - V-P (Intl), Gordon Guaranty Trust Co. of New York, 23 Hall St., New York 10008 - Res: 23 Midwood Dr., Kendall Park, NJ 08824
        U.S. Chamber of Comm. on Import Trade Policy, Chrm
        Import Expansion Comm. of the Bankers Assn. for Foreign Trade, Mem
        National Overseas Trade Council, Inc., Dir

ENTRY FROM STANDARD & POOR'S REGISTER OF CORPORATIONS, DIRECTORS, AND EXECUTIVES VOLUME 2—DIRECTORS AND EXECUTIVES (FICTITIOUS DATA)

EXHIBIT 24.5

affiliations and activities. This biographical information is very valuable in that it can be used with your grants advisory committee to uncover links and expand corporate relationships. For example, in the sample entry we can see that William S. Chasel Jr. graduated from Dartmouth College. Therefore, if you have an advocate or grants advisory committee member who is a graduate of Dartmouth, you will be wise to take that individual with you when you make preproposal contact.

In addition to these national reference books, your library should also have *Who's Who in America* and other books on outstanding individuals in your geographic area. The more you know about the people you will be approaching for a grant, the more prepared you will be to create a powerful appeal that motivates the grantor to award you funds. Corporate leaders have much more written about them than federal bureaucrats, and your local librarian can show you how to use free resource tools to learn more about corporate grant prospects. Check the List of Resources in this book for commercially available materials that you will find helpful in your search for corporate funding sources.

Profits are the bottom line in corporate philanthropy. If there are no profits there is little incentive to donate money to reduce taxes. Since corporate contributions depend on a company's profitability, your corporate research should include information on revenue. There are several ways to obtain accurate data on profitability. You can:

- access a corporation's Web site to learn about their new products and plans

- track a corporation's stock prices on the DOW, NASDAQ, or AMEX

- include a stockbroker on your advisory group to help you monitor corporate profits

- include a corporate executive on your advisory group who subscribes to Dun & Bradstreet's financial services and ask him or her to request a Dun & Bradstreet report on your prospective corporate grantor. This report will rate the fiscal stability of the company and give you a sense of the company's ability to support your proposal. (A corporate person will also understand the values of corporations, and may have linkages to companies you are interested in pursuing for grant support.)

- purchase a few shares of stock in each publicly held company in your area. If you receive a dividend check, you will know the company made money! Using this technique , you will also receive corporate reports, proxy statements, and up-to-date information on top corporate administrators and board member changes. You might even make some money, and if you get rejected by a corporation you can always sell their stock for revenge!

Doing your homework on corporate grantors can be more frustrating than researching federal or foundation sources. You will find much less information available on corporate grants awarded by companies that do not use a foundation to make their grants, and the information you do find will be much less reliable. The reason for the lack of sound data on corporate giving is that there are no laws allowing public review of corporate contributions programs. Companies must record their corporate charitable contributions on their IRS tax return, but no one, not even a stockholder, has the right to see the return.

Except for the portion of corporate grants that are awarded through corporate foundations, corporate data are not subject to validation and hence the reporting is not always accurate. The data on corporate giving are derived from self-reported, voluntary responses to surveys and questionnaires. Even the corporate contributions data reported to *Giving USA* (published by the AAFRC Trust for Philanthropy) are based on a voluntary survey conducted by the Conference Board, a nonprofit organization with a reputation for keeping corporate responses confidential.

Irrespective of the difficulties in obtaining accurate corporate granting information, the corporate research strategies recommended in this chapter will at least provide you with the ability to gather the name, address, e-mail address, fax number, and/or phone number of the corporate contact person; information you will find necessary to take the next step in your grant-winning strategy step—contacting a corporate grantor before submission.

CHAPTER 25

Contacting a Corporate
Grantor Before Submission

J ust as with private foundation grantseekers, corporate grantseekers who discuss their projects with the appropriate corporate funding officials before submitting their proposals increase their success rates dramatically. A fivefold increase in success was found when preproposal contact was made with private foundation funding sources. Experience leads me to believe that the impact of preproposal contact on success rate is much higher in the corporate marketplace, and could approach a tenfold factor.

Often it is difficult for grantseekers to make preproposal contact with corporate grantors. This is because it takes more time to make profits than it does to grant the 1 percent of net earnings before taxes that most corporations award. In a sense, it costs the corporate grantor even more money to make grants when their time would be better spent on making more profits.

Staff cutbacks also contribute to pre proposal contact difficulties. For example, from 1986 to 1996, IBM community relations staff went from 77 to 19. From 1991 to 1996, Bell Atlantic's corporate contributions staff went from 7 to 2, and Digital's from 14 to 4. There will most likely be even more staff cutbacks in 2003 in corporate departments that oversee philanthropy.

Corporate webbing and linkages become critical here (see chapter 7). It pays to figure out who may know who, and who would be willing to make an appointment or open a door for you. If you do not have a linkage to any of your prospective corporate grantors, consider creating one by inviting selected corporate representatives to take part in your advisory group.

Your initial point of contact may not always be the individual listed in your research as the corporate foundation contact or the chair of the corporate contributions committee. Your initial contact person could be a salesperson for the corporation, parents of your students who are employed by the corporation, clients of your organization who works for the company, and so on. Many corporations pay special attention to proposals that can be linked to employees that are volunteers of the prospective grantee's organization.

One big difference between private foundation grantors and corporate grantors is that the corporate grantor has an office or a facility. Even so, corporate grantors have a multitude of responsibilities and cannot spend unlimited amounts of time with grantseekers. Therefore, it is imperative that you follow the formal instructions your research uncovers. If you uncover a name and an e-mail address and/or a phone number, assume that you can contact the person listed. If your research states no contact except by letter or application, then follow those instructions. However, *informal* contact through an advisory committee member, advocate, or linkage is still advised. In these instances, the important thing is that *you* are not the one making the contact. If your advisory committee member, advocate, or linkage can orchestrate a conference call or preferably a face-to-face meeting, go with him/her. If you are instructed to request current guidelines or an application package, you can use the sample corporate inquiry letter/e-mail shown in exhibit 25.1.

Contact by Telephone

If contact by telephone is encouraged, call to discuss how your project relates to the corporation's interests. Let them know that you have done your homework. If it is a corporate foundation, use the information you obtained from their tax return (IRS form 990-PF) to show your knowledge of their past granting interests. If the corporate grantor seems interested in your project, do not be afraid to inquire about the possibility of a face-to-face meeting. If a visit is out of the question, then discuss the same issues over the phone as you would in person.

The Visit

While often the most anxiety producing, a face-to-face visit is usually the best way to discuss your project and to gauge the interest of the corporate grantor.

Who Should Go. It is advisable for you to take either an advocate, linkage, or an advisory committee member with you. A good listener who can summarize and reflect back the grantor's position is a good choice. Successful corporate people are skilled at making sales calls and they will expect you to try to be so when asking for their money. You do not want to appear as a fast-talking used car salesman, but your approach should be well rehearsed and professional, and your appearance should be conservative, imaging that of the corporate official's as closely as possible.

Name
Title
Address

Dear _____:

I am developing a project which deals with _____ and provides benefits to [or in]
_____. My research indicates that this area is an important concern of the
[name of corporation or corporate foundation].

Please use the enclosed label to send me your current priority statement and information on your
desired format for proposals or other guidelines. I would also appreciate it if you could add us to
your mailing list so that we could receive your annual reports, and any other materials you think
might be useful to us as we work on this and related projects.

Thank you for your cooperation.

                                                                    Sincerely,

                                                                    Name/Title
                                                                    Organization
                                                                    Address

SAMPLE INQUIRY LETTER/E-MAIL TO A CORPORATION

EXHIBIT 25.1

Materials to Bring. Your proposal development workbook (Swiss cheese book) will be a great confidence builder, since you will most likely be able to open it right to the areas of question. Also bring a short video or a CD that you can play on your laptop to document the need, as well as the unique qualities you and your institution bring to the solution. Use your battery to power your short two- to three-minute presentation so you do not require any plugs or adapters.

If the corporate representative asks you to join his or her colleagues in a conference room, you may need to set up your audiovisuals on the corporation's equipment. Make sure you know how, and have an extra CD to use with their data projection system.

What to Discuss with a Corporate Grantor. Review the following topics of discussion and tailor them to your particular situation and prospective corporate funding source. Remember that the purpose of these discussions is to verify the information you gathered through your research, and to gain more insight into how to produce a proposal that the prospective grantor will find impossible not to fund.

1. Discuss the need for your project/research and then introduce your solutions. Briefly explain the various approaches you are considering to solve the prob-

Complete one of these forms after each contact with a corporate grantor.

Funding Source: _____

Funding Source Address: _____

_____

Funding Source Contact Person: _____

Telephone Number: _____ Fax: _____ E-mail: _____

Contacted On (Date): _____

Contacted By (Name): _____

Type of Contact: Phone _____ Visit _____ Other (Explain) _____

Objective of Contact: _____

_____

_____

_____

Results of Contact: _____

_____

_____

_____

Follow-up: _____

_____

_____

_____

CORPORATE GRANTOR REPORT FORM

EXHIBIT 25.2

lem and then ask if they prefer any one approach over the others. Asking for their input is often a good way to start.

2. Verify all information you have on the corporation's granting programs and patterns. Show them you have looked at their annual reports or corporate foundation tax returns by the comments you make and the questions you ask. For example, "I can see from my research that this area is important to your corporation because it represents 50 percent of all your granted projects. My research indicates that your board is very educated and sophisticated in this field. Will they be the group that reads and selects the proposals for approval?"

Corporate Grantor Report Form

Whether you, your advocate, linkage, advisory member, or staff person makes contact with the prospective grantor, make sure that *who* was contacted and *what* was discussed is documented. Complete a corporate grantor report form (exhibit 25.2) after each contact with a corporate funding source whether the contact was made in person, over the phone, or through an e-mail.

CHAPTER 26

Applying for Corporate Funds

M any of the corporate grantors you will approach for funding have had experience developing applications for use with government grant programs they are eligible for, and with contract and procurement programs as bidders and contractors. They strive to put together succinct and well-written proposals, sales and marketing materials, and presentations for their sales prospects. They value e-mail and correspondence that is effectively written. Of all the grantor types, they are probably the most critical and demanding audience you will encounter in your grants quest.

Construct your corporate proposal as outlined in this section, and have a quality circle or mock review of your proposal performed by corporate individuals from your advisory group. While you have chosen to make the nonprofit world your base of operation, you must recognize that your values glasses are different from those who have chosen the for-profit world as their primary frame of reference, and that you must adjust your proposal writing style accordingly.

When I asked a corporate vice president what the biggest mistake was in proposals from the nonprofit world, he said, "The vocabulary." When I asked him to clarify, he said that nonprofits should never use the "g" word. I asked him if he meant "g" for "grants" and he said, "No, 'g' for 'give.'" Proposal writers had repeatedly asked his company to *give* them funding. He suggested to me that they use "I" word, or "*invest,*" instead. Considering what you learned about corporate self interest in chapter 23, this should make sense to you. To be successful in the corporate grants marketplace, you must be able to convince the prospective grantor that it will get a *return on their investment* if they fund your project.

The fact that only a few of the larger corporations have staff members dedicated to contributions, and that most do not rely on outside readers or peer reviewers to evaluate submitted proposals, means your proposal will probably be read by individuals on the corporate foundation board or the corporate board, research and development types, salespeople, and/or marketing representatives. Corporate contributions' committees are often comprised of a mix of these types of individuals.

As with the private foundation marketplace, you will fail miserably if you take the "one size fits all" approach and blanket the corporate community with the same proposal that starts with, "We want _____. Please send a grant." To make matters worse, the corporations you approach with this method are likely to never forget the poorly developed proposal you submitted to them.

The successful corporate letter proposal follows the same basic order as the proposal to a private foundation. The main components are

- an introductory paragraph stating the reason for writing
- a paragraph explaining why this grantor was selected
- a needs paragraph
- a solution paragraph
- a uniqueness paragraph
- a request for funds paragraph
- a closing paragraph
- signatures
- attachments, if allowed

INTRODUCTORY PARAGRAPH

If you have a linkage to the corporation use it here. For example:

> When this exciting project to increase the technology skills of educators was discussed with John Smith, the vice president of your corporate board, he suggested we ask the Jones Corporation to consider a role in increasing teacher competencies.

You could also mention a volunteer connection in your opening paragraph. This is a particularly good idea since many corporations will not invest in a local non-profit organization unless their employees are voluntarily involved with it. Consider using your introductory paragraph to refer to the commitment of their employees to your cause. For instance:

> Will Olsen, your Region Four supervisor, and I have discussed Oak Computer's role in increasing the performance of our students through the use of applied technology. As chairperson of our school advisory committee, Mr. Olsen has donated over 100 hours of time and has been instrumental in making our computer lab a reality.

In the case of a research related project, you might refer to an employee linkage who has served on your advisory committee, given a talk or lecture to your staff or students, served as a mentor, or allowed students to shadow workers to gain insight into the corporate marketplace.

Always check with your linkages before submitting your letter proposal, and provide them with a draft copy of the section that refers to them to be sure that they are agreeable. If you do not have a linkage that you can refer to in the opening paragraph, start your letter proposal by focusing on the grantor.

WHY THE GRANTOR WAS SELECTED

This paragraph presents you with another opportunity to express your knowledge about the grantor. The purpose of this section of your letter proposal is to establish that the similarities between what they, the grantor, value and what you value are why you selected them. Align your organization with the values of the grantor by saying something such as:

> As the Jones Corporation has become an international leader in innovative technology related to energy conservation; the Jonathan Smith Laboratory has dedicated its research to the same field of study.

NEEDS PARAGRAPH

This section of your corporate proposal must establish that you have a command of the knowledge in the field. You must convince the reader/reviewer that you know what exists now in your field of expertise, and that you know what needs to happen to close the gap between what is and what should be. The gap provides the reason why your proposal cannot be rejected. If the corporate grantor is truly interested in the area and in contributing toward solving the problem, then they must keep reading your proposal, and ultimately fund your project.

The following example illustrates the proposal writer's expertise in the field, and identifies the gap.

> The problem is simple, the solution is not. Current accepted theory used to explain the energy expended in the X reaction does not account for Y. The inability to predict Y costs our energy conservation effort billions of dollars in the United States alone.

Make sure that you do not mention your proposed solution or your organization in the needs section of your letter proposal except if you need to make reference to your own studies or findings. One way to insure that you do not make this mistake is to include a transition sentence or two that enables you to move smoothly from the problem to your solution. For example: "What must be done to address and close this gap? We propose a solution!"

SOLUTION PARAGRAPH

The purpose of this paragraph is to provide a short summary of the methodology that will be employed to solve the problem.

Corporate executives are accustom to using spreadsheets to analyze the steps and costs involved in planning and evaluating just about every thing they do in the corporate world. Therefore, if space allows (you need to be able to submit at least three pages) it is a good idea to include a one-page project planner/spreadsheet (see chapter 12) as page two of your corporate proposal. Refer to this project planning aid as a one-page summary of your more detailed plan. Make mention that you have several more pages of project planners that detail the methods summarized on the page included in your letter proposal, and that you would be happy to provide them on request. Remember that corporate people are likely to ask for more detail, might visit you, and could ask you to come to them. While they may not designate a specific amount of time to grants, they do have an office and a travel budget.

UNIQUENESS PARAGRAPH

The corporate grantor wants to be assured that you, your organization/institution, and your project are the right investment choice for them. Most nonprofits reflect on their organization's mission and their history when creating this section. While this may work with private foundations to demonstrate commitment to the field of interest, corporate grantors want facts, data, statistics, and examples of winning characteristics. While they will probably want to know that you have been a grant winner before, what really matters to them is the breakthroughs your institution, program, or lab have made in the field, and the competency and productivity of your staff. If your key personnel are exceptional, tell them so. While you may have written the proposal, you will probably not be the individual to sign it. Therefore, it is okay to refer to yourself in this paragraph as the qualified leader to carry out the plan.

Think of this paragraph as part of a corporate marketing brochure. For example, what convinces you to buy a particular product from one company over another? It's probably their credibility, the proof that they are behind their product, and their commitment to quality! These are the same attributes that corporate funding sources want to see in their grantees.

REQUEST FOR FUNDS PARAGRAPH

As in all proposals you must ask for the money. If you are targeting a corporate foundation, you will have access to their 990-PF IRS tax return and can use the data provided on that form to decide how much to request. However, it is difficult to know how much to request from a corporation that awards grants through a

June 8, 2003

Lawrence Blaine, President
Blaine Corporation
811 Cold Spring Highway
Appleton, OH 25891

Dear Mr. Blaine:

I would like to take this opportunity to invite you to join our school district in initiating an exciting new program. .We know your company is particularly interested in education because you generously support elementary and secondary schools, are an enthusiastic partner in the Adopt-A-School Program, and encourage your employees, like Leon Smith and Marilyn Jones, to volunteer at our local schools.

As a matter of fact, Mr. Smith and Ms. Jones are currently involved in helping our district address the problem of declining math and science skills and the growing inability of our students to transfer these skills from the classroom to the work place. Our students rank _____ in the country and score in the _____ percentile on standardized math tests, but we are not the only ones to recognize the problem.

- A ____ study conducted by the Educational Testing Center showed that American 13-year-olds placed 14th among 15 industrialized countries on standard math tests.

- A ____ Scans Report indicated that the average American high school junior spends 30 hours a week on school work; the average Japanese junior spends 60.

Although there is some evidence that our students' mathematical scores are improving, the demand for mathematical skills is not remaining constant. It is growing, and we have already graduated individuals with inadequate skills.

You may have read about the Will-Burt Corporation of Orrvile, Ohio (*Profile*, August 20_). They recently found themselves in a terrible situation. Their company employees were producing inferior products. In fact, they had a 35 percent rejection rate, massive product recalls, and 2,000 hours per month of "re-work." Their employees ' lack of basic math skills was found to be one of the main culprits. After setting up a school in the plant to teach math skills, the company's rejection rate decreased to 2 percent, but the Will-Burt Corporation discovered that while remedial training was an effective solution it was also a costly one.

It is estimated that over $25 billion is spent annually on remedial training in this country! We must do better. Our schools must provide our students with the skills necessary to meet the challenges of the twenty-first century. An April 20_ article in *INC.* magazine reported that

SAMPLE LETTER PROPOSAL TO A CORPORATION

EXHIBIT 26.1

contributions program because of the lack of available public information. If you are unable to decipher an appropriate amount through preproposal contact, you will have to guess. As you learned in chapter 8, most grantseekers think that corporate grants account for $60 to $75 billion dollars per year, when it is actually $5 billion. With this in mind, you might want to scale down your request. Anything over $100,000 is a very large corporate commitment.

If you are forced to divide your project into several fundable pieces, explain that in this paragraph. Also name-drop any of the grantors who have already granted you funds. You and your project are a junk bond until someone else with a good reputation buys in. Then you become a blue chip stock.

even today's modern corporations want employees who can and will think about innovation, quality service, and using advanced techniques such as statistical process control.

Our school district has been developing several solutions to deal with declining math and science skills, including parental involvement in education, less television, and more valuable homework. However, we also need to apply new techniques - techniques we cannot afford in our regular budget. For example, we know that individualized instruction and self-paced learning materials could make a big difference if we only had the funds to provide for and purchase these resources.

Our parents advisory committee, teachers, staff, and volunteers are very excited about implementing SUCCESS-MAKER, a computer assisted learning program designed to help teachers develop and individualized instructional approach that will allow:

- remedial students to catch up,
- average students to excel, and
- gifted students to leap beyond.

The SUCCESS-MAKER elementary package in math is particularly interesting to us. It would allow our teachers to place students on computers to improve skills in number concepts, computation, problem solving, and math applications in science. The students' progress would be continually recorded and a report would be developed for the student, teacher, and parents. Our objective would be to increase our district's math competency by __ percent. Other districts that have used this approach have not only documented an improvement in skills but also significant increases in parental involvement.

Our district is ready to accept the challenge that SUCCESS-MAKER offers. Our teachers have already volunteered their time for in-service training, and our district has dedicated $____ in resources to support the project. Everything is ready, but we need you.

A grant of $____ from the Blaine Corporation equates to an investment of $____ per student who will benefit. I have enclosed a spreadsheet [or project planner] that outlines exactly how your funds will be put to use. I am sure you will agree that we need to move now before another group of students becomes another group of American workers needing remedial training. Your support will be an important catalyst in insuring the strength of our country's future work force and the growth of companies such as the Blaine Corporation.

We think of this project as an investment with a tremendous return and we hope you will too. We promise to stand accountable and to share all results of the program with you and your company. Please contact my office or [name] at [phone number] with any questions you may have. If you would like, we can provide you with support materials and a videotape that describes SUCCESS-MAKER in greater detail and includes comments from educators who have used this approach.

Sincerely,
Melissa Appleton, Ed.D.
Superintendent, Friendship Heights School District

SAMPLE LETTER PROPOSAL TO A CORPORATION *(continued)*

EXHIBIT 26.1

Your project planner should help the corporate decision maker evaluate the appropriateness of your request. If you must present a budget, avoid dedicating a whole page to this purpose. Use a paragraph form budget instead and refer to the column totals on your project planner.

You can refer to the return for their investment by dividing the total cost by the number of people the project will serve. In a research proposal, compare the requested amount to the benefits that may occur as a result of answering the research question and closing the gap in the field of knowledge, and suggest what

---

Corporate Contributions Guidelines

How to Apply

Kodak does not have a formal application form. A cover letter accompanying the proposal should state the mission of the organization, the grant amount requested, the purpose of the grant, and the legal name of the organization (which must be identical to the name used on IRS form 990). Note any previous Kodak support, including dates and amounts.

Proposals must not exceed five single-spaced typed and numbered pages. (Do not use binders.) Provide the following information in this order:

- Proposal summary (a 1-to-2 page description of the entire proposal)
- Mission of the organization
- History of the organization
- Need for the project, in view of related work by others
- Project description
- Audience served
- Goals, objectives, and action plan
- Expected quantifiable outcomes or results
- Method of evaluation of proposed outcomes
- Other sources of support for the project
- If appropriate, the plan for continuing the activity beyond Eastman Kodak Company's support

Attachments must include:

- Financial information (most recent organizational financial statement and income-and-expense budget; list of other current and projected sources of funding for the project).
- Most recent completed form 990 submitted to the IRS, which includes the federal taxpayer identification number and the legal name of the organization.
- List of Board of Directors and their affiliations.

SAMPLE CORPORATE CONTRIBUTIONS GUIDELINES: EASTMAN KODAK COMPANY

EXHIBIT 26.2

---

this may lead to in the future. Both of these approaches are quite successful with corporate grantors.

CLOSING PARAGRAPH

Do not start this paragraph off by stating that you would like to meet with them; they already know you would. Instead, invite them to meet with you and your key personnel, and to visit your institution, organization, laboratory, and so on. Be sure to express your desire to provide any additional information and request that the prospective grantor contact you (or the individual responsible for the project) to provide that information and/or to answer any questions.

SIGNATURES

Corporate people expect your proposal to be signed by an administrator or officer who holds rank and responsibility within your organization/institution. This is viewed by the corporate grantor as institutional commitment and endorsement. More than one signature or the signature from your consortia partner(s) is also impressive to them.

ATTACHMENTS, IF ALLOWED

While most corporations do not *encourage* attachments, they may be *allowed* in proposals for research grants. In these instances, project planner spread sheets detailing your protocol are recommended over text.

Corporate applications instructions for other types of grants (nonresearch) will usually restrict the use of any attachments. For example, when applying for a $200,000 grant from the Bell South Foundation, the application instructions received by my institution specifically stated that letter proposals were restricted to five double-spaced pages and that no attachments were allowed. The guidelines also stated that the foundation would request further information from a select group of applicants from which one-half would be funded. We eventually received a letter stating that our proposal had made the first cut and that of the total 200 applicants we were one of the 20 under consideration. Along with that letter came of list of 10 questions that the reviewers had regarding our proposal. We were required to answer these questions, limiting our responses to a total of three double-spaced pages.

Review the sample corporate proposal in exhibit 26.1. This sample includes the main components of a letter proposal outlined in this chapter. While you are encouraged to develop your own style, you should still include these integral parts in any letter proposal you submit. Even when provided with specific corporate contributions guidelines such as those in exhibit 26.2, try to incorporate the concepts suggested in this chapter into your proposal. For instance, in the needs section, you should work in the fact that through your research you are aware of the company's strong commitment to resolving this problem. And, after the section outlining your solution, you could slip in a few sentences in telling the prospective corporate funding source why you are a unique grantee and the best choice to implement the solution.

CHAPTER 27

Proposal Submission, the Decision, and Follow-Up
Corporate Grantors

B efore submitting your proposal to a corporate grantor, put it through a quality circle (see chapter 13) that resembles the actual review process as closely as possible. The purpose of this exercise is to get an unbiased first expression of your proposal from individuals who view it from the perspective of enlightened, corporate self-interest.

Ask two or three of your colleagues and two of your corporate advisory committee members, or a professor from your local college's business school, to participate. Have two of the individuals role-play corporate executives. Unless you have other information, inform all of the participants that the real reviewers will be corporate executives who read your proposal in less than five minutes. They also should be made aware of the fact the real reviewers (the corporate executives) will not follow any specific scoring or rating system, and will not provide any comments to the applicants. The whole exercise should take less than one hour.

SUBMISSION

Since only a few corporate grantors allow online submittal, you will most likely be sending a print copy of your proposal to the contact person listed in your research. Even when you submit online, print your proposal out to be certain the font and/or graphics are not altered, and send a hard copy of your proposal to the funding source just in case they do not receive the electronic version. Submit the proposal a few days before the deadline using the United States Postal Service, United Parcel Service, or Federal Express. Make sure you send your proposal as certified mail, requiring a proof of receipt, and by a carrier that can guarantee next-day delivery.

Send copies of your final proposal to your corporate linkages so that they know you finally submitted your proposal and are aware of exactly what you requested. Thank them for the assistance they provided up to this point, and for the assistance they may provide in the future to help get your submitted proposal funded.

THE DECISION

Corporate grantors may only provide an outcome to those to whom they award grants. They may fail to notify those they reject. In any case, your research will provide you with the dates that the corporate board meets, and from these dates you can approximate when you should hear from the grantor.

Rejected

If you do not hear by six months after the deadline date, your proposal was probably rejected. If you do receive a rejection letter, you also may receive little in the way of constructive criticism, redirection of your efforts, and/or reapplication rules. Some corporate grantors do not allow you to resubmit immediately. For example, I was once told by a corporate foundation that I could not resubmit for three years. Other grantors may advise you never to resubmit because of new restrictions and/or changes in their priorities and philosophy. Learn what you can from the grantor, your advocates, and/or your linkages, and reapply when it is allowable and advisable.

Always send a thank-you letter that acknowledges the time the funding source invested in the selection process, and your gratitude for their foresight in dedicating profits to impacting these problems and their areas of interest.

Awarded

If your proposal is funded, send the same thank-you letter as outlined above, but include an invitation to visit your institution/organization to see the important work you are conducting and the unique qualities you mentioned in your proposal. You should also request any comments they may have that would help you improve on a future proposal to them or another corporation. However, do not expect a response.

FOLLOW-UP

Whether you are successful or not in your corporate grants quest, try to maintain professional contact. Like you, corporate decision makers are trying to keep up on the advances in your mutual field of interest. Send them an interesting article that your research uncovers, or even an article of yours that is scheduled for publication. Let them know you are alive between the deadline dates. Seek them out at conferences and meetings, and ask them questions about their next grant opportunities.

Persistence and the maintaining of a professional interest in their area of concern will pay off. You will improve your relationship with them, and have chances to learn of their upcoming grant priorities. Just remember that being persistent is different than being a pest! Keep your relationship focused on the need for your projects and research, and their opportunities for involvement.

The best approach to grantseeking is to develop a long-term and mutually beneficial relationship among you, your organization, and the grantor. This relationship should be based on honesty and a sincere concern for the grantor's needs. Saying thank you is a crucial element in building such a relationship.

Thank you for purchasing this book, and I am confident that you will be rewarded for practicing the strategies outlined.

LIST OF
RESOURCES

You may wish to look at copies of these recommended grant tools before you purchase them. Many of the resources listed include locations where you can find the materials and get assistance from helpful staff. Many institutions have developed joint or cooperative grants libraries to reduce costs and encourage consortium projects.

The list of resources is divided into the following sections:

- Government Grant Research Aids
- Foundation Grant Research Aids
- Corporate Grant Research Aids
- Government, Foundation, and Corporate Grant Resources
- Electronic Resources

GOVERNMENT GRANT RESEARCH AIDS

Tips

1. Each congressional district has at least two federal depository libraries. Your local college librarian or public librarian will know where the designated libraries are and will advise you on the availability of the resources listed in this section.
2. Many federal agencies have newsletters or agency publications. You can ask to be placed on their mailing lists to receive these publications.
3. Contact federal programs to get the most up-to-date information.
4. All of the government grant publications listed here are available through your congressperson's office.

Government Publications

Catalog of Federal Domestic Assistance (CFDA)

The *Catalog* is the government's most complete listing of federal domestic assistance programs, with details on eligibility, application procedures, and deadlines, including the location of state plans. It is published at the beginning of each fiscal year, with supplementary updates during the year. Indexes are by agency program, function, popular name, applicant eligibility, and subject. It comes in loose-leaf form, punched for a three-ring binder.

Price: $63.00 per year

Order from:

Superintendent of Documents

P.O. Box 271954

Pittsburgh, PA 15250-7954

(866) 512-1800 or (202) 512-1800 in DC metro area

Available online at <http://www.cfda.gov>

Congressional Record

The *Congressional Record* covers the day-to-day proceedings of the Senate and House of Representatives.

Price: $434.00 per year

Order from:

Superintendent of Documents

P.O. Box 271954

Pittsburgh, PA 15250-7954

(866) 512-1800 or (202) 512-1800 in DC metro area

Available online at<http://www.access.gpo.gov/su_docs/aces/aces150.html>

Federal Register

Published five times a week (Monday through Friday), the *Federal Register* supplies up-to-date information on federal assistance and supplements the *Catalog of Federal Domestic Assistance* (CFDA). The *Federal Register* includes public regulations and legal notices issued by all federal agencies and presidential proclamations. Of particular importance are the proposed rules, final rules, and program deadlines. An index is published monthly.

Price: $764.00 per year with indexes

Order from:

Superintendent of Documents

P.O. Box 271954

Pittsburgh, PA 15250-7954

(866) 512-1800 or (202) 512-1800 in DC metro area

Available online at <http://www.nara.gov/fedreg/>

National Science Foundation Bulletin

Provides monthly news about NSF programs, deadline dates, publications, and meetings, as well as sources for more information. The material in the print version of this publication is also available electronically on STIS, NSF's Science and Technology Information System. There is no cost for this service.

To subscribe: <http://www.nsf.gov/cgi-bin/ebulletin/mailit.pl>

NIH Guide for Grants and Contracts

NIH Guide is published weekly and there is no subscription fee. Electronic access to the Guide is now available.

To subscribe: <http://grants1.nih.gov/grants/guide/listserv.htm>

United States Government Manual

This paperback manual gives the names of key personnel, addresses, and telephone numbers for all agencies, departments, and so on that constitute the federal bureaucracy.

Price: $49.00 per year

Order from:

Superintendent of Documents

P.O. Box 371954

Pittsburgh, PA 15250-7954

(866) 512-1800 or (202) 512-1800 DC metro area

Available to order online at <http://bookstore.gpo.gov/>

Other popular government Web sites:

National Endowment for the Humanities—<http://www.neh.fed.us>

National Institutes of Health—<http://www.nih.gov>

National Science Foundation—<http://www.nsf.gov>

Department of Education—<http://www.ed.gov>

Department of Housing and Urban Development—<http://www.hud.gov>

Commercially Produced Publications

Education Grants Alert

This weekly publication gives quick access to federal and private funding opportunities available for education.

Price: $486.00 softcover

Order from:

Aspen Publishers, Inc.

7201 McKinney Circle

Frederick, MD 21704

Phone: (800) 638-8437

Fax: (310) 417-7650

<http://www.aspenpublisher.com>

Federal Directory

The *Directory* includes names, addresses, and phone numbers of federal government agencies and key personnel.

Price: $375.00 print version

Order from:

Carroll Publishing

4701 Sangamore Rd.

Suite S-155

Bethesda, MD 20816

(800) 336-4240

<http://www.carrollpub.com>

Federal Grants and Contracts Weekly

This weekly contains information on the latest Requests for Proposals (RFPs), contracting opportunities, and upcoming grants. Each issue includes details on RFPs, closing dates for grant programs, procurement-related news, and newly issued regulations.

Price: $489.00 softcover, $489.00 online

Order from:

Aspen Publishers, Inc.

7201 McKinney Circle
Frederick, MD 21704
Phone: (800) 638-8437
Fax: (301) 417-7650
<http://www.aspenpublishers.com>

Federal Yellow Book

This directory of the federal departments and agencies is updated quarterly.
Price: $342.00
Order from:
Leadership Directories, Inc.
104 Fifth Avenue, 3rd Floor
New York, NY 10011
Phone: (212) 627-4140
Fax: (212) 645-0931
Or order online at <http://www.leadershipdirectories.com>

Health Grants and Contracts Weekly

Price: $459.00 softcover, $459.00 online
Order from:
Aspen Publishers, Inc.
7201 McKinney Circle
Frederick, MD 21704
Phone: (800) 638-8437
Fax: (301) 417-7650
<http://www.aspenpublishers.com>

Washington Information Directory, 2002/2003

This directory is divided into three categories: agencies of the executive
branch; Congress; and private or "nongovernmental" organizations. Each
entry includes the name, address, telephone number, and director of the or-
ganization, along with a short description of its work.
Price: $120.00
Order from:
CQ Press
Customer Service and Order Dept. WEB2

1255 22nd St., NW, Suite 400

Washington, DC 20037

Phone: (866) 427-7737 or (202) 729-1900 in DC metro area

Fax: (202) 729-1923

FOUNDATION GRANT RESEARCH AIDS

Tips

Many of the following research aids can be found through the Foundation Center Cooperating Collections Network. If you wish to purchase any of the following Foundation Center publications, contact:

The Foundation Center

79 Fifth Avenue, Dept. ST

New York, NY 10003-3076

(800) 424-9836

Fax: (212) 807-3691

Internet: <http://www.fdncenter.org>

Corporate Foundation Profiles, 12th edition, March 2002, 723 pages

A Foundation Center publication, this book contains detailed analysis of 187 of the largest corporate foundations in the United States. An appendix lists financial data on hundreds of additional smaller grant makers.

Price: $155.00

Order from: The Foundation Center

The following five directories can all be ordered by mail or fax (no telephone or credit card orders accepted) from:

Research Grant Guides, Inc.

P.O. Box 1214

Loxahatchee, FL 33470

Fax (561) 795-7794

Directory of Building and Equipment Grants, 6th edition

Profiles on 950 foundations that provide support for buildings, equipment, and/or renovations.

Price: $69.00

Order from: Research Grant Guides, Inc.

Directory of Computer and High Technology Grants, 4th edition

Includes 750 foundation profiles to help you search for funds for computers and software.

Price: $69.00

Order from: Research Grant Guides, Inc.

Directory of Grants for Organizations Serving People with Disabilities, 11th edition

Profiles of 700 foundations with specific interests in this area.

Price: $69.00

Order from: Research Grant Guides, Inc.

Directory of Operating Grants, 6th edition

Profiles on 1,000 foundations receptive to proposals for operating grants (salaries, rent, overhead, etc.)

Price: $69.00

Order from: Research Grant Guides, Inc.

Directory of Program Grants, 2nd edition

Profiles of 800 foundations interested in programs and projects that help meet community needs.

Price: $69.00

Order from: Research Grant Guides, Inc.

Foundation and Corporate Grants Alert

Price: $383.00 softcover, $383.00 online

Order from:

Aspen Publishers, Inc.

7201 McKinney Circle

Frederick, MD 21704

Phone: (800) 638-8437

Fax: (301) 417-7650

<http://www.aspenpublisher.com>

The Foundation Directory, March 2003, 2,533 pages

The most important single reference work available on grant making foundations in the United States, this directory includes information on foundations having assets of more than $2 million or annual grants exceeding $200,000. Each entry includes a description of giving interests, along with address, telephone numbers, current financial data, names of donors, contact person, and IRS identification number. Six indexes are included: index to donors, officers, and trustees; geographic index; types of support index; subject index; foundations new to edition index; and foundation name index. The index to donors, officers, and trustees is very valuable in developing links to decision makers.

Price: $215.00

Order from: The Foundation Center

The Foundation Directory Part 2, March 2003, 1,995 pages

This directory provides information on 10,000 mid-sized foundations.

Price: $185.00

Order from: The Foundation Center

The Foundation Directory Supplement, September 2003, 1,000 pages

The *Supplement* updates the *Directory*, so that users will have the latest addresses, contacts, policy statements, application guidelines, and financial data.

Price: $125.00

Order from: The Foundation Center

Foundation Grants to Individuals, 13th edition, 1,117 pages

This directory provides a comprehensive listing of over 4,300 independent and corporate foundations that provide financial assistance to individuals.

Price: $65.00, available on CD-ROM for $75.00

Order from: The Foundation Center

Foundation News and Commentary

Each issue of the *News* covers the activities of private, company-sponsored, and community foundations, direct corporate giving, government agencies and their programs, and includes the kinds of grants being awarded, overall trends, legal matters, regulatory actions, and other areas of common concern.

Price: $48.00

Order from: Council on Foundations

1828 L St., NW

Washington, DC 20036

(800) 771-8187

The Foundation 1,000, October 2002, 3,056 pages

The 1,000 largest U.S. foundations are profiled by foundation name, subject field, type of support, and geographic location. There is also an index that allows you to target grant makers by the names of officers, staff, and trustees.

Price: $295.00

Order from: The Foundation Center

Foundation Reporter, 36th edition

This annual directory of the top 1,000 private foundations in the United States supplies descriptions and statistical analyses.

Price: $525.00

Order from:

Gale

P.O. Box 9187

Farmington Hills, MI 48333-9187

Phone: (800) 877-8238

Fax: (800) 414-5043

<http://www.gale.com>

Grant Guides

There are a total of 12 Grant Guides available in a variety of subjects including: arts, culture and the humanities; children and youth; elementary and secondary education; environmental protection and animal welfare; foreign and international programs; higher education; libraries and information services; mental health, addictions, and crisis services; minorities; physically and mentally disabled; religion, religious welfare and religious education; and women and children.

Price: $75.00 each

Order from: The Foundation Center

Guide to Funding for International and Foreign Programs, 6th edition, May 2002, 358 pages

This guide includes over 1,300 funding sources that award grants to international nonprofit institutions and projects, as well as over 8,900 grant descriptions.

Price: $125.00

Order from: The Foundation Center

Guide to Grantseeking on the Web, September 2001, 775 pages

Includes information on hundreds of grant maker Web sites and a variety of related nonprofit sites of interest.

Price: $29.95, also available on CD-ROM for $29.95

Order from: The Foundation Center

Guide to U.S. Foundations, Their Trustees, Officers, and Donors, April 2003, 4,235 pages

Includes information on over 65,000 U.S. private, corporate, and community foundations, and an index to the individuals who establish, manage, and oversee these foundations.

Price: $295.00

Order from: The Foundation Center

National Guide to Funding for the Environment and Animal Welfare, 6th edition, June 2002, 527 pages

Includes over 2,900 sources of funding for environment- and animal welfare–related nonprofit institutions and projects, as well as over 7,200 grant descriptions.

Price: $115.00

Order from: The Foundation Center

National Guide to Funding in Arts and Culture, 7th edition, May 2002, 1,138 pages

This guide includes over 7,500 sources of funding for arts- and culture-related nonprofit organizations and projects, as well as over 16,500 grant descriptions.

Price: $155.00

Order from: The Foundation Center

National Guide to Funding in Health, 7th edition, May 2001, 2,447 pages

This guide includes over 10,763 sources for health-related projects and institutions and over 15,960 grant descriptions.

Price: $155.00

Order from: The Foundation Center

National Guides from the Foundation Center are also available in the following areas:

AIDS, $115.00

Libraries and Information Services, $115.00

Religion, $155.00

Private Foundation IRS Tax Returns

The Internal Revenue Service requires private foundations to file income tax returns each year. Form 990-PF provides fiscal details on receipts and expenditures, compensation of officers, capital gains or losses, and other financial matters. Form 990-AR provides information on foundation managers, assets, and grants paid or committed for future payment.

The IRS makes this information available on aperture (microfiche) cards that may be viewed for free at the reference collections operated by the Foundation Center (New York, San Francisco, Washington, DC, Cleveland, and Atlanta) or at the Foundation Center's regional cooperating collections. You also may obtain this information online at <http://lnp.fdncenter.org/finder.html>, <http://www.guidestar.org>, and <http://www.grantsmart.org/search.html>.

Directories of State and Local Grant Makers

Visit the Foundation Center cooperating collection (see chapter 19) closest to you to determine what directories are available for your state and surrounding region. The following eight regional guides are available through the Foundation Center:

- *Guide to Greater Washington, D.C. Grantmakers on CD-ROM*, $75.00
- *New York State Foundations*, $180.00
- *Directory of Missouri Grantmakers*, $75.00
- *Guide to Ohio Grantmakers*, $125.00
- *The Michigan Foundation Directory*, $70.00, CD-ROM $80.00
- *New York Metropolitan Area Foundations: A Profile of the Grantmaking Community*, $24.95
- *California Foundations: A Profile of the State's Grantmaking Community*, $24.95
- *Southeastern Foundation II: Profile of the Region's Grantmaking Community*, $19.95

Visit the Rural Information Center at <http://www.nal.usda.gov/ric/ricpubs/funding/funding1.htm> for a comprehensive listing of available state directories. Please note that some directories are updated on a regular basis, but many are not.

Other popular foundation related Web sites:

> The Council on Foundations—<http://www.cof.org>
> Philanthropy News Network Online—<http://www.pnnonline.org>
> The Foundation Center's homepage—<http://www.fdncenter.org>

CORPORATE GRANT RESEARCH AIDS

Corporations interested in corporate giving often establish foundations to handle their contributions. Once foundations are established, their IRS returns become public information, and data are compiled into the directories previously mentioned under Foundation Grant Research Aids.

Corporate contributions that do not go through a foundation are not public information, and research sources consist of:

- information volunteered by the corporation
- product information
- profitability information

Corporate Contributions in 2000

> The results of this annual survey include a detailed analysis of beneficiaries of corporate support but do not list individual firms and specific recipients.
> Price: $45.00 for associates; $180.00 for nonassociates
> Order from:
> The Conference Board
> 845 Third Avenue
> New York, NY 10022
> Phone: (212) 759-0900, general information
> Phone: (212) 339-0345, customer service
> Fax: (212) 980-7014

Corporate Giving Directory, 2002, 25th edition

> This directory provides detailed entries on 1,000 company-sponsored foundations.
> Price: $505.00
> Order from:
> Gale
> P.O. Box 9187
> Farmington Hills, MI 48333-9187
> (800) 877-8238
> <http://www.gale.com>

Dun and Bradstreet's Million Dollar Directory, 5 volumes

The five volumes list name, addresses, employees, sales volume, and other pertinent data for the largest businesses in the United States. Available in hard copy and as part of the *Million Dollar Directory Suite* accessible by database subscription.

Call company for pricing.

The D&B Corporation

103 JFK Parkway

Short Hills, NJ 07078

(800) 234-3867, customer service

http://www.dnb.com/

The National Directory of Corporate Giving, 8th edition, August 2002, 1,165 pages

Information on over 2,100 corporate foundations, plus an additional 1,300 direct-giving programs, is provided in this directory. An extensive bibliography and seven indexes are included to help you target funding prospects.

Price: $195.00

Order from:

The Foundation Center

79 Fifth Avenue, Dept. FJ

New York, NY 10003-3076

800-424-9836 or in New York State, (212) 807-3690

Fax: (212) 807-3677

Internet: <http://www.fdncenter.org>

Standard and Poor's Register of Corporations, Directors and Executives, three volumes

This annual register is made up of three volumes: volume 1 provides information on both public and private corporations, volume 2 contains biographical information on corporate executives and directors, and volume 3 contains indexes.

Available in print and electronic versions; call customer service for pricing.

Standard and Poor's Corporation

55 Water St.

New York, NY 10041

(800) 523-4534, customer service

North American Industry Classification System Manual, 2002

Developed for use in the classification of establishments by type of activity in which they are engaged.

Price: printed version $45.00, $32.50 hardcover; CD-ROM version $60.00

Order from:

National Technical Information Service

Springfield, VA 22161

(800) 553-6847

<http://www.ntis.gov>

Who's Who in America, 2003 edition

Known for its life and career data on noteworthy individuals. The 2003 edition has three volumes. Available in hard copy and on the Web.

Price: $629.10 for print version, first time orders

Order from:

Order Dept.

Marquis Who's Who

P.O. Box 31

New Providence, NJ 07974

Phone: (800) 473-7020

Fax: (800) 836-7766

<http://www.marquiswhoswho.com>

Other corporate related Web sites:

The Insider Trading Monitor—<http://www.wealthid.com>

Hoovers—<http://www.hoovers.com>

Business Journal's Book of Lists—<http://www.bizjournals.com>

Securities and Exchange Commission (SEC)— <http://www.sec.gov>

GOVERNMENT, FOUNDATION, AND CORPORATE GRANT RESOURCES

Many of the following research aids can be purchased from Greenwood Publishing Group online at <http://www.greenwood.com>, or by phone at (800) 225-5800.

How to Evaluate and Improve Your Grants Effort, 2nd edition

Provides information on the roles and responsibilities of an effective grants office. Particularly useful for those in the process of setting up a new grants office or evaluating an existing one.

Price: $39.95

Order from: Greenwood Publishing Group

Directory of Biomedical and Health Care Grants, 2003, 17th edition

This directory provides information on biomedical and health care-related programs sponsored by the federal government, corporations, professional associations, special interest groups, and state and local governments. Published annually.

Price: $84.50

Order from: Greenwood Publishing Group

Directory of Grants in the Humanities, 2002/2003, 16th edition

Current data on funds available to individual artists and art organizations from Corporations, foundations, and professional associations as well as from the NEA, NEH, and state and local arts and humanities councils.

Price: $84.95

Order from: Greenwood Publishing Group

Directory of Research Grants, 2003

Information on government, corporate, organizational, and private funding sources supporting research programs in academic, scientific, and technology related subjects is included. Published annually.

Price: $135.00

Order from: Greenwood Publishing Group

Funding Sources for Community Development and Economic Development, 2003

Description of programs that offer funding opportunities for quality-of-life projects at the community level are included. Funding programs sponsored by both local and national sources are listed, including state, local, and federal government sources, nonprofit and corporate sponsors, foundations, and advocacy groups. Published annually.

Price: $64.95

Order from: Greenwood Publishing Group

Funding Sources for K–12 Education, 2002

Descriptions of programs that offer funding opportunities for classroom instruction, teacher education, art in education, general operating grants, and equipment from federal, state, corporate, and foundation sources.

Price: $49.95

Order from: Greenwood Publishing Group

Giving USA 2002

Annual report on philanthropy for the year 2001.

Price: $65.00

Order online or from:

AAFRC Trust for Philanthropy

Fulfillment Dept.

P.O. Box 1020

Sewickley, PA 15143-1020

Phone: (888) 544-8464

Fax: (412) 741-0608

<http://www.aafrc.org>

ELECTRONIC RESOURCES

There is a wealth of information available through online subscription databases and CD-ROMs. Check with your librarian and your grants office to locate those electronic resources you may already have access to.

Academic Research Information System, Inc. (ARIS)

ARIS provides a database of funding information in the arts, humanities, social sciences, natural sciences, and biomedical sciences. For information, contact:

Academic Research Information System, Inc.

2940 16th Street, Suite 314

San Francisco, CA 94103

Phone: (415) 558-8133

Fax: (415) 55808135

<http://www.Grantsinfo.com>

Community of Science (COS) Funding Opportunities

COS *Funding Opportunities* database is a comprehensive source of funding information available on the Web. It contains more than 23,000 records, representing over 400,000 funding opportunities, worth over $33 billion.

Price: COS *Funding Opportunities* is included with fee-based membership in the Community of Scholars. Other institutions may purchase access to COS *Funding Opportunities* for a fixed annual subscription fee. Subscription pricing is determined by the amount of external research funding your institution manages. Contact customer inquires for further information:

COS

1629 Thames Street, Suite 200

Baltimore, MD 21231

Phone: (410) 563-2595 X302, customer inquiries

Fax: (410) 563-5389

<http://www.cos.com>

Congressional Information Service Index (CIS Index)

CIS covers congressional publications and legislation from 1970 to date. Hearings, committee prints, House and Senate reports and documents, special publications, Senate executive reports and documents, and public laws are indexed. *CIS Index* includes monthly abstracts and index volumes. CIS publications are available in print, microfiche, and microfilm formats. Pricing information is available from customer service.

LexisNexis Academic and Library Solutions

4520 East West Highway

Bethesda, MD 20814

Phone: 800-638-8380, customer service

Fax: (301) 657-3203

<http://www.lexisnexis.com/academic/CISPubs/>

DIALOG OnDisc Grants Database

DIALOG OnDisc Grants Database lists approximately 8,900 grants offered by federal, state, and local governments; commercial organizations; professional associations; and private and community foundations. Each entry includes a description, qualifications, money available, and renewability. Full name, address, and telephone number for each sponsoring organization is included as available.

Price: $850.00, includes bimonthly updated CD-ROM

Order from:

DIALOG Corporation

11000 Regency Parkway, Suite 10

Cary, NC 27511

(800) 334-2564

Fax: (919) 468-9890

<http://www.dialog.com>

Federal Business Opportunities FedBizOpps

A government database listing notices of proposed government procurement actions, contract awards, sales of government property, and other procurement information over $25,000.

Federal Business Opportunities

(877) 472-3799

Available online at <http://www.fedbizopps.gov/>

Foundation Center Databases/CD-ROMs

The Foundation Center offers several grant related electronic resources. For further information on these products, visit <http://www.fdncenter.org/marketplace>, or call (800) 478-4661.

Foundation Directory Online Subscription Plans. The Foundation Center has several different online subscription plans including, *The Foundation Directory Online Platinum*, *The Foundation Directory Online Premium*, *The Foundation Directory Online Plus*, and *The Foundation Directory Online Basic*. The basic subscription allows you to search the nation's largest 10,000 foundations and the names of over 60,000 trustees, officers, and donors, starting from $19.95 per month or $195.00 per year. Contact the Foundation Center for information and pricing for the other plans.

FC Search: The Foundation Center's Database on CD-ROM. This CD-ROM provides information on over 70,000 U.S.-based foundations, corporate givers, and grant making public charities. It also contains additional information on defined program areas for 1,000 top funders, expanded application guidelines for 6,700 funders, and links to over 3,900 grant maker and corporate Web sites. It is updated semi-annually in April and December and costs $1,195 for a single-user disk. This price includes a free Fall Update disk and a 100-plus-page printed manual. Contact the Foundation Center for network prices.

Other CD-ROMs available through the Foundation Center include:

- *Foundation Directory on CD-ROM*—$295 for the single-user disk
- *Foundation Directory 1 and 2 on CD-ROM*—$495 for the single-user disk
- *Foundation Grants Index on CD-ROM*—$165 for the single-user disk

GrantSelect

This database is available on the World Wide Web, and provides information on more than 10,000 funding opportunities. Grantseekers can subscribe to the full database or to any one of seven special segments offered: children and youth, health care and biomedical, arts and humanities, K–12 schools and adult basic education, community development, international programs, and operating grants. An e-mail alert service that notifies grantseekers of any new funding opportunities within their area of interest is also available.

For questions on registration and pricing, information for consortia, and questions about content, contact: grantsadmin@greenwood.com

Oryx Press

A Division of Greenwood Publishing Group

88 Post Rd. West

Westport, CT 06881

Phone: (202) 226-3571

Fax: (203) 222-1502

<http://www.greenwood.com>

Illinois Researcher Information Service (IRIS)

The *IRIS* database of funding opportunities contains records on over 8,000 federal and nonfederal funding opportunities in all disciplines. It is updated daily.

Price: *IRIS* is a subscription service. It is available to colleges and universities for an annual subscription fee. For more information on the subscription policy and/or an *IRIS* trial period, contact:

Illinois Researcher Information Service (IRIS)

University of Illinois at Urbana-Champaign

128 Observatory

901 South Mathews Avenue

Urbana, Illinois 61801

Phone: (217) 333-0284

Fax: (217) 333-7011.

<http://www.library.uicu.edu/iris/>

The Sponsored Programs Information Network (SPIN)

This is a database of federal and private funding sources. Price depends on the institution's level of research and development expenditures.

For pricing, more information, or to order, contact:

InfoEd

1873 Western Avenue

Guilderland, NY 12203

Phone: (800) 727-6427

Fax: (518) 464-0695

<http://www.infoed.org/>

DAVID G. BAUER ASSOCIATES, INC. ORDERING INFORMATION

Order the following grantseeking and fundraising materials directly from David G. Bauer Associates, Inc. Prices do not include shipping charges and are subject to change without notice.

Call toll free (800) 836-0732, Monday–Friday, 9–5 Pacific Standard Time

GRANTSEEKING MATERIALS

Technology Funding for Schools—Techniques schools can use for obtaining funding for their technology related goals. $38.00.

Creating Foundations in American Schools—Techniques for creating school foundations. $49.95.

Grants Time Line—Pad of 25 worksheets for developing time lines and cash forecasts. $3.95 per pad; 10 or more pads $2.95 each.

The Teacher's Guide to Winning Grants—A systematic guide to grantseeking skills that work for classroom leaders. $29.50.

The Principal's Guide to Winning Grants—Strategies principals can apply to support grantseeking at their schools. $32.00.

Project Planner—Pad of 25 worksheets for developing work plans and budget narratives. $8.95 per pad; 10 or more pads $7.95 each.

Proposal Organizing Workbook—Set of 30 Swiss cheese tabs. $9.95 per set; 10 or more sets, $8.95 each.

Successful Grants Program Management—Practical tool for the superintendent or central office administrator to assist in developing a districtwide grants support system. $35.00.

FUND RAISING MATERIALS

Donor Pyramid—three-fold visual depicting various levels of donor activities and volunteer involvement. $9.95 per pyramid; 10 or more $8.95 per pyramid.

Fund Raising Organizer—Pad of 25 spreadsheets for planning and analyzing fundraising events. $8.95 per pad; 10 or more pads $7.95 each.

Fund Raising Organizer Activity Cards—Pack of 25 cards that summarize resource allocation, costs, and net funds. $3.95 per pack; 10 or more packs $2.95 each.

The Fund Raising Primer—112 pages that provide basic information on various fundraising strategies. $24.95.

VIDEOTAPE PROGRAMS

For more information or to order, call (800) 228-4630, Monday—Friday

Winning Grants 2—Proven grant-winning system on five videocassettes. Produced by the University of Nebraska Great Plains Network. $495.00

How To Teach Grantseeking To Others—Two-hour video providing the essential know-how to instruct others in the strategies and techniques of successful grantseeking. Comes with a companion text and computer disk that provide detailed support and supply all necessary forms and checklists. $189.00

Strategic Fund Raising—Five 60-minute videocassettes designed to help nonprofit organizations increase board and staff involvement and understanding of basic fundraising principles and the development of a funding plan. $495.00.

SOFTWARE PROGRAMS

For more information or to order, call (800) 836-0732, Monday–Friday, 9–5 Pacific Standard Time.

Grant Winner—IBM-PC or compatible software package that organizes grantseeking techniques and stores four proposals and the worksheets found in *The "How To" Grants Manual*. $189.00.

Winning Links—IBM-PC or compatible software package providing a database that records the contacts of your board members, staff, and volunteers. $139.00

SEMINARS AND CONSULTING

Public Seminars—Call (800) 836-0732 for information concerning David Bauer's public seminars held in major cities throughout the United States.

In-house Seminars and Consulting—David Bauer gives seminar at your institution or organization to increase your staff and/or board members' skills and interest in the following areas: federal grantseeking, foundation and corporate grantseeking, fundraising, evaluating your grants and/or fundraising system, motivation/productivity, and team building. He also provides grants system audits and analyses. For more information on these services, call (800) 836-0732.

INDEX

About the Author

DAVID G. BAUER is highly sought after as a speaker on grantseeking. He is president of David G. Bauer Associates, Inc., a consulting firm created in1981 to provide educationally based grantseeking and fund raising seminars and materials. Bauer has taught more than 25,000 individuals the keys to grantseeking and fund raising. He has recently served as the director of development for the Center for Educational Accountability and Associate Professor at the University of Alabama at Birmingham School of Education. David Bauer is also author of 10 books on winning grants and administering grants programs, some having appeared in several editions. He has developed several videotape series and two software programs in this field as well.